MUIRHEAD LIBRARY OF PHILOSOPHY

An admirable statement of the aims of the Library of Philosophy
was provided by the first editor, the late Professor J. H. Muirhead,
in his description of the original programme printed in Erdmann's
History of Philosophy under the date 1890. This was slightly modified in subsequent volumes to take the form of the following
statement:

'The Muirhead Library of Philosophy was designed as a contribution to the History of Modern Philosophy under the heads:
first of Different Schools of Thought—Sensationalist, Realist,
Idealist, Intuitivist; secondly of different Subjects—Psychology,
Ethics, Aesthetics, Political Philosophy, Theology. While much
had been done in England in tracing the course of evolution in
nature, history, economics, morals and religion, little had been done
in tracing the development of thought on these subjects. Yet "the
evolution of opinion is part of the whole evolution".'

'By the co-operation of different writers in carrying out this plan
it was hoped that a thoroughness and completeness of treatment,
otherwise unattainable, might be secured. It was believed also that
from writers mainly British and American fuller consideration of
English Philosophy than it had hitherto received might be looked
for. In the earlier series of books containing, among others,
Bosanquet's *History of Aesthetic*, Pfleiderer's *Rational Theology
since Kant*, Albee's *History of English Utilitarianism*, Bonar's *Philosophy and Political Economy*, Brett's *History of Psychology*,
Ritchie's *Natural Rights*, these objects were to a large extent
effected.

'In the meantime original work of a high order was being produced both in England and America by such writers as Bradley,
Stout, Bertrand Russell, Baldwin, Urban, Montague, and others,
and a new interest in foreign works, German, French and Italian,
which had either become classical or were attracting public attention, had developed. The scope of the Library thus became extended into something more international, and it is entering on the
fifth decade of its existence in the hope that it may contribute to
that mutual understanding between countries which is so pressing
a need of the present time.'

The need which Professor Muirhead stressed is no less pressing to-day, and few will deny that philosophy has much to do with enabling us to meet it, although no one, least of all Muirhead himself, would regard that as the sole, or even the main, object of of philosophy. As Professor Muirhead continues to lend the distinction of his name to the Library of Philosophy it seemed not inappropriate to allow him to recall us to these aims in his own words. The emphasis on the history of thought also seemed to me very timely; and the number of important works promised for the Library in the near future augur well for the continued fulfilment, in this and in other ways, of the expectations of the original editor.

H. D. LEWIS

MUIRHEAD LIBRARY OF PHILOSOPHY

General Editor: H. D. Lewis

Professor of History and Philosophy of Religion in the University of London

The Analysis of Mind by BERTRAND RUSSELL 8th impression

Brett's History of Psychology edited by R. S. PETERS

Clarity is Not Enough by H. D. LEWIS

Coleridge as a Philosopher by J. H. MUIRHEAD 3rd impression

The Commonplace Book of G. E. Moore edited by C. LEWY

Contemporary American Philosophy edited by G. P. ADAMS and W. P. MONTAGUE 2nd impression

Contemporary British Philosophy first and second Series edited by J. H. MUIRHEAD 2nd impression

Contemporary British Philosophy third Series edited by H. D. LEWIS 2nd impression

Contemporary Indian Philosophy edited by RADHAKRISHNAN and J. H. MUIRHEAD 2nd edition

The Discipline of the Cave by J. N. FINDLAY

Doctrine and Argument in Indian Philosophy by NINIAN SMART

Essays in Analysis by ALICE AMBROSE

Ethics by NICOLAI HARTMANN translated by STANTON COIT 3 vols

The Foundations of Metaphysics in Science by ERROL E. HARRIS

Freedom and History by H. D. LEWIS

The Good Will: A Study in the Coherence Theory of Goodness by H. J. PATON

Hegel: A Re-examination by J. N. FINDLAY

Hegel's Science of Logic translated by W. H. JOHNSTON and L. G. STRUTHERS 2 vols 3rd impression

History of Aesthetic by B. BOSANQUET 2nd edition 5th impression

History of English Utilitarianism by E. ALBEE 2nd impression

History of Psychology by G. S. BRETT edited by R. S. PETERS abridged one volume edition 2nd edition

Human Knowledge by BERTRAND RUSSELL 4th impression

A Hundred Years of British Philosophy by RUDOLF METZ translated by J. H. HARVEY, T. E. JESSOP, HENRY STURT 2nd impression

Ideas: A General Introduction to Pure Phenomenology by EDMUND HUSSERL translated by W. R. BOYCE GIBSON 3rd impression

Imagination by E. J. FURLONG

Indian Philosophy by RADHAKRISHNAN 2 vols revised 2nd edition

Identity and Reality by EMILE MEYERSON

Introduction to Mathematical Philosophy by BERTRAND RUSSELL 2nd edition 10th impression

Kant's First Critique by H. W. CASSIRER

Kant's Metaphysic of Experience by H. J. PATON 3rd impression

Know Thyself by BERNADINO VARISCO translated by GUGLIELMO SALVADORI

Language and Reality by WILBUR MARSHALL URBAN 3rd impression

Lectures on Philosophy by G. E. MOORE edited by C. LEWY

Matter and Memory by HENRI BERGSON translated by N. M. PAUL and W. S. PALMER 7th impression

Memory by BRIAN SMITH

The Modern Predicament by H. J. PATON 3rd impression

Natural Rights by D. G. RITCHIE 3rd edition 5th impression

Nature, Mind and Modern Science by E. HARRIS

The Nature of Thought by BRAND BLANSHARD 3rd impression

On Selfhood and Godhead by C. A. CAMPBELL

Our experience of God by H. D. LEWIS

Perception by DON LOCKE

The Phenomenology of Mind by G. W. F. HEGEL translated by SIR JAMES BAILLIE revised 2nd edition 5th impression

Philosophy in America by MAX BLACK

Philosophical Papers by G. E. MOORE 2nd impression

Philosophy and Religion by AXEL HAGERSTROM

Philosophy of Whitehead by W. MAYS

The Platonic Tradition in Anglo-Saxon Philosophy by J. H. MUIRHEAD

The Principal Upanishads by RADHAKRISHNAN

The Problems of Perception by R. J. HIRST

Reason and Goodness by BLAND BLANSHARD

The Relevance of Whitehead by IVOR LECLERC

Some Main Problems of Philosophy by G. E. MOORE 3rd impression

The Theological Frontier of Ethics by W. G. MACLAGAN

Time and Free Will by HENRI BERGSON translated by F. G. POGSON 7th impression

The Ways of Knowing: or the Methods of Philosophy by W. P. MONTAGUE 6th impression

Values and Intentions by J. N. FINDLAY

𝔐uirbead 𝔏ibrar𝔶 of 𝔭bilosopb𝔶
EDITED BY H. D. LEWIS

GIFFORD LECTURES

———◇———

THE TRANSCENDENCE OF THE CAVE

*How odd
Of God
To choose
The Hindoos*

THE TRANSCENDENCE OF THE CAVE

(*Sequel to* THE DISCIPLINE OF THE CAVE)

GIFFORD LECTURES
GIVEN AT THE UNIVERSITY OF ST ANDREWS
December 1965–January 1966

BY

J. N. FINDLAY

M.A., PH.D., F.B.A.,

*Professor Emeritus of Philosophy in
the University of London
Clarke Professor of Moral Philosophy and Metaphysics
Yale University*

LONDON: GEORGE ALLEN & UNWIN LTD
NEW YORK: HUMANITIES PRESS INC.

PRINTED IN GREAT BRITAIN
in 11 on 12 point Imprint type
BY UNWIN BROTHERS LTD
WOKING AND LONDON

To

CLARE

Chè, come sole in viso chè più trema,
così lo rimembrar del dolce riso
la mente mia di sè medesma scema.
DANTE, *Paradiso*, Canto xxx, ll. 25–27

PREFACE

The lectures in the present volume continue the themes of my 1964–65 Gifford Lectures entitled *The Discipline of the Cave*, though only the last five lectures deserve the new title of *The Transcendence of the Cave*. In the opening lectures I have sketched an ontology, an axiology and a theology which are purely phenomenological, which do not describe any object otherwise than as it is constituted in and for our present, this-world experience. In the lectures which follow I have definitely 'stuck out my neck', and attempted to construct a picture of transcendental experiences and their objects based solely on the premiss that such experiences must be such as to resolve, at a higher level, the many philosophical surds that plague us in this life: the philosophical perplexities, e.g., concerning universals and particulars, mind and body, knowledge and its objects, the knowledge of other minds, etc., etc. What I have tried to work out could have been documented and confirmed by an immense amount of mystical and religious literature and experience, but I have not appealed to such support. While I do not accept any form of the widely-held dichotomy between logical and empirical truth, I do not wish, as a philosopher, to contribute to the merely empirical treatment of anything. If there is not an element of necessity, of genuine logical structure, in the construction of higher spheres of experience and their objects, they are for me without interest or importance. I stand and fall, further, by the assumption, not only that such a logical structure is discoverable, but that it is inseparable from *any* logical structure whatever. These large claims go beyond what I can claim to have established in the present lectures, but to the extent that I have been able, I have tried to move in this direction.

J. N. FINDLAY

London,
July 1966

CONTENTS

FOUNDATIONS OF THE REALM OF REASON AND SPIRIT

This evening I am to start the second series of my lectures on what I have called the human cave, taking over a term and a picture from Plato and using both for my own fairly similar purposes. The first series of my lectures was called *The Discipline of the Cave*, and I have had to rekindle a possibly declining or extinct interest by giving the present series the mildly sensational title of *The Transcendence of the Cave*. In my first series, I seem to suggest, I was dwelling only on the difficulties and restrictions of a life of intellectual and moral bondage, but now, it would appear, I am introducing you to the heady excitements of a new life of liberation and perfected insight. In reality, my change of title is misleading. I am really pursuing the same steady revisionary ascent from views of things that have shown themselves up as inadequate to views of things that seem likely to prove more adequate. I have been carrying on with my mixed phenomenological-dialectical programme, faithfully trying to describe the world as it shows itself to us at different levels of abstraction, and making at first no attempt to transform the phenomena into anything that embraces more or goes deeper, and *then* showing up the deep flaws and radical discrepancies in the overall view just arrived at, and so rising to a revised view that dissolves all those flaws and discrepancies. Half of the present series of lectures will only be a stage on the progress towards true notional adequacy; we shall try out the solvent power of a conception of radically immanent teleology that is largely a borrowing from Hegel. Only in the second half of the series shall we aspire, not at all confidently, to that finality of insight and utterance that can consider itself a transcendence of the limitations that make up what we call the human cave. And we shall end our whole study by voluntarily returning to those limitations, by seeing whatever ecstatic perspectives we may have introduced as doing no

B

more ultimately than perhaps adding a new, glorious dimension to our ordinary talk and experience.

In the present lecture I intend to do little more than review the positions reached in the first series of lectures, seeing them all more comprehensively than was possible when I was struggling with detailed issues. What we saw generally was that the world of our experience, shaped and articulated as it comes before us for practice and utterance, is such as to reveal the brooding dominance of certain major forms or *ideas*—each a self-contained would-be absolute—the spatial, the temporal, the inertly bodily, the living, the conscious, the social, etc.—which work themselves out in a whole system of interrelated features and connections. All of these interrelated features show an inherent affinity for one another and a mutual belongingness which enables us to pass from one to another more or less smoothly. Space, with its indifference to occupancy, and its free openness to variations of size, shape, and motion, is a major idea having the requisite self-sufficiency to count as a fit object for the kind of examination now in question, one that lies hidden under the incredible detail of varied geometries: we can set forth its basic characters, we can see how it fits in with other basic notions, we can see everything in the world— time, body, mind, etc.—in relation to it. In the same way body, with its occupancy of space, its indifference to perception, together with its free self-exhibition to all comers and viewers, with its simplicity of basic character and its endless proliferation of qualified, slanted appearances, represents a major idea, an absolute that can be chosen for special eidetic examination, and that will develop into a whole system of interrelated, coherent aspects: everything in the world, as is well-known, can be seen in relation to the solid material basis without which it would elude our efforts to trap it or to tie it down. The same applies to the idea of the single conscious mind, comprehending all actuality, possibility and impossibility in the range of its radiating intentions, and going so far towards multiplicity and hard separateness in one direction as it goes towards fluid fusion and interpenetration in another. It certainly is a major idea, capable of putting its seal on everything, and becoming the central source from which all other things acquire lucidity, while it itself retains full notional self-sufficiency, and requires nothing external in terms of which it could be better understood. The same obviously applies to the social world of mutually communicating persons, to the ideal world of abstract meanings, to the realm of values, and so on. Some of these have not engaged us so far, and will only be dealt with in our present series.

Such major conceptions, such organizing ideas, are not ones which emerge from the examination of ordinary discourse without some struggle. They lie hidden under a wealth of ancillary expressions, whether adverbial, participial, conjunctive or merely inflectional. To bring them out from the many points at which they serve, and to erect them into more or less clearly outlined abstracta, requires the penetration, the re-assembling skill of philosophy. The sketching of a major idea in the full context that it abstractly demands and that it expands into, is the task of those eidetic sciences mentioned by Husserl, of which phenomenology, the development of the notion of intentionality, of conscious reference, is the most fundamental. All these sciences involve a suspension of interest in what actually exists or does not exist, and a replacing interest in what notions permit or do not permit, what they intrinsically favour or do not favour; they are, in short, studies of intrinsic possibilities, necessities, plausibilities and unplausibilities. But though thus modal in approach, it is not by a wanton metaphor that they are spoken of as 'descriptive'. For there is nothing merely 'analytic' in their exploration, no mere setting forth of what we arbitrarily have *put* into a notion or meaning. The possible combinations permitted or favoured by a notion, and the extensions it rules out or frowns upon, often affect us with the same shock of surprise as do the shades and contours of an observed object, even though the latter is revealed by ordinary sight, and the former by what we may call a 'seeing' use of language. That a body should be indifferent to the existence of observers yet none the less intrinsically likely to appear to their senses, that it should be simpler in character than its appearances but likely to reveal its basic characters the more variously it is examined: all these are connections of essence which our instinct follows unhesitatingly, but which are so far from being merely analytic that those who make this their touchstone might well question their truth. In the same way it is profoundly surprising that every densely packed interior mood should necessarily unpack itself into quite precise forms of response and setting, and the latter condense itself into the former, and so far is all this from being merely obvious that even a philosopher like Wittgenstein thought it merely factual and contingent.

The necessary being the necessary and not the trivial, necessary truths of essence may constantly shed fresh light on notions already had or defined, and so serve to delimit or describe them. The notion of description is also valuable as stimulating that 'seeing' use of expressions which alone gives philosophical research a direction, and prevents it from fumbling among trivialities.

Human experience and language are therefore swayed by powerful directive ideas each of which generates a systematic, extensible order into which the detailed deliverances of individual encounter may be fitted: such ideas are *a priori*, not in the sense of merely adding to the ideas derived from individual encounter, but in the sense of providing the framework for individual encounter and for ideas derived from it. Having them involves more than having notions which may or may not apply to the details of individual encounter; it is having the further confidence, not absolute nor unmodifiable, that we shall be able to apply such notions, that the world even in its unseen and unknown aspects will fit them. Each such *a priori* notion therefore dictates a pattern of future detailed experience, a pattern that can be imagined as unfulfilled, and even experienced as breaking down in some cases, and so always positively significant. We can study such ideas at work in our talk, whether ordinary or philosophical, but we can also study them at work in 'the appearances', in the actual phenomena, in the world as it comes before us and actually seems to us. This last is the best way since it brings out what is important and central, and what otherwise would remain hidden under trivialities and minutiae.

We here, however, come up against a central feature of life and experience: that the various directive ideas in terms of which the phenomena are ordered and articulated do not always square, that the pattern or order which one of them sets before us as a guiding framework runs athwart the pattern another sets before us, and that even in the pattern dictated by what may be called a single idea there are possibilities of alternative development, confusions of direction that make orderly extensions difficult. Antinomy, in other words, is an all-pervasive phenomenon in the experienced and interpreted world, and becomes more and more acute the more we attempt to focus phenomena clearly, to see them in an unshifting, fully revealing light. It is this all-pervasive presence of antinomy in the world of experience that makes us find the world a queer place, and that led Plato and ourselves to describe it as a cave. The all-pervasive antinomy of the world is far too serious and too deep to count as a merely formal contradiction, though it *can* be forced into that form if we choose. Nothing is easier than to rid oneself of such a formal contradiction: one can do so by simply specifying a respect or sense or manner in which one statement is true, and another in which its seeming contradictory is true. But such devices do nothing to remove the real conflicts involved, which are more like the discrepancies in a person's character, or in a statesman's policies, or in the story told by certain witnesses, which are not done away with by the mere fact that they are not flatly contradictory. The line here taken by most modern philosophers is an accommodation which pares or reduces or argues away one or other of the discrepant fundamentals. It is conceived to be the obligation of philosophers to make sense of experience as it actually stands, and to adjust fundamental concepts to meet it, rather than to modify or extend experience to fit such concepts. It is not seen that a clear division between experience and interpretative concepts is unfeasible, and that the best accommodation is the one that does the fullest justice to all the notional claims involved, intensifying them rather than watering them down, and being ready to extend experience in highly novel directions rather than remaining in hidebound contexts. All use of concepts like body, space, social mind, etc., goes beyond the immediate data in respect of the order it projects into experience, and there is no reason why, in quest of a deeper harmony, there should not be a much more revolutionary going beyond the data than is ordinarily practised. The accommodations we seek are at least accommodations that must live in the full consciousness of the antinomies it is their task to heal: they must explain rather than explain away such antinomies.

Before we attempt such explanations, it will be best if we run through some of the basic antinomies which emerged in the course of our first series of lectures. There were first the varied difficulties connected with the two great media of space and time, in which all bodies and conscious and unconscious organisms have their place, media which at one moment seem mere backgrounds for the coloured, figured, bulky things and occurrences displayed in them, but which can at any moment, by a figure-ground reversal, become themselves the substantial stuff of the world, in which things and occurrences are mere gaps and interruptions. This perpetual reversal, in which the full constantly becomes the vacuous, and the vacuous the full, embodies no idle aesthetic change in the look of things, but a change in our whole manner of conceiving them, on which many profound theoretical and practical consequences attend. To make the great media of the world mere extensions of the arrangements of the data that point them up for us, extensions like that of Adam's imagined ancestry, or the unfilled 'posts' in a projected secretariat, flatters our love of clear content at the expense of our deeper understanding. For hard, clear data are so fragmentary as to afford absolutely no firm foundation for the vast confidence we repose in the power of spatial and temporal arrangements to be moved and repeated without change, as also for our faith in the possibility of lines of unbroken communication, direct or indirect, between anything that has a place and a time and anything else that also has a place and a time. 'Empty' space and time are not only the most obdurately haunting, but also the most hard-worked of categories, representing as they do the 'permanent possibilities' of all that makes the 'external world' capable of effective handling, possibilities fortunately so much part of the phenomena that the maddest empiricism seldom tries to question or, more dangerously, to justify them. But to believe in the great media and their mute, background presence is obviously also to embark on the perilous ascent along which one absolute darkly succeeds another, and in which the test of authentic being is not so much making a difference, as being the inescapable presupposition of all differences. Tied up with these conflicts in regard to the relation of the great media to their occupants, go conflicts in regard to the modality of these relations. Sheer accident would seem to govern the relations of occupying events and objects to the great media of space and time, it being of their essence that they freely permit any and every filling or lack of filling. Yet, on the other hand, it is only in the free, undistorted, continuous behaviour of things and patterns, that the grand indifferences of space and time make themselves plain, and their dependence on such contents seems no mere issue for *our* verification, but an issue of *their* being. There are deep puzzles in this extraordinary dependence-in-independence which will again and again meet us in the human cave.

A further tension arises from the fact that the great media in question alternatively show themselves as the very type of the divisive and discrete, and then again as the very type of the continuous. Seen in one regard, nothing is so separative, so inviduating, as differences of spatio-temporal position: even in a monotonously repetitive wall-paper world, full of symmetrically placed identities of pattern continued *ad infinitum*, there remains the separateness of the this and the that, the here and the there, the now and the then, despite all indiscernibility of general description, and it is by the separateness of the zones that things continuously occupy, or the epochs through which they extend, that we are able to pin them down as *these* individual things, identified and reidentified on many occasions, and oppose them to *those* individual things which occupy a different place in the whole ordered picture. In the absence of temporal and local signature, individuation and identification might assume some wholly new and difficult form, as comes out in the speculative sound-world of Peter Strawson or in the angelology of St Thomas. And countless abstract matters assume manageable clarity by being set out side by side in the externality of an imaginary space. Yet these types of the discrete are also the very types of the continuous, the holding together, so that it is always artificial to imagine one can deal with one region, one period, in clear separation from another, that one can keep it from spilling over into its environment and untidily incorporating the latter in itself. We should like the parts of space and time to be separated by gulfs or fences, thick no-man's barriers that firmly keep them apart, but they are unhappily only separated by boundaries, which means that they are not really separated or kept apart at all. We can, if we like, take advantage of our own finitude and firmly distinguish where and when we are from where and when we are not, but even as we speak movement and the passage of time erode our clearly fixed delimitations. That everything is what it is and not some other thing, is an unexceptionable maxim, expressive of certain modes of understanding which it is profitable to apply in all or most of our first-order discourse. But second-order reflection shows that our maxim is unexceptionable precisely because it can never fit anything real, certainly nothing in which space and time play a part. Nowhere can we really perform the neat excision that would give us just this individual thing here and now placed, and distinct from that other individual thing. Each thing shades off into something that shades off into something, so that before one knows where one is, one is somewhere quite different, as everyone who has painted a large wall or been involved in a

live piece of argument well knows. Space and time point to two
wholly different types of treatment, the phenomena show themselves in two radically different ways, one of which leads to the
admirable fixities of Zeno and their working out by Dedekind,
Weierstrass and others, and the other of which leads to the 'infinite' of the Pythagoreans or the 'Great and Small' of Plato in
which nothing can be kept firmly within bounds but always pushes
on indefinitely in the direction of the ever greater or the ever less.
Our modern philosophy of mathematics has built on the πέρας, the
principle of Limit, which dominates most of ordinary discourse,
and has arrived at the transfinite and the continuous through this.
It might just as well have followed Plato and some of our ordinary
talk and built itself on the ἄπειρον, the principle of indefinite,
extensible continuity, and arrived at the natural numbers and other
clear abstractions through this. Certainly the two great media
which contain all phenomena evince both of these trends, and
evince them quarrelsomely and without final reconciliation. The
world at one moment falls apart into things or phases which have
nothing to do with one another, as at another moment its things
and phases melt tantalizingly into each other.

If the internal quarrels just indicated are common to the two
great media under examination, they are exacerbated to the last
extremity in the case of time. Our stress on phenomenology rather
than dialectic perhaps led us to underplay these quarrels in the
lectures of the previous session; we may therefore make brief
amends in this place. In the inner structure of time we have
extreme exclusiveness always alternating with extreme inclusive-
ness, absolute priority confessing itself to be most utterly derivative, permanence declaring itself in and through the sheerest
impermanence. Time is nothing without the plain distinction
between what now is, with its ineffable, final prerogative, and what
only enjoys the modally qualified status of *having* been or of being
about to be, which are no more instances of simple being than
probable, possible or putative being can be regarded as such. Yet
not only do we find the content of what *is*, without cease passing
from what merely *will* be to what *has* been, even as we try to lay
hold of it, only permitting us to grasp it in large, indefinite fashion,
but we see further, once the rough conventions of ordinary
language are disturbed, that the whole content of what now is or is
the case, is made up in equal and unlimited parts of what definitely

has been up to that moment, and of what possibly *will* be after it, with only a boundary, which really does not divide, between them. Here the past and future avenge themselves on the present, making its non-modal immediacy depend puzzlingly on their second-order status, so that it becomes obscure where the notional priorities lie, or if, indeed, we can fix them anywhere. And while, on the one hand, the order and distance of the points of time seems to be a mere frozen reflection of the order and intensity of the rush of happening through the present, it seems impossible, on the other hand, to give sense to either such order or intensity of 'rush' except in terms of such a contained reflection, so that the priorities are again confused. There is, further, the extraordinary asymmetry in virtue of which what is about to be may cover alternative possibilities, all but one of which become total impossibilities once the 'issue is decided', whereas no such alternatives obtain in the past, an asymmetry so extraordinary as to afford justification for those perverse constructions, often wrongly buttressed by formal logic, in which the future is given the settled character of the past or the past less readily given the unsettled character of the future. If to these real puzzles, which are part of the essential phenomenology of time, we add the unreal puzzles to which the abstract manipulations of mathematics give free rein, and allow them to override any and every difference of category—time being assimilated throughout to space—it is plain that the second of the great media is by far the shiftiest thing in our experience, and the most protean in its transformations. It can be reduced to relative fixity by a flat refusal to follow out any of the notional pressures that beset ordinary language, as I myself once tried to reduce it in a much reprinted article,[1] but the tendency of 'phenomena' to change and develop is as deeply characteristic as any first form revealed by them to unreflection.

If the great media of the phenomenal world are beset with fundamental antinomies, so too are their contents, the bodies which occupy them and change in them, and the intelligent minds which look out upon them from variously placed, animated bodily standpoints. Bodies, on the one hand, come before us as having or being something which enables them to fill or occupy space and prevent other bodies from tenanting the same space, and this

[1] 'Time: a Treatment of some Puzzles.' See *Logic and Language*, Series I, ed. Antony Flew (Basil Blackwell).

something is presupposed by all merely qualitative features, or by all possibilities of acting on other bodies or being acted on by them. Yet this the basic presupposition of bodily occupancy remains obdurately obscure, and resembles a 'wall' created by hypnotic suggestion or by a magical taboo. This puzzle of solidity concerns us at the macroscopic level, but it is not exorcized at the microscopic level, nor by letting a mere vocabulary of energy, wielded without categorial grasp, supersede one of bulk or stuff. Equally Janus-faced is the manner in which bodies come before us as undoubtedly single and individual, even if spread out over a region, and as therefore possibly having modes of action which appertain to them as *wholes*, and not necessarily to their parts, yet again as hanging together in some wholly external and in the last resort incomprehensible way, and as necessarily having *no* characters or modes of behaviour which are not a complex consequence of the modes of behaviour of their constituent parts. The idea of body is at once such as to demand and also to exclude mechanization, to demand explanation in terms of parts of parts without end, and yet to resist this self-destruction; this two-sided absurdity is practically resolved by an equally absurd compromise resting on the dubious warrant of experience. We find our 'irreducibles', our 'wholes', at what level seems most feasible, though the exponents of other sciences never think we have done so properly.

Implicit in the divisive, mechanistic way of considering bodies lies the impossibility that they should do more than obey some extremely austere set of laws of motion, moving and resting according to the simplest of formulae, and interfering with one another's rest or motion only by acts of pushing governed by formulae of similar simplicity. The seventeenth and eighteenth centuries developed all these demands in their purity, and adjusted them to the empirical detail actually encountered, in a manner now so overlaid by theory and experiment, that we hardly have an idea, austere or relaxed, of what bodies are or of what they may be capable. Implicit, however, in the totalistic way of considering bodies lies the possibility, not only that their parts should move and behave in consonance with one another and with the total pattern they form, but also, by an easy extension, that they should respond to remote bodies and bodily configurations in the manner characteristic of gravitational and other types of 'field'. There will always also be a tendency for the scandal of field-phenomena to resolve itself into some concealed form of pushing, but the push-philosophy, being ultimately incoherent, may very well have to come to terms with the field-philosophy or to give way to it.

Implicit in the field-philosophy is, however, the presence of what we have called physical intentionality, that analogue of conscious reference, in which a body's reactions are adjusted, and so are in a manner 'sensitive', to remote bodily facts which are, from the standpoint of the body concerned, absent and non-existent. From the possibility of adjusting to what is physically actual but remote, there is only a step to the possibility of adjusting to what is not yet, or, perhaps, never will be, physically actual, and hence of that immanent teleology which, once admitted as within the bodily repertoire, soon affords countless instances of its actual presence. Such teleology, however, never stably reveals itself as a simple bodily phenomenon: if at one moment it seems to explain rather than require explanation, at another moment it seems plain that it merely masks complex field-phenomena or even cases of mere clock-work. It remains deeply difficult, even absurd, that a body should adjust its behaviour to what exists *nowhere* in the bodily world, and we therefore have recourse to any way of regarding the matter which makes it merely *appear* that an ideal end is shaping the drift of development, while in reality this is entirely shaped by the unvaried behaviour of intricately inter-acting parts. The same tension becomes extreme when, as in complex physical systems like the brain, we constantly find the guidance of bodily change by remote resemblances, complex mathematical and logical relationships, etc., in the absence of any accompanying consciousness, and where the phenomena challenge us to see nothing in their changes beyond the quite unintelligent transformations possible to a thinking-machine. What we have to see in all the phenomena just set forth is a deep tension in the very notion and being of body, a tension between a readiness to transcend the immediate and the actual in a quasi-conscious, 'intentional' manner, and a tendency to slip back into being just where and when one is, into responding to nothing remote, nothing abstract, nothing that is not part and parcel of one's sheer spatial occupancy. This tension is felt by us 'in our bones', in what we know, despite surface-appearances, is really there, but it seems also to be present in bodies themselves, whose power to maintain complex integrations, and to be continuously guided by attenuated, abstract lines of relevance and affinity, is liable to be disrupted or weakened by death, fatigue or many forms of enfeeblement.

The difficulties we have so far dealt with are all on the purely corporeal plane, but it is, further, clearly in the repertoire of body, suitably organized and in action, to refer us 'inwards' to phenomena of higher order which, though concerned with bodies or 'of' bodies in some direct or remote manner, thereby successfully evince, not their bodily, but their intractably non-bodily character, and so create an opposition of the most trying sort, in which either member seems at once to require and yet also to exclude and repel the other. Thus the bodies which come before us and declare themselves to sight, touch and our other senses, can also, by a sort of inversion of their deliverances, make us aware of the manners in which *we* are sensitively affected by them, manners which not only bring into view unnoticed perspectival variations, which have to do with *us* and *our* relation to the bodies in question, but which also have that overallness, that reduction to felt singleness, which characterizes the interior life of mind, and is quite foreign to the dispersed, uncentred life of bodies. The 'inversion' in question as readily takes place in the case of other sensitive organic bodies as of our own: we 'know' how someone else feels the coldness of some marble surface on which his bare arm rests almost as clearly and as directly as we know how *we* feel in such a situation. It is not necessary that we should reflect on the way in which cold, that phenomenal feature of objects, is brought home to *us* in our feeling, in order to know how it is brought home to others.

The inversion in question works also in the case of the reactive tendencies, emotional and unemotional, exploratory or practical, which are operative and can become evident in each experient's phenomenally central organism, or in the remote organisms of other creatures. These tendencies can make themselves evident in external fashion, as modes of behaviour having the same 'outness' and distance as those of a glacier or a falling stone, but they can also make themselves evident in the condensed, personal form of an attitude lived through or felt, a feeling-ready-for or feeling-ready-to-do this or that, whether directly by the person who has them or 'sympathetically' by some bystander. In the same way the purely physical intentionality which we credit to the goal-directed organism or to a nerve-centre functioning unconsciously, refers us inwards to that mental directedness to things present and absent, things immediate and remote, things concrete and things abstract, of which there can at times be a direct reflex givenness and an inviolable certitude, and which can be given as the secret sense of the behaviour and signs of other living creatures and ourselves. In all these respects the purely physical extended phenomenon and the condensed interior phenomenon have the profoundest inner affinity and mutual fit: the one seems naturally to flow over into the other, the one is the correlate of the other in another medium, as it were, it is through the one that we know and know of the other, and that through a key which experience uses rather than fabricates. The full reasons for the apriorism we are adopting need not be rehearsed here.

Yet in all this affinity of the two media before us, disparateness and exclusiveness still make themselves felt: neither on reflection requires, or has a place for, the other. The physical medium has nowhere a place for that summing-up in unity of what lies dispersed, nor for that gesturing towards what is remote, abstract and not necessarily actual, which the other medium allows: it can at best offer us phenomena which *seem* to spring from such an interior source, but which yield us no convincing or understandable foothold in the latter. And the interior medium, in its turn, has no need for the exterior physical one, since the directedness of mind to this or that real or imaginary object seems a matter of the mind's own internal economy, and has no test that is not also an interior test. A state of mind is neither more nor less directed to a certain object because there is or is not such an object, or because it is or is not an object to other minds as well as one's own. There can likewise be no test of the reality of such an object which does not entirely fall within the experience of each person who has hazarded hypotheses as to its existence. One can indeed prove something to be real by appealing to the experience and testimony of others, but the existence of such experience and such testimony, and of such others, must be something whose tests lie, or could lie, in a man's own experience, and of whose validity he alone is the final judge. A number of persons can entertain and verify some hypothesis in a co-operative manner, performing the same experiments, witnessing their outcome and drawing the same conclusions, but they can do so only because each, with his experiences, is given in the experiences of each other, so that, while all carry out common tests, the tests are also carried out by each man severally. Each man, there-fore, in a sense inhabits his own intentional cosmos, in which other men and their concurrences occur as intentional objects, and so far is this from refuting an ordinary realism that it is a necessary con-dition of its truth: a conscious being cannot be said to inhabit a world which is not also, in all relevant particulars, a world for him. In a deep sense, further, all discourse with others must also be dis-course with self, since it is we who must interpret and evaluate all that others do and say: a reference to others can only take us out of our subjective quandaries if *we* decide that it does so. In a sense, therefore, a public language with agreed rules is only a particular sort of private language, and this is not so much a paradox as a simple truism. The very grammar of our talk of experience there-fore involves the limiting possibility, gratuitous perhaps but still genuine and indefeasibly 'part of the language', of a set of Cartesian minds each living in the experience of a world which has no being beyond the perceptions and references of the mind in question, which need not be a similar world to the world inhabited by an-other Cartesian mind, and which need not contain any true givenness of such another mind. That in such a limiting situation, which we perfectly understand, the discrepancy of the intentional worlds would be wholly undiscoverable, merely refutes the view which confounds the understandable with the discoverable, or meaning with validation.

What all of this involves is that, while the world of personal interiority is understandably tied up with the world of bodies in space, and so indirectly linked up into a system of mutually com-municating persons, there is still something not wholly under-standable in this understandability. A mind being a complete personal cosmos, it is sometimes not clear why the 'world' of its personal perception, belief and concern should in any way reflect the structure of a world with which it can stand in no real relation, from which it even differs radically in category. The world as perceived or believed by me is confusedly said to coincide with the world as it actually is, at least at some points and times, but this on reflection can seem as absurd as supposing that the characters of some fictional narrative could stray out of fiction and take their place among real persons. Once the infinite categorial gulf between the merely bracketed status of an object perceived or thought of, on the one hand, and an object *simpliciter*, on the other, has been adequately plumbed, it is no longer plain that there must tend to be some sort of coincidence or correspondence between them, and we no longer feel it probable that things must tend to give us ideas that are *of* them or of something like them. In the same manner once the infinite categorial gulf between other persons as given to us through sympathetic personal extension, however unlearnt and ultimate, has begun to yawn before us, we no longer feel confidence in any probable 'coincidence' or 'correspondence' of the former with the latter, nor even entire clarity as to what such a coincidence or correspondence might involve or mean.

We have dwelt rather sketchily on a wide range of philosophical issues in all of which there is a strange blend of dependence and independence, of requirement and indifference, of the supremely obvious and the totally mysterious. It is as wrong to dwell merely on the clear, gnostic side of these issues, to make philosophy merely analytic or descriptive, as it is to dwell, in traditional fashion, on the insoluble problems of philosophy, in quest of an explanation or justification whose very form eludes us. The suggestion we are to explore in the first half of these lectures is the suggestion that all these opposed ways of regarding things have their common ground in something of which we do not ordinarily form much notion at all, or which we tend to think of as in the last degree dependent and derivative: the life of common meanings and aims which conscious beings have with one another, the life which consists in intercourse, discourse and co-operation among persons and with the things which form an irremovable part of such intercourse, discourse and co-operation. This common conscious life we hold to be related to all the factors in the world, and the varied ways of seeing them, as an immanent end which all subserve, and not as anything underlying them or coming before them or causally responsible for them. This end is, moreover, not the end of anything or anyone, nor does it exist otherwise than as an ultimate fit, involving many impediments, among the factors in the world, or in an ultimate drift towards secure and intimate communication, in which it itself, the end, as the 'sense' and 'truth' of the world, will ultimately make itself manifest and evident. Our understanding of the world and its manifold opposi-tions depends, accordingly, on the abandonment of ways of thinking which look to elements and origins and defined ways of working, for one which sees in all these factors only constituitive moments of a single pervasive end which, however much it may be fully declared and lucid to self only in its final outcome, must none the less be thought of as including and wholly explaining all the elements, circumstances and ways of working which we say lead up to it. Our end must be 'infinite' in the Hegelian sense of being implicit in and including all its instrumentalities, and so being self-realizing and self-explanatory.

The deep paradox of this mode of conceiving, its almost wilful subversion of established distinctions and thought-procedures, need not be gainsaid: its justification lies in the sheer impotence of any other approach to steer clear of antinomies, as much as in the sheer logical power with which it makes conflicts redound to its own credibility. For we can understand how the media of space and time, on the one hand, and their occupants on the other, can play their queer game of dependence-in-independence, if we see the essence of each in the role it plays in conjunction with the other in forwarding an ultimate lucidity, the great media precisely permitting that contingent occupancy, that limited separateness and independent mobility, which provide manageable, manipulable 'pieces' for theory and practice to play with, while they also firmly place all such pieces on a continuous world-board, permit their behaviour and surroundings to be appropriately extrapolated, and enable the players to confront each other on a common field or territory. The great media and their diversified occupancy are indeed perfectly tailored to suit the emergence of that enquiry, that constructive spontaneity, that zestful sparring and co-operation, and that final victorious self-consciousness and self-enjoyment, in which rational, social mind consists.

If we now turn to the multiple antinomies of totalism and mechanism, of physical intentionalism and its reductivist negation, of the interior-exterior double-aspect view which, entirely understandable in its living, imaginative use, breaks up into various surd dualisms on the jagged rocks of 'clear ideas', as well as all the epistemological antinomies according to which the manner in which nature regularly meets our cognitive anticipations is at one moment a thing entirely likely and understandable, while at another time it assumes the character of a perpetual, uncovenanted miracle—all these antinomies show some signs of dissolving when we cease to look for a factor or factors responsible for the sides of the conflict and their coming together, or cease to think in terms of existences which underlie other existences and manifestations, and begin instead to think in terms of an interior programme in the light of which all these disparate things have a function and a role. If we follow this line, we can see in the tendencies towards mere inertia, mechanism and simple location which characterize phenomenal nature throughout, the necessary foil to the unitive, teleological, intentional, inward-pointing and inward-outward-accommodating tendencies which are equally necessary to it. It is, we may say, precisely in overcoming mere inertia, etc., that organic being exists, and were the problems of self-maintenance, self-replenishment, adjustment to environmental resistances, reproductive continuity, etc., removed, there could be no life as we know it. Inert, non-living matter must not, however, be thought to be *used* organically by some outside agency, spiritual or otherwise, but as merely fulfilling its own role when with creaks and groans it gets impressed into organic service. It is life in the sense of a goal of actual livingness which here has the explanatory priority, not any bodily or spiritual agency which either has or can impart life. In the same way the complex behaviour of bodily realities in the scientific situation, their initial coy opacity, their flouting of countless approaches and their sudden, astonishing yielding to others, their ready breakdown when subjected to questions and tests often based on models and formulae of childlike simplicity, as well as their final, teasing retention of residual mysteries which may demand total reorientations when all seemed lucid and secure: all these facts show bodies as having an intrinsic destiny, a making-towards, the manipulations of the laboratory and the lucidities of the scientific paper, and with exactly the right amount of resistance and friction that will ensure the strength and perpetuity of the scientific endeavour. If they were insolubly enigmatic or carried their secrets on their faces, there could be no science, and it is as inherently oriented towards the possibility of science, that they do neither. Scientists may not like to confess these articles of faith, but they unhesitatingly act on them. To say all this is emphatically *not* to say that anything thus oriented things, whether a conscious divine scientist or an unconscious scientist immanent in nature: this would in fact replace radical teleology by a form of causality. It is only to say that bodies are inherently accommodated to the scientific process even if they have to wait for millennia to fulfil their role in it, perhaps

c

vainly, and just as it is the complementary role of other minded bodies, perhaps frustratedly, to be witnesses, experimenters and theorists in such a process. Science, in short, is no peripheral function of the natural world, but its 'sacrament of the altar', a proceeding more central to it than, say, entropy. The same can be argued to hold, *mutatis mutandis*, of the practical transformation of the world to suit rational convenience, and its aesthetic transformation to minister to rational delight. What we are saying has, of course, its own profound absurdities, but the absurdities we are only too ready to see in it are largely its mere difference from the laughably absurd ways of viewing things which were abolished in our first series of lectures. The unprompted hurrying of disparate things towards a common co-operative assignation, which, like Mohammed's coffin, hangs suspended over them in the ether of the unrealized, may have its own incredibility, but this is as nothing compared with the incredibility of the dualisms and pluralisms studied in our previous series.

If we now turn to the strange problems of accessibility and inaccessibility, knowability and total unknowability, which confront us in the relations of an ego to other egos, and even in the relations of an ego to itself, we are faced with the supreme test for the radical teleology we are considering. We may say that the rational, shared life of mind, and its capacity for parallax and cross-illumination, all stem from the ground-level separateness of individual minds, and would be impossible without this. Wittgenstein's famous strictures upon the possibility of a private language may have the imperfectly worked-out character of all his ideas, but they stress the need for confirmation from a wholly outside source to give a precious note of authentication to our notions and assertions. We may say that we are greatly set apart *in order that* bridges of understanding may be built among us, this 'in order that' not being anything that presupposes ourselves and our apartness nor indeed anything else at all, but which totally explains all circumstances of our apart existence as well as their transcendence. The explanation of course goes further than the field of cognition and covers all those forms of co-operative endeavour, emotional, practical, religious, etc., which are not so much human, rational and spiritual as they are humanity, rationality and spirituality themselves. So much at least is the lesson of the great German idealistic classics of which Fichte's *Wissenschaftslehre* and Hegel's

Phänomenologie des Geistes are the greatest. And all the dizzying antinomies of the graspable ungraspability of different egos to one another, and even of an ego to itself, and again of their total perspicuity, not only to themselves but to one another, all show up as devices through which our common spiritual life gains and maintains what may be called its 'transcendental' character, and through which, as having this function, these devices are themselves made part of this common rational spiritual life itself. It is the open sky and its light which form the inescapable upper zone of our variously partitioned chambers, but its being a sky and open depends on those lower partitionings which at its own level vanish.

In the next four lectures we shall try to bring out the logical power and fruitfulness of these essentially Germanic notions, the 'Germanic Theology' as we may call them, only to pass on, in the last five lectures, to a transcendentalism and a theology which are only marginally Germanic in spirit.

THE REALM OF NOTIONS
AND MEANINGS

———————

At our present stage of consideration, as our last lecture sought to explain, we are to look at the phenomena of cave-life, of human existence in this world, from an extraordinarily remote, general elevation: if we have not succeeded in getting outside of the cave, we shall at least be floating about in its upper regions, above its many sharp divisions. At this elevation we come to be among all sorts of new detached phenomena—qualities, forms, relations, types, categories, requirements, values—all cut loose from their original moorings, and as much interlinked and intertangled *with one another* as with the phenomena at levels beneath. The phenomena of these higher levels are the abstracta, the entities of reason, the true idols of the cave, the overarching second nature which, one is tempted to say, the communicating minds of men educe from the particularities and immediacies of the first nature around them and within them, inject into their language, and erect into a common frame of reference in terms of which the world and themselves can be seen and understood and spoken of. Only to speak in this way would be to espouse the empiricist legend and the particularist or individualist ontology, both of which are gravely unequal to portraying the phenomena of the human cave. For, though our approach to them may be difficult and indirect, and a product of much verbal education, entities of reason are undoubtedly part of the phenomena of developed experience: we understand and fathom what it is to be painful, proud, purple, unique, related in more ways to one thing than to another, etc., etc., as much as we understand and fathom the particular plants, people, domestic utensils and environmental hazards and facilities that lie around us. They are, in fact, in many ways clearer phenomena, better lighted and presented, than the confused, dark, multiply suggestive particularities of sense-perception: like models in some brilliant fashion-show, they take the stage, bow, doff or don this or that, flutter their skirts generally and depart. And if our grasp of their specificity is often dry and blunt, as in all prosy forms of thought and discourse, it may assume any degree of impassioned engagement as our understanding of poetry and imaginative literature abundantly shows.

At the level of our consideration, the phenomena of the upper cave are not, in fact, secondary and derivative at all. They are part and parcel of the shared life of understanding, which is for us, for the time being, the primary phenomenon, the explanatory point of absoluteness in the human cave, the phenomenon in their bearing on which all other phenomena are viewed, and in terms of which they are to be understood. For a long course of antimony has made us cease to think merely in terms of the bodies and spaces and times and embodied intelligent egos of the lower regions of the cave, according to one or other of *them* some sort of ontological priority over the others. Thought that operates in terms of mere foundations, existential priorities, will never, we have decided, sustain itself adequately: we must look to some outcome, some unifying end, in relation to which all these competing priorities can play a part or have a role. That outcome, that end, we have seen in the rational life of communicating persons. The separateness of persons, with its moments of metaphysical anguish and darkness, is basically a *device* that makes this rational, communal life possible, as the merely material world, with its overloaded detail and dizzying mixture of regularity and anomaly, provides the stage-scenery and properties among and through which this rational communal life can be conducted. It is 'for us men' and our rational education that this complex machinery is there at all, though it has not, on our view, been put there by anyone, whether human or superhuman. The radical teleology with which we are now working, has, we may be sure, its own brand of absurdity and incredibility, but this will at least be quite different from the older types of absurdity and incredibility that we found so unenlightening. We shall therefore not question our radical teleology till we come to our fifth lecture. What we shall do in the next few lectures will be to explore the peculiarities of the hypostatic activity through which creatures of reason are summoned up for us and come to be built hierarchically on one another. We shall be concerned, in successive lectures, first with the products of ordinary abstraction, next with the special products of value-hypostatization, and then, lastly, with the level of religious projection, of theogony, the three zones into which the upper reaches of the cave may most conveniently be divided.

The phenomenology of the upper reaches of the cave may best be approached by way of the notion of 'conscious light' or 'angle'. It is, as we saw, the essence of the conscious life of an ego to be *of* a thing or class of things or a situation or class of situations, which perhaps, but not necessarily, have a place in the order of things to which we give the preferred status of 'realities'. All conscious life is referential, though the word 'referential' must not be given the modern implication of involving an actual referent, a circumstance necessary only to the *success* of a reference, which involves matters going beyond the features which make it referential. Confusion would be avoided if we distinguished between the 'reference' or 'referential character' of a conscious state, and the *application* which constitutes the success of its reference: a reference which applies, e.g., to an object, is like a bowshot which hits its target, whereas a reference that lacks application is like a bowshot that shoots wide of its mark. Quite distinct from the referential dimensions of conscious life are the dimensions to which reference is irrelevant: here, as sketched in a previous lecture, we have the dimensions of the focally and the marginally given, the dimensions of the illustratively, 'seeingly', and the non-illustratively, 'emptily' given, and finally, and for our present purposes most importantly, the infinitely diversified dimension of 'conscious light.'

What we have in mind are the remarkable differences in which it is as much *we* who approach our object differently as it is *our object* which impresses us differently, which comes before us in a different respect or regard, differences which are as readily given a subjective as an objective colouring and attachment, being in fact among the differences in which the whole subjective-objective distinction itself first comes to light. An object seen or thought of can be seen as being thus or thus qualified, or as being thus or thus knit together or related to other objects, it can be seen or thought of as *there*, existent, and not replaced by a corresponding gap or absence, it can be seen as involving these or those lacks or deficiencies, these or those open possibilities, these or those elements of fixity and invariance, and so on. In each of these cases we see or think of our object or objects, or our situation, in this or that 'light',

and the 'light' in which we see it floats ambiguously between ourselves and the thing or situation seen or thought of, so that it is as
much a part of our individual personal life as of the parcelled,
divided world of things around us, while at other times it seems to
be broken by what it connects into two wholly diverse, if correlated
aspects: the seeing or conceiving of something *as*, e.g., a rather
washed out red cushion, on the one hand, and its simply *being* such
a washed out red cushion, on the other. What we are here dealing
with is the sort of primary abstraction of seeing or thinking of
something only *qua* this or *qua* that, or seeing or thinking of it, in
Berkeley's phrase, so far forth and no further, an abstraction which
would seem to be part of all conscious reference, as opposed to
those merely facultative confrontations in which, not making anything of what lies before us, it is only by courtesy that we can be
said to have anything before us at all.

Differences in conscious light of course acquire systematic fixity
in language and its forms: it is in language and language alone that
we can refer to something as being about to happen the day after
tomorrow, as reversing a policy that had been pursued over a long
period, and so on. But it would be gravely misguided to think that
there were not many differentiations of 'light' which preceded and
conditioned linguistic usage: the simple tense-distinctions, for
example, the distinction between presence and absence, the distinctions of readiness and unreadiness, etc., etc. The basic linguistic differences between sense, reference and application have a
pre-linguistic basis, and the 'light' in which things are seen or
thought of first provides the sense of an expression which is used
to refer, and, if successfully used, to apply to such things. It is
further clear that it is part and parcel of conscious experience that
the seeing or thinking of things in varying lights should have
behind it an ever enriched marginal or dispositional background:
what we now see in this light, is what we have seen in that light and
in that light, and what we are again ready to see in all the lights in
question. Also part of conscious experience is a vaguer background
of open possibilities: what we have seen in certain specified lights
is what we shall or may see in countless further unspecified lights.
All this is reflected in the subject-predicate structure of language,
in which there is always an open possibility of further predication,
as well as an identity of subject or subject-matter that will persist
through it.

It is important here to note that through all this variation of conscious light there may be seen to run a vein of deep generality or community: any light in which anything is seen or thought of is a light in which *other* things could have been seen or thought of, and it is also a light in which the same or other things could be seen or thought of on many occasions and by a diversity of persons. In other words, while there may be particularity in the objects of our references, and particularity in the occasions and performers of such references, there is always unfettered generality in the lights in which the references are made. This is the foundation of the perhaps exaggerated Hegelian doctrine of the universal character of *all* features and factors in thought and discourse, even of such as are avowedly demonstrative and tied to the here, now, and the exclusive personal 'I'. Obviously a general predicament lurks even in reference to such immediacies and particularities. It is in a sense always *we*, an unboundedly variable subject, that is in *this* unboundedly variable situation, and in it *here* and *now*, even if we think we can give such free variables a not further describable precise value on each occasion of their use. It is also the foundation of the somewhat exaggerated denial of the possibility of a private language: for what this doctrine really amounts to is that nothing in a reference apart from certain necessarily unshared particulars, is intrinsically unshareable and incommunicable. If, owing to some oddity or defect of sensibility, there is a light in which an object is seen by A in which it cannot be seen by B, this is plainly an accidental failure in communication. *A could* have had senses which would have shown him objects just as they appear to B, and all ordinary discourse proceeds on the assumption that it is in fact inherently likely or 'normal' that this should be the case, that while we can understand that it should *not* be so, either normally or at all, what we thus understand represents something quite gratuitous, something in which we shall never have the slightest *reason* to believe. This strange mixture of absolutely understanding a possibility that we reject with almost equal certainty, is part of the unquestioned phenomenology of the situation. In the same way, if there is some posture of the mind which A can take up to an object, and which does not fall within B's repertoire, this too is given as a merely accidental limitation: every access of clearness, illustration and conscious light of which A is capable, is also given as one of which B is intrinsically capable. That a thought *can* be communicated in all but the point of particularity from which it originates, or to which it applies, is part of what we understand by a thought. And even, as we have said, the incommunicable individuality of our references is in a *general* manner communicable, since *everyone* is necessarily this one, i.e. an individual, and lives through references non-recurrent and particular, and which may have points of attachment which are also so. However we look on things in experience and thought, and however we look on our own selves and their experiences, is therefore intrinsically a common, a shareable matter, and can accordingly be given a fixed form and currency in the use of some particular expression.

What we are, however, further maintaining is that to see things in any conscious light is in a sense to rise above one's own personal particularity and the sheer particularities of one's environmental position, and to enjoy a life that is in principle common: language, with its fixed rules and its fixed points of attachment and ostension, merely serves to ensure and regularize the publicity, the commonness of intent and import, which is the essence of thought as such. Which must not, however, be distorted into the doctrine that the particular circumstances in which we learn languages, and the environmental oddities to which such learning is attached, set limits to the range of what can be communicated and built into linguistic usage. Some things, e.g. the red and the blue, enter into the sphere of discourse because we are shown instances of them, other things, e.g. mental apartness, enter the sphere of discourse even though it is quite impossible to show instances of them, and yet other things, e.g. certain basic categories, enter the sphere of discourse because, however much we try, it is impossible to find anything which is *not* an instance of them. The function of ostension is often as much to direct our thought *away* from what comes before us as to direct our attention to what is there, or to direct our attention to what is so all-pervasive that it cannot, except in general contrast with what can be as much presented as *not* presented, be brought before us at all.

The common life of thought we have been sketching, with the language which gives it content and currency is, at the stage at which we (and the 'phenomena') have now arrived, a more important and logically central feature than the particularities, personal and environmental, from which it takes its rise. It is, as we have said, in a sense peculiar and ultimate, *for the sake of* this common thought-life that these particularities can be held to exist or to be there at all. The thought-life in question is, however, capable of a further impressive performance, or endless series of performances, in virtue of which its sphere of objects can be indefinitely augmented, thereby acquiring a riches which can only through confusion be found embarrassing. The performances we are to deal with are those of hypostasis, or of abstraction in the strict sense of the word, the passage from something red to red*ness* as such, from the situation in which *both* Jane and Mary are washing to the general possibility of something's being true of *both* of two things, and so on. Such performances plainly involve language; from a non-substantival, synsemantic way of talking, we proceed in a regular manner to a substantival manner of talking, and it is not easy to imagine such a performance being carried out without the help of the thing-like, substantival suggestions of separate words and phrases. But it is easy to pass from this admission to a view according to which the step is largely misguided and misleading, according to which it only serves to people the world with fictions, and springs from the basic confusion of imagining that every expression that *helps* in reference has also an independent referential function, that there is some object or objective feature it brings before us, and of which it can rightly be regarded as a name. Whereas it may be argued against all this that the step involved in hypostasis genuinely serves to bring to light phenomena infinitely more varied and interesting than the lowest-order population of the world, and that it, moreover, brings logical power and richness into the phenomena which cannot be discovered by any mere scratching about on the logical ground.

The nature of hypostasis will be best seen by considering one or two examples. Let us imagine that I see someone in the marketplace at Pella and remark 'There goes the teacher of Alexander'. I shall then have directed my mind to a particular individual present to my senses, and shall further have seen him in a particular light, as being one who teaches, and who exercises this function in regard to the local crown-prince, Alexander. The intentionality involved in this relatively simple reference craves a carrying-out and a carrying-further by a vast family of further intentions, some of which will also *fulfil* or illustrate it in various ways, as, e.g., by presenting us with situations in which Aristotle is shown *with* Alexander, and as actually instructing him. But my reference is limited in the sense that in it I do not refer to Aristotle in *every* respect in which it would be possible to refer to him—I may not, for instance, even have heard that he is a pupil of a famous Athenian Professor called Plato—and that while he comes before me as something which can be teased out into dizzying complexity, involving much border-line obscurity, this yet cannot be teased out into more than a thin excerpt of all that could be asserted of Aristotle the man. My reference, in other words, has a fairly limited sense or scope, even if it leaves room for indefinite additions, and to conceive of someone as the teacher of Alexander is to fall vastly short of conceiving him as *all* that he is or could be.

So far we have a case merely of the angular purblindness essential to all consciousness, not anything that properly merits the title of abstraction. It is however, possible for us as thinking persons to reflect on our previous act of reference, or on the way in which it was directed to its theme of concern, and on that theme of concern *to the extent* that it was made the target of our reference. What this means is that we can achieve a remarkable feat of retractation in which the open becomes the closed, the loose rigid, the developing frozen, and where we deliberately, on one pretext or another, stay confined in this scope of our previous reference and refuse to budge beyond it, thereby achieving that astonishing conceptual death, that separation of the essentially inseparable, which Hegel describes in the Preface to the *Phenomenology*, and which he sees as the necessary prelude to the highest forms of rational, conceptual life. The kind of retractation we are considering can be very various: it can take the form of considering only the scope of the approach represented by the phrase 'The teacher of Alexander' or, alternatively, the objective coverage of this phrase, the object intended *to the extent* that it is so intended. We can consider, in other words, what precisely it means for someone to think of Aristotle as a teacher of Alexander, its cash-value in terms of personal awareness, and we can consider, what is the same thing seen by a kind of projective turning-inside-out, what it means for Aristotle to be thus characterized. We shall leave undetermined which of these senses, the subjective or the objective, corresponds to the *Sinn*, the sense, which fulfils so important a role in Frege's semantic theory. In general, our act of retractation or abstraction can bring to light a large number of differing abstracta, particularly if different groups of words are selected: we can consider the meaning or sense of the various expressions 'There goes the teacher of Alexander', 'the teacher of Alexander', 'teacher of Alexander', 'teacher of', 'of Alexander', 'of', 'Alexander', etc. We can consider what exactly it is for the teacher of Alexander to go by, what exactly it is to be *the* teacher of Alexander or *a* teacher of Alexander, or to teach Alexander, or to be the teacher of anyone, etc. In talking of 'meanings' or 'senses', we are, on the whole, looking at the matter non-objectively, as is not the case when we speak of '*being* a teacher of Alexander', etc. This appears in the fact that it would be somewhat unnatural to say that being a teacher of Alexander was a meaning or sense, whereas it would be quite natural to say that it was a property, an abstract something, possessed by Aristotle, and so forth. If the sense of an expression represents the direction of a verbalized intention, its 'intentional object' represents the object of that intention artificially limited by the direction in question. The notion of limitation, of an artificial stopping-short, of a cutting adrift, is part and parcel of all the entities that are now under consideration. A non-abstract reference has a limited scope, but it is also *open* in its limitation: in thinking of Aristotle as a teacher of Alexander, I am at least ready to think of him as a son of a specific person, the pupil of a specific person, or as born in a specific place, etc. But in thinking of such abstracta as the sense of the expression 'Aristotle was a teacher of Alexander', as the property of being a teacher of Alexander, or the proposition that Aristotle taught Alexander, as the intentional object *Aristotle the teacher of Alexander*, etc., all this openness vanishes. While what I have before me may have rough edges and gaps to be filled, it is no longer permissible to fill them. The sense of 'being a pupil of Plato' falls quite outside of the sense of 'being a teacher of Alexander', outside of the scope of what it is to teach Alexander, outside of the content of the proposition that Aristotle taught Alexander, outside of the intentional object present in my reference when I recognized Aristotle in the market-place. And, being thus abstractly cut short, the abstracta in question are necessarily *new* objects, separate from the old ones from which they were derived, and better describable in separatistic and Platonic, than in Aristotelian terms. Locke was, moreover, perfectly right in seeing the absurdity in some of the abstracta thus constituted, and in seeing them, in all their absurdity, as part of the real phenomenology of the situation. The triangle as such has an incompleteness of specifiable character incompatible with its status as a triangle, and even being triangular is absurd in its abstract divorce from context.

That the hypostasis or abstraction just mentioned—the turning of a reference with limited but open scope, into a reference which freezes its scope at the previous point of limitation—is a psychologically genuine and epistemologically important process, would, of course, be questioned by many. Many would doubt whether there is, or can be, a precise specification of inner experience answering the sense of a phrase like 'being true of both of two objects', whether anything *could* correspond to it but the *use* of more natural phrases which its abstract form travesties. No one, however, for whom it was a momentous issue whether or not *both* of two possibilities were realized, and who then, looking across the room, saw that *both* were, can doubt that there is a uniquely specific interior realization of 'bothness', or of any other abstract feature, however formal and incapable of separate exemplification. Phrases of the form *what it is for something to be such and such* plainly indicate something of which there may be a vivid interior realization, directed precisely to what the phrase covers and nothing beyond, and this as much in the most rarefied, higher-order formal case, as in the case of the separable features of objects which seem ready to drop off like ripe plums into our hand.[1] And that the interior realization is pragmatically fruitful lies in the fact that it permits us to deal unconfusedly with the innumerable lights in which things show themselves, and to see these lights in higher-order lights and so on *ad infinitum*, in a manner which would be impossible without reification or hypostatization. It is, for example, only because likelihood or probability has been reified or hypostatized, and not left in the synsemantic state of a merely modal qualification of other verbs ('It will probably rain', etc.), that the vast conceptual structures built upon it have become possible at all. True, these structures have confused many, and have led to a search for probabilities among the first-order characters and relations of objects, but for the wise they have made possible the running up and down of the conceptual ladder in which all true science consists. Only empiricism and the dictates of certain works on English usage have made it seem respectable and enlightening

[1] The point of the above passage is, in part, to attack the attack on abstraction in Peter Geach's *Mental Acts*.

to run *down* the conceptual ladder and never to run up it, whereas the rising to an embracing abstraction, and the due and solemn naming of it, is as essential to understanding, as is the constant running down from it to the applications which fall under it.

Here too a much misunderstood dictum attributed to William of Ockham has played its deplorable part, making us forget that, while certain conceptual multiplications, particularly in natural science, may well be a dangerous redundancy, the very essence of thought is in a sense to multiply entities, every light in which things are seen being the foundation for further critical and assessing lights, and so on *ad infinitum*. Such infinity terrifies only because we fail to realize that it is an infinity of intentionality, an infinity no more noxious than that of the endless images formed in two mutually confronting mirrors. The meanings, propositions, universals, intentional objects, etc., which are thus generated only need enjoy a bracketed, intentional inexistence: they need be there only in the sense that there are, or may be, higher intentions directed upon them, which never entails or permits us to make of them genuine subjects of predications. And their merely intentional status permits them to have a summary and an illuminative use which is not nullified by the inherent absurdity involved in the refusal to specify them completely.

The common life of mind consists, therefore, in seeing the particularities of personal and environmental existence in lights that are universal and common as among objects, and likewise universal and common as among thinking persons, and it consists, further, in the use of these lights, by way of the words which give them a seeming thinghood, for the setting up, the hypostasis, of an endless hierarchy of abstractions, which preside, like a panel of magistrates, in their public majesty, even when what falls under their jurisdiction is variable and altogether lacking. These abstractions are, of course, of various sorts—types, classes, characters, relations, relational properties, numbers, negations, disjunctions, truth-values, variables, tenses, modalities, etc.—and the setting up of each is the subject-matter of a special study such as is to some extent found in the various writings of Husserl, as well as in some fine parts of the *Logics* of Bradley and Bosanquet, where the origins of such things as negations, hypotheticals, etc., is treated with some care and brilliance. It is not our task in the present lectures to do any of this detailed constitution-theory: suffice it to say, in general, that the mind is capable of seeing things or thinking of things in a great number of conscious lights, simple and complex, and that further it is capable, through self-retractation, of employing these lights to present truncated, abstract, artificially frozen objects which stay within the precise coverage of the lights in question, which need have only an intentional inexistence, but which have profound value both in lending precision and distinctness to the coverage of each conscious light, and so enabling us better to understand the cases we see in terms of it, and also by making the coverage of the light the subject of new, higher-order comparisons and predications, thus gaining an ever deepening grasp of the whole eidetic territory.

What it is important, further, to stress is that, even at the highest level of abstraction, it is always possible to undo whatever damage may have been done by the truncation or freezing involved in all abstraction. We can reintegrate abstractions into abstractions of any degree of interior richness and complexity as when, for example, we combine separate characters into some highly complex characterization or description, and propositions into a complex propositional system, or a fictional narrative or even a science. It is here important that we should keep in mind the difference of two modes of procedures which belong to quite different types of discourse: the procedure in which we deal with first-order material in a variety of conscious lights, describe an object to ourselves, utter or hear a connected narrative, study a science which deals with some special field in the real world, e.g. the past of man or of the earth's rocks, and the second-order procedure which deals with such descriptions, narratives, sciences, as an ordered assemblage of abstract characterizations, propositions, etc. There are two senses, for example, of every science, every 'ology', a sense in which it embraces a field of phenomena in the real world, and a sense in which it embraces only a set of propositions, definitions, concepts, etc., which are to be found in books, lectures and other modes of communication. There is a geology which embraces the rocks on the ground-floor of the cave, and a geology which floats in the upper regions of the cave, and consists only of propositions about rocks. One can pass from one geology to the other much in the manner in which one can pass from looking at the world through elaborately coloured, engraved spectacles to taking off the spectacles and considering the colours and engravings upon them.

Everything, however, detailed and particular, that is present on the lower floor of the cave, can in fact be taken up into its upper reaches: even the contents of a trivial day's diary, full of nugatory events, constitute an eternal meaning, all stateable in general terms that all men at all times can understand. Plato in later life was beginning to be worried by the way in which the turbidities of the world of sense could not be kept from filtering through into the world of forms: we, on the other hand, may be pleased by such infiltration. For, provided one has some relatively clear, tone-setting members in the conceptual field, it does not matter how many turbid, ragged, squalidly empirical members one also admits.

Here, however, we have to direct attention to a science which holds sway in the highest reaches of the cave, and which holds sway, not as some frozen set of propositions (though it can also be presented in this form), but as a science which concerns itself with abstracta and with manipulating and transforming them. This science of second intentions can be given various names, but in the present lecture I propose to give it the ancient, well-established name of 'logic', though perhaps the titles 'meta-logic' or 'philosophical logic' or 'philosophy of logic' might suit it better. I shall now for the remainder of this lecture be concerned to make a few unusual statements about this logic, statements which will disturb you only because the true purport and implications of the science have been utterly lost sight of. I shall try to show in this logic, properly understood, nothing beyond a higher expression of the pervasive rational teleology among all objects in the world and the communicating minds which have to deal with them. Logic is an expression of the existence of everything for a mutually recognizant society of minds which has become for the moment our explanatory absolute.

Logic, as I propose to understand it, is first of all concerned with the *categories* of abstracta (and of the conscious lights they abstract from) which we shall admit into our discourse, and with the principles which tell us how they could fulfil their role in the propositions which are in some sense the units of understanding and communication. Among these categories there is unquestionably that of the *first* subjects of discourse, the thematic *things* that can be seen in various conscious lights and, at a more sophisticated level, brought under corresponding abstractions (e.g. as being red or as being instances of redness). Objections might be made to treating these first subjects of discourse as themselves abstract, but from the point of view of understanding and communication this is what they are: they are the mere first termini, the points of attachment of discourse, the things shown in various communicable lights. It is important to stress that though the mere forms of discourse *say* nothing about these first subjects they *presuppose* much regarding them: that they are many and diverse, that they are identical and identifiable in many contexts, and by many speakers and thinkers, that they have unique places in some total order which makes their picking-out possible, that they are points of attachment of countless characterizing and relational lights which attach also to other prime subjects, that none of these lights quarrel or conflict with one another, that the prime subjects are exhaustively characterizable and definite in every respect, etc., etc. It is obvious that these prime subjects of discourse are the ordinary population of the bodily world or of some similar first-order system, and that in default of some such subjects there could be no abstract category as that of prime subjects at all. Other subjects of discourse will arise in indefinite numbers: things abstract and momentary and subjective and metaphysical and monistically absolute in all their varieties, and there is absolutely no reason why some of these may not, in a revised, deepened form of diction, come to occupy the position of prime subjects from which they were originally remote. Characters may arguably end, as in Platonism, in becoming more substantial than their instances, or our original subjects may end, as in Spinozism, by becoming mere modes of a single absolute prime subject. All these new subjects must stand, however, in some original relation to those straightforward first subjects of which bodies are the paradigm, and the latter can only be demoted from their prime position if they have first held it.

It will be necessary for us to say much regarding the other higher categories and their necessity for understanding and communication. Characters, e.g., must not be indefinitely diverse nor belonging in all cases to single individuals, if they are to fulfil their role of sorting things out, of placing them in an understandable order of kinds. Propositions are, further, among the particularly important abstracta which thoughtful retractation sets up as new intentional objects: having seen A, a logical subject, in a certain conscious light, and having replaced that conscious light by an abstract character

D

or relation or other determination, we can conceive just what it is for A to have that character or to stand in that relation or other determination, and are then framing the new and valuable abstraction of the λεκτόν or proposition. Among such propositions no distinction is more important than that of the asserted, the given as true, on the one hand, and the unasserted, the not so given, on the other, whether or not we represent assertion or 'truth' by a special sign, or merely show it by the non-subordinated occurrence of a sentence, the form of its verbs, etc. Yet this distinction is not one that is understandable until merely cited, subordinated occurrences of propositions can be opposed to independent ones, and this in turn can have no meaning if we could not start from the compulsively fulfilling experience of sense-confrontation, the same for others as ourselves, which by fulfilling all our meanings, utterly differentiates the imaginary from the real, and unless there were also that widely-ranging, systematic interconnection of things, whether by space and time or by special links of causality, which enables us to admit one propositional unit as 'fitting in' with the total pattern of things, while another gets bracketed as embodying an illusion or an error, and is only as such incorporated in the total picture. In default of the compulsively fulfilling shareable experiences of the senses, and in default of the discoverable interconnection just mentioned, and the more or less monistic character of the system they generate, there could be neither truth, nor belief (which is the claim to have truth) nor knowledge (which is the well justified claim to possess the same). Truth, belief and knowledge range, of course, over territories remote from the bodily and the sensuous: they cover the abstract, the interior, the possible, the transcendently metaphysical. Perverse belief is further possible in what is absurd and groundless and unintelligible simply *because* it has these belief-repellent characters. But such extensions and perversions of the believing attitude all point back to ordinary belief, and this presupposes the possibility of compulsive, public, sensory fulfilment, and far-reaching coherence among what is thus compulsively given, as well as our unlearnt power to use the notion of intentional bracketing. These notions may be modified beyond all recognition as we deepen our phenomenological insight, but such deepened insight always builds upon and incorporates its origins. All these immense phenomenological and ontological commitments, with their revisionary extensions, lie concealed beyond the simple formal use of p, q, r in an ordinary propositional calculus.

A large number of ontological and phenomenological commitments come out in our ordinary approaches, though they have not as yet received full acceptance and elaboration in the systems of symbolic logicians. The essence-accident distinction, for instance, lies deep in ordinary language and in the procedures of science, as well as in the logic of Aristotle: there is a vast distinction between the *sort* of thing something basically is, which it could not without absurdity be thought of as not being, and the various properties that, as a specimen of that sort, it may or may not have. In the same way, distinctions of tense have a place in the logic of ordinary speech, in which having been ill, or being about to be ill, do not count as cases of being ill at all, and in which merely having existed or being about to exist are sufficient to remove a term from among genuine subjects of predication. Ordinary approaches, likewise, use the notion of existence in such a way that it is possible to say of individual objects—e.g., this table before me—that it exists and might not have existed, and they regard existence as something presupposed by, but not identical with, the possession of properties. It is clear, further, that the logic of ordinary speech admits the use of sentences and descriptions in oblique contexts, thereby making room for all the phenomena of intentionality, and it is clear, further, that ordinary speakers are not all unready, in their more detached, contemplative moods, of talking in terms of 'deeper identities' which override or underlie ordinary surface differences and separatenesses and even embrace incompatibilities, in a manner which many logicians would condemn as essentially illogical and mystical. Symbolic systems have not, until quite recently, thought it worth their while to disturb their own artificial smoothness by trying to accommodate all these complicating features.

What we are in general maintaining is that the notion of a quite uncommitted, emptily formal, wholly topic-neutral logic is entirely inadmissible. By the forms which our thought and our symbolism accept, and accept in full seriousness, they presuppose the existence of orders and categories of things variously related, even if they explicitly assert the existence of none of them. Though the scheme they decide on may ideally represent the *only* possibility, other schemes having merely an abstract feasibility, they none the less decide among what are for us, and for our imperfectly developed reflection, genuine alternatives. And by excluding suitable forms in which certain sorts of objects and states of affairs can be talked of, they certainly try to legislate them out of existence. A perverse logic has certainly been employed to prove that there can be no relations, that the thought of what is non-existent or false is impossible unless preposterously analysed, that what will be tomorrow is as definite as what was yesterday, that the notion of a single, necessarily existent, all-pervasive absolute is senseless, etc., etc. What we are here maintaining is that the categories and the forms of propositions that are to be admitted into a satisfactory logic demand a deep-going examination of the requirements which make a world of objects understandable to us, both severally and collectively, which render possible the emergence of the shared life of rational mind. In every age there is a science which prepares its own downfall by its overweening hubris: physics, biology, psychology, economics have been such sciences in the past, but in our own day the supremely hubristic science is symbolic logic. It is our plea that the forms of discourse should not be formulated without a full consideration of what we can understand, of all that we can understand. What logic will emerge from the examination in question cannot be specified in advance, and is in its higher reaches necessarily and permanently controversial.

The higher ether of the cave not only contains a logic which determines the ultimate categories of our concepts, and their possibilities of integration in propositions or unities of sense: it also contains a logic of transformation, of legitimate inference, resting on formulated or unformulated relations of necessitation, exclusion or probabilification. These rules of transformation are of very various sorts, some rising to a high 'formal' indifference to the sorts of things we are dealing with, and that we might encounter in individual experience, some depending on specificities, e.g. colours, that we could only know of through individual cases, some only arising out of repeated encounter with specimens of certain natural kinds, some, lastly, depending on our deep understanding and experience of particular individuals. Necessitation, exclusion and probabilification do not differ in kind because known formally, or intensionally, or inductively, or by individual understanding: they are always the same notions, the most ultimate and important in philosophy. And all these rules of transformation in a sense lead us from the same to the same, they illuminate an identical area of existence, even if only problematically, and so are in a very wide sense tautological. Thus one is entitled to go from conceiving of something as blue and sweet to conceiving it as sweet and blue or as not being either, and one is entitled to do so because, despite differences in conscious light, one is, and must be, laying hold of the same real items in either case, that are items for everyone and with a fixed place in the real world. In the same manner one is entitled to go from conceiving of something as purple to conceiving it as nearer to red and blue than to green in colour, because again one is laying hold of the same real items despite all profound differences in conscious light. In the same manner one is entitled to pass from conceiving of something as having a certain molecular constitution to conceiving of it as readily entering certain combinations since one is laying hold of the same substances or sorts of substance in either case. One is even entitled to pass from conceiving of a thing as the morning star to conceiving of it as the evening star because of a deep but discoverable identity underlying the the two manifestations. None of the transformations just considered is, however, emptily tautological in the manner of 'There is a blue thing here, so there is a blue thing here'. This is *obviously* true in the cases where the necessitation, etc., belongs to the sphere of the *a posteriori*, and it is necessary to encounter things falling under the conscious lights in question in order to establish a connection among such lights. It is true, but less obviously true, in cases like that regarding the relationships of colours just mentioned, where the conscious lights are much closer together, and where the leap from one to the other can be made with complete confidence after seeing or imagining a *single* case, or even by merely savouring the senses of words used and not seeing or even imagining cases, But to pass from 'That is blue and sweet' to 'That is sweet and blue' involves a change in conscious light so minimal and so indifferent to the specific characters it concerns, that one is tempted to think that it involves no change in conscious light at all. There is, however, a genuine change in conscious light even in most purely formal transformations, and a blue, e.g., to which sweetness has been added is a differently conceived matter from a sweetness to which blue has been added. Strict synonymy, we may hold approvedly, hardly ever exists: even faithful translation into another language brings subtle changes in conscious light. There is an indefinable differ-

ence, reflecting the whole spirit and attitude of two cultures, between *deux mains sales* and two dirty hands. Strict tautology is a
degenerate, useless case of inference, and inference is more truly
inference the more it departs therefrom. This is plainest where the
inference in question is ampliative and problematic, as in all cases
of analogy and extrapolation, whether in science or philosophy.

We may hold, finally, that the whole of logic is presided over by a
number of values and disvalues which are seldom explicitly acknowledged, and hardly ever argued about. To do so would be felt
to bring a note of emotional persuasion into the serene air of logical
conception and reasoning, it being forgotten that serenity is
nothing if not an emotional attitude. These values have been presupposed in much that has been so far said, and like all values they
lie in very varied directions, so that there are often relations of
practical antinomy among them. We have in the first place the
familiar value of the definite and the unchanging, the goals of most
rigorously formulated and controlled thinking, to which, however,
may be opposed the less obvious value of the open and changing,
the sort of value that characterizes a good discussion as opposed to
a rigorous demonstration on prearranged lines. We have, in the
next place, the familiar value of the contradiction- and conflict-
free, a value hedged about with dire warnings, quite groundless in
practice, as to the ruinous consequences of admitting even a single,
trivial contradiction into one's thought: freedom from contradiction is indeed an ultimate desideratum, provided it is not achieved
by adopting conceptions of a too one-sided or ground-level type.
And what we have said stresses the less familiar dialectical value of
a contradiction, the sort of value that produced, for what they are
worth, the theory of types or Goedel's theorem. We have, in the
next place, the value of the exhaustiveness of determination
wrongly supposed to be implied by the logical law of excluded
middle, and the violation of this exhaustiveness which characterizes, e.g., many illuminating intentional objects, including the
content of the anticipated future. We have the value of the simply
uniform and the value of the diversified and richly complex. We
have the value of the luminously necessary and the value of the
imaginatively or empirically contingent. There is, finally, largely
unrecognized in logic as usually treated, the all-pervasive value of
'truth', capable of large number of degrees, to the compulsive
deliverances of experience in the sense of individual encounter. It

is the general possibility of applying one's logical forms to such deliverances, of finding material that fits them, that gives value to all these logical forms, and the whole methodology of enquiry further revolves around the need of adjusting one's theoretical notions and assertions so that they precisely fit the detail of individual encounter, and so that the slightest change in that detail would throw them out of gear. All treatments of the crucial instance from Bacon to Popper are here in place, even if, on our view, the lax treatments of earlier thinkers did better justice to the ontology and phenomenology of the situation that the would-be exactitudes of later ones.

To write about logical values is somewhat terrifying: they are childishly limpid and indefeasible, yet so long relegated among the indecencies of philosophy. Any sort of nugatory technicality or paradoxical manipulation is discussable in preference to such concepts as those of simplicity, harmony and truth to experience. The study of the values of logic is not, however, merely edifying: we must be able to show how such values stem from the basic endeavour of the mind to burst the springes of its merely personal subjectivity, and to achieve understandings with its fellows concerning the common world which compulsively confronts them all. This endeavour is none other than thinking mind itself, and all the subordinate goals it involves are simply different aspects of thinking mind. And, on the view we are adopting—which we hold to be the secret persuasion of all who engage in science—the world and its objects is geared to satisfy this endeavour, and to oppose only such resistance to it as will make of it a brighter, more sustained effort. The eternal life of thought is its own end, and all its conditions are, by teleological seepage, made part of itself.

THE REALM OF VALUES AND
DISVALUES

Last time we were dealing with one type of suspended furnishing found in the upper reaches of the cave: the entities of reason in their various styles and guises—predicates, propositions, definitely pinned down but not necessarily characterized particulars, particulars not definitely pinned down and hence enjoying an indefinite or variable status, relations, collections, generally characterized types of varying degrees of determinateness (the so-and-so, a so-and-so, etc.), mental directednesses of varying types, meanings, negations, alternations, notes of assertion or existence, and countless other classes of abstracta. These furnishings are all secondary appearances, matters not given in our primary exploration of the world, in which that world's furniture certainly comes before us in a variety of 'lights'—as being so-and-so or such-and-such, or not this or that, etc.—but in which there is no introduction of floating or abstract entities to which they stand in a number of formal relations, e.g. of being characterized by, of being a member of, of being the intentional object of, etc. These abstracta have been introduced into experience, made part of the phenomena, by various remarkable acts which concerned us in the last chapter, and which have never been adequately studied by philosophers. These are acts in which, instead of employing a conscious light as something in which other primary objects are seen, we use it in a new manner to present only so much of those objects as those lights themselves illuminate, in which, in short, a new truncated world of objects comes into our ken, of objects determined only in certain precise ways and not in others, which *cannot* (as ordinary objects can) be given a larger and richer content, though we may make many *external* comments regarding them and relating them to ordinary objects and to one another.

The introduction of these higher-order objects, products of the mind's self-truncation, into experience, is, moreover, in a sense, no introduction at all, since we are not compelled to regard them as more than intentional objects, things to which conscious references can be directed, but not as things that can, except by a legitimate but readily misleading act of pretence, be treated as genuine subjects of predicates. A man can think of just what it is *not* to be something not further specified, and we can say if we like that what it is *not* to be something, is exemplified in James who is *not* a mathematician or in Andrew who is *not* a lover, that it is a not-further analysable determination of objects, etc. etc., but in such discourse there is, or should be always, a side-long reference to the thinking persons capable of performing relevant abstractions and so multiplying the lights in which common-or-garden objects can be seen. Not-being-something-or-other is exemplified in James who is not a mathematician, only in the sense that those who see James in the latter light and who have been trained to conceive things in the truncated manner in question, can see James in a peculiar relational light involving the abstractum in question, which, since it involves a relation to what is merely intended, is itself a merely intended relation. That it can be right and true to conceive James in this manner, means that this is how a suitably trained mind will view the matter: if there is a 'correspondence with fact' in all this, this merely reflects the property in question. What we have said merely justifies by a plea of sheer innocuousness the valuable analyses which Meinong and the early Russell devoted to the variety of higher-order objects which diversify the phenomenal scene; Russell's subsequent descent into 'logical constructions', 'incomplete symbols' and other nominalistic doctrines, was all an unphenomenological confusion, springing from an incapacity to distinguish between an object in the sense of what completes the description of a conscious reference and an object in the sense of what is also a logical subject or real subject of predications. It spring, in short, from an inability to use the notion of intentionality in the artificial context of a formalized language.

I pointed out, further, how all the richness, the many-sidedness and even the smudgy unclearness of the lower world could, if we chose, be carried up into the upper reaches of the cave. We could frame abstractions, if so Hegelian a phrase can be tolerated, of any degree of concreteness. And, presiding over the cave's whole upper region, and so indirectly over all the phenomena in the cave, was a science which we chose to call 'logic', a science which prescribed the forms of abstracta and their relations to one another, and to the particular existences beneath them, as well as their transformations into other abstracta which covered the same range of existence and possibility. At the heart of this logic we were further made aware of what we called the presiding logical values, the values of the clear, the consistent, the simple, the empirically exhibited and tried out, the publicly recognizable, as well as, very strangely, values lying in quite opposite directions, the values, e.g., of the never fully clarified which pervades all philosophy, the values of what always involves a differentiation of meaning which rules out strict consistency-procedures, the values of the inexhaustibly complex and various, the values of what can never be straightforwardly exhibited and tried out, or what can never, in its full individuality, be shown to another, and so forth. These points of value, and the corresponding points of disvalue—which could only by a confusion be identified with the antithetical points of value just mentioned, there being, e.g., both a pregnant and wholly empty obscurity—can themselves be erected by our minds into separate goals of reason, in which contemplated character is one with a note or urgency or suasion, but which are alike cut adrift from particular occasions and subject-matters, and so stand for mere general desirabilities and undesirabilities in the field of thought and knowledge. These desirabilities and undesirabilities are not arbitrary or changeable, but are all sides of our basic endeavour not to live immured in the yielding medium of private fancy and sensation—if that were in fact possible—but to submit ourselves to hard, 'objective' tests of various sorts, which will be as hard for others as they are for ourselves, and which will provide the firm basis of rational commerce about which all veils of personal privacy and mystery can be draped.

If these values of theory reign supreme over the variations of conscious light, and the bracketings and unbracketings of our acts of belief, disbelief and mere entertainment, they may now serve to introduce another set of values and disvalues, which are rather connected with the objects and states of affairs that we thus envisage or bracket, than with the personal acts that thus envisage or bracket them. And in so far as these values and disvalues *are* concerned with our personal acts, they are concerned with such personal acts as either bring things into being or remove them from being, or which work in such a direction, with acts in short which belong to the active, causal segment of our nature. That there are such values and disvalues, and that they pervade the whole or almost the whole of the cave, is a simple matter of phenomenological observation. Hardly ever, in fact, and then only when we make a somewhat artificial exertion, do things come before us in that special, neutral light, neither attractive nor repellent, not pressing us to *do* anything about them nor to approve of anything done or undone, which some have regarded as the normal or original posture of the human mind, upon which sentiment, interest and linguistic confusion then raise up a phantasmagoric creation. What we see before us, or conceive in our private thoughts, has ideals, requirements, defects, standards built into it: it should be a little wider or longer, it is just right as it is, it is horribly inappropriate and so forth. And some of the ideals, requirements, etc., thus built into things impress us as having the same sort of remoteness from ourselves and our interests, and the same sort of neutral compulsiveness that we cannot help feeling must compel others as much as ourselves, that we find in our sense-encounters with material objects as in the transformations of strict logical thinking. And as, in non-valuational thought, we can perform an act of self-retractation, so that what comes before us stops short at a certain point, and is a mere unsaturated fragment of possible being, so in the field of values we can perform a similar retractation, which brings before us such abstract desirabilities as being fair to persons in situations unspecified, as having whatever we want and find satisfactory, as being free to pursue and obtain what we want, as being zealous and energetic in the realization of things on some further ground found desirable, and so on. A firmament of abstracted values and disvalues, which are given as being values and disvalues for *anyone* whatever, which may be attenuated and empty, but which still set bounds to what can be concretely desired and pursued, and whose force is not felt as the force of anyone's interests or personal preferences, is certainly part of the phenomenology of the human cave, whatever analysis or explanation we may choose to give of its evident presence. And, however little we may wish to give such detached values a status beyond that of intentional objects, they remain indefeasibly fixed points of the compass by which our practical navigation may be shaped and guided.

Certain points in the phenomenology of values and disvalues here require special emphasis. Each value-phenomenon as it comes before us, does so as a standing refutation of the Humean diremption of fact and value, or of any contemporary diremption of descriptive and evaluative meaning, or of most of the literature which is so complacently clear about the 'naturalistic fallacy'. (Moore himself never wrote thus superficially and complacently, but believed in *a priori* synthetic connections in this field.) In each value-phenomenon what is commonly called descriptive content comes before us as in close logical marriage with an axiological and prescriptive element, and as only abstractly separable from the latter: being or doing such and such has a baseness, a disvalue which not only *must* accrue to it, but which is peculiarly *adjusted* to to it, and is precisely the baseness *of* being or doing such and such. Just so having this or that may have an excellence about it which is just its own untransferable excellence, to which the thought of it necessarily and logically leads, and without which it would not be completely understood. A general transferable goodness or badness, unspecified by the sort of feature it is the goodness or badness of, and which could meaningfully have belonged to quite a different sort of thing or not belonged to what it actually belongs to, is a senseless abstraction, even if we can, for some purposes, form the notion of a goodness or a valuableness logically tied to some content unspecified. Even in the grossest value-experience the value of, e.g., reading poetry is not something that could have belonged to the performance of an act of heroism or to the adjustment of reward to desert: even states and performances and characters that are closely similar are often felt to be excellent or base in a wholly different 'way'. And that the true worthwhileness which invests certain activities should be removed or changed by a mere change in the attitude of the man who finds them worthwhile, is in plain contradiction with their ever having been worthwhile at all. It brackets the whole phenomenon of value, not merely in the legitimate manner which applies to all things abstract, but in the manner which makes it an abstraction without possible instances, and moreover internally at war with itself. What we therefore have before us are not descriptive characters neutrally characterizable, to which a uniform evaluative character mysteriously attaches, but values and disvalues *in the plural*, from which descriptive characters can only be separated by an abstraction, which would become

quite sense-destroying were it thought that the descriptive character could be present without the value or *vice versa*. The relation of
fact to value is the clearest case of phenomenological necessity,
which does not, of course, mean that it is a necessity that will
sustain itself through all phases of deepened examination. We
therefore are not ashamed to speak of justice, pleasure, etc., as
'values', i.e. forms into which the generic intentional object *value*
specifies itself, rather than as mere 'grounds of value', as they
usually are spoken of in contemporary British discussion.

It is easy to defeat Hume, that worst of phenomenological
observers, phenomenologically: in experience fact and value come
before us as married and not isolated, and in many cases they come
before us as logically, necessarily married, not brought together by
an arbitrary link of taste or decision. The indissoluble character of
the marriage is in the cases mentioned—it would be tedious and
contentious to cite detailed examples—absolutely part of the
phenomenon: to imagine it dissolved is to assert that it was merely
apparent, that it never really existed. The link is not, of course, a
case of trivial formal entailment: it is a case where a one-sidedly
viewed phenomenon completes itself into a full phenomenon which
alone is seen to have true self-sufficiency. But, though all this is so,
the difficulties which lead to Hume's unphenomenological diremp-
tions are not thereby banished: we have still to face the issue of
evaluative conflict and disagreement, which is not removed by the
mere *claim*, present in all our consciousness of value, that the conflict or disagreement in question is not or should not be there.
These difficulties are not removed by the mere fact that reflective
disagreements on value-questions, in fact, fall within much
narrower limits than superficial theory and observation have
thought possible, and that here, as elsewhere, the arguable falls
within a general framework of the unarguable, within which alone
it is possible. We differ as to the detailed shape of just allocations
and assignments, but not as to the need of *something* wearing the
egalitarian, proportionate face of justice, we differ as to the prefer-
ability of a deepened grasp of truth over a deepened grasp of
sensuously shown order or character, but not as to the desirability
of either, we differ as to the absolute stringency of certain obligations rather than as to the general undesirability of overriding
them and so on. Certain valuations, as that nothing is so important
as the indefinite multiplication of boots and shoes, or that the

destruction of the whole world is preferable to the scratching of one's finger, bear so plain an index of absurdity upon them, that none but a philosopher could countenance them for an instant. Nor are they removed by the many strong arguments which expose the fallacy of the argument from disagreement: that it rests very largely on arguing that, because A and B are existentially and practically incompatible, and represent two contrasted modes of life and existence, there must also be an incompatibility between them from the point of view of value, an incompatibility between the excellence of the one and the excellence of the other. Or again that it rests on the *blindness* to the worth of A which is readily induced in those keenly alive to the worth of the practically incompatible B, or on the narrow bounds and on the consequent 'wandering' of the focus of our value-consciousness, it being well-nigh impossible to be vividly conscious of the worth of too many quite diverse alternatives. It is not even removed by the immense success of those mappings of the value-firmament by such moral philosophers as Moore, Rashdall, Ross, Scheler and Hartmann, a success vainly belied on the grounds that they fail to yield results of a practical precision which the very character of their cloudy material in principle excludes, or on still more suspect, wholly unphenomenological views as to the nature of evaluative references and discourse. That many quite discussable questions are raised in the works in question, and that their discussability precludes all chaotic divergence, shows that we are here dealing with a valid and viable enterprise, even if it does not enable us to say just *why* and *how* it is thus valid.

The difficulty lies of course in the close marriage of values and disvalues, not merely with the descriptive contents that seem to go with them, but with emotional and dynamic drifts which are part of the developmental and causal, rather than the merely referential and inferential part of our conscious life. Our conscious life not merely involves manifold forms of sentience, and makes use of these, in a not further analysable manner, to be *of* various objects, and to be of them in varying 'lights' and manners, and it not merely learns to 'bracket' some of what it intends as having a merely intended, thought of status, while to other parts it accords an unbracketed or 'real' status: it also has characteristic drifts or trends in various directions, some involving no more than a change in outlook or angle of vision, and so classed as merely 'cognitive', while others involve gross change in grossly given environmental situations and in a man's own gross body, and so count as *practical* changes in which something is *done* by a man to the world around him. These drifts, whether cognitive or practical, and whether fully carried out or arrested, necessarily give rise to changes in our personal sentience and to more or less lucid references to the drifts from which they sprang. We *feel* alert, frustrated, smoothly progressive, wearily effortful and so on, and we may be *conscious* of ourselves as subject to the drifts in question. These feelings and inwardly turned awarenesses enjoy a phenomenological immediacy and simplicity which is far from revealing the complex reference back to origins which a more probing phenomenology soon lays bare in them. Such drifts in experience and behaviour, and the conscious poses that sum them up, have obviously a more than merely contingent relation to the value-phenomena we have been considering. To feel a conscious drift towards a situation in which an object would be given in fulfilled reality, and to have and feel this drift operating in one's own bodily musculature, is, except in some compulsively perverse situations, to see worthwhileness in the goal of one's conscious causality, just as to see worthwhileness in such a goal is to have and feel the conscious drift in question. In other words to want or feel positively about a thing, and to see it as worthwhile, are internally related, and the same holds of not-wanting or negative feeling and the seeing of something as detrimental or evil. Yet this internal relation when stated, at once creates a tension with the other internal relation given as part of 'the phenomena', the relation between the moment of valuableness or disvaluableness in general and the moment of descriptive content with which it is phenomenologically united. If valuableness is always given as the valuableness of some specific content, with which it is has a relation of necessary 'fit', valuableness is also given as necessarily related to feeling and wanting, and these are phenomena which do not appear to have the same *close* relation to descriptive content that we think obtains in the case of valuableness. In other words, there is a looseness of fit in the relation of feeling and wanting to their objects that does not match the tight relation of the value-moment to its descriptive specifiers: people, it seems, may have feelings and wants infinitely more various than the distribution posited in the case of value-moments. This looseness of relation goes together

with an *actual* variability in value-phenomena which assorts ill
with the *claim* to be necessary and invariable. Whenever we want
anything strongly, or feel positively about it, we tend to see a
worthwhileness in it that we feel *must* be apparent to others: not
only do we *desire* others to share our attitudes, but we also *expect*
them to do so. 'Surely you must realize, how wonderful, horrible,
important, reprehensible, etc., all this is!' is a most frequent
utterance: our first reaction tends to be one of incredulity when the
attitude or realization is disavowed. Nothing is, further, more
disillusioning and more destructive of the claim of a necessary
tie-up between descriptive and evaluative moments, then the
manner in which this connection loses its cogency with a slight
change in our attitude. The scales drop from our eyes, and the
unquestionably precious turns into unquestioned dross: there are
transvaluations of values, not only at the major cross-roads of
existence, but at every falling in and out of love with someone or
something. It is these revolutions of outlook and attitude, not the
stilted moves of a logic concerned to prohibit any genuine inferential advance, which give a justification to Hume's diremption
or reason and sentiment, and the consequent schism between the
'is' and the 'ought'.

The phenomena of value further involve a tangled difficulty
which the wit of the whole eighteenth century found itself unable
to resolve: the difficulty of the relation between values and disvalues as *overtones* added to the things in the world, overtones as
much 'out there' in the objects as the characters which we say
describe them, and capable of being considered with quite as much
dispassion as the latter, and the feelings and prescriptive pressures
with which, we held, they have an internal connection. The
perverse wrongness of certain attitudes and lines of conduct—
those, e.g., of the Marquis de Sade—seems as much a character
written on their faces as the characters which, in the narrowest
sense, describe them, and we can recognize its presence quite
coolly and without striking any attitude ourselves. Yet we recognize too that it is only because we at some time *have* been or at
least *could* be outraged by such actions and attitudes, that their
overtones of evil can be given to us as clinging to them. We are
not uttering a merely inductive discovery if we say that a man incapable of such outrage would also be incapable of 'seeing' the
wrongness in question. The problem now stands in two alter-

native forms before us, both rooted in the actual phenomena on hand. How, if the prime thing in valuations are our own emotional and practical attitudes, can such matters of internal sentiment help to 'gild and stain' all natural objects with borrowed colours, as Hume in the Appendix to the *Inquiry concerning the Principles of Morals* rightly maintains that they do? Or how, on the other hand, if the prime thing in values and valuation are the notes of fittingness, goodness, etc. which we simply recognize as attaching to objects and consequent upon their other characters, do such notes compel attitudes in us other than those of recognition and belief, attitudes of approval and disapproval, of attraction and repulsion, of decision for or against? We can, if we like, say with Richard Price, that there is a *necessity* in the connection between certain recognized characters and certain affections, but as long as such a necessity is merely postulated *ad hoc*, it entirely fails to meet the difficulties of the case. In Scheler and Hartmann, the most gifted modern mappers of the firmament of values, the whole problem becomes verbally misted over. We are told of feelings, and of a 'logic of the heart', that will enable us to discern values that none the less enjoy some sort of Platonic self-existence. How feelings, being attitudes *towards* things, could help us to discern characters *in* things or beyond things, is not anything which all this turgid talk really makes clear. The facts of value-experience are undoubted, and their deliverances far from lost in ambiguity, but these facts themselves raise questions of internal possibility which a more penetrating insight has to resolve.

The solution has been in part provided by Meinong's valuable later work on 'emotional presentation'.[1] He has argued persuasively that, just as sense-experience is essentially two-sided, having both a side of 'content', of personal affectivity, and another quite different side of objective, presented quality, the former being intrinsically, and not merely contingently, such as to introduce or present the latter, so too, in the realm of emotion and desire, how we are affected can serve, and that not accidentally, to introduce us to certain higher-order predicates that Meinong spoke of as 'dignitatives' and 'desideratives'. Revulsion can set things before us as revolting, terror as terrible, pleasure as pleasant and so on: the principal dignitatives are, however, the agreeable,

---

[1] *Über emotionale Präsentation*, Proceedings of the Imperial Viennese Acadamy, 1916. See my *Meinong's Theory of Objects and Values*, pp. 302-12.

E

the beautiful, the true (or valid) and the good, corresponding to four subtly distinguished genera of feelings, while the principal desideratives are corresponding 'oughts' or imperatives of (as we may say) a voluptuous, aesthetic, scientific or axiological sort. What is interesting in the doctrine is the repudiation of any causal analysis of the dignitatives or desideratives postulated: the pleasant is not what makes us feel pleased nor the terrifying what makes us feel afraid, the attractive is not what attracts nor the desirable what is or could be desired, despite all verbal suggestions to the contrary. The pleasant, terrifying, etc., are rather seeming characters in things which we are aware of *in* being pleased or terrified, etc., we do not need to reflect on our own pleasure or terror in order to see these characters in things. And the valuable or good is, in Meinong's view, a character of things that comes before us in so far as we have the attitudes called 'existence-love' towards such things, or of 'existence-hatred' towards their absences, in so far, that is, as we delight in their being and deplore their non-being, and are practically concerned to bring them into being or to preserve them in being or to preserve them from non-being. These attitudes do not, however, enter into the analysis of value or goodness, but are only essential to the *presentation* of the latter. It is in virtue of being thus and thus emotionally and desideratively affected, and that not by some merely empirical law, that we come to see objects in a corresponding value-tinged 'light'.

Meinong's theory goes far towards abolishing the mystery and difficulty of value experience by making it merely carry one stage further that *use* of the personally interior to mediate a reference to what is external and objective which characterizes all our inter-personal, conscious life, and which has been so often misrepresented as involving a causal inference from one thing to another, or as the seeing of some object as causing a change in ourselves. The immediate, felt commerce between our unified, personal being and the dispersed, impersonal being that contrasts with it, is no doubt one of the sources, probably the main source, of our awareness of causality, of the causality we exercise or that we to seem exercise upon things and that they exercise or seem to exercise upon us. Hume's musings on these matters are entirely wide of the mark, for we certainly seem to do something to objects when we discharge our feelings on them just as they certainly seem to do something to us when they excite us or appal us, etc. But that commerce is not in its origins an awareness of ourselves as personally responsive to some object, nor of some object as provoking a personal response in ourselves: it is the seeing of an object differently in virtue of our own personal response to it, without seeing that it is in virtue of such a response that we see it in this light. The further puzzling fact that, while personal feeling is necessary to the deeper, more authentic experiences of value and disvalue in things and situations, value and disvalue can still be present to us, and that not merely verbally, when we are *not* deeply affected or committed, is merely another case of the contrast between fulfilled and unfulfilled modes of experience which runs through the whole of our conscious life. We can entirely understand and believe something while yet not *realizing* our understanding and belief in the full vividness and detail of imagination, perception and action: in the same way we can and must in detached moods see things in a favourable or unfavourable or imperative light without needing to give our experience all the flesh and blood of actual feeling or practical endeavour. The higher achievements of deliberation are in fact dependent on this remarkable power, but they do not establish the non-practical, non-emotional character of their foundations. In some absolute sense it remains true that διάνοια οὐθὲν κινεῖ ἀλλ' ἡ ἕνεκὰ τοῦ καὶ πρακτική, but what must be added to this is that it is never possible to separate the one sort of διάνοια from the other, and that it is correspondingly impossible to separate the descriptive or cognitive characters of things from their valuational overtones. The world comes before us as a graded world, and the attempt to see it in a wholly ungraded manner cannot be entirely successful. (At least it will involve seeing it in a peculiar set of abstractly cognitive gradings.) The further movement from values as lights in which particular objects or types of objects are viewed, to values as abstracta, e.g. purity, freedom, kindness, etc., uniting a descriptive and an evaluative side, is but another instance of the development studied in the case of other abstracta. The mind cuts off edges that are blurred and free in ordinary thought, and so raises a new creation of intentional abstractions.

To solve the problem of value-presentation is not, however, to solve the problem of value-judgment. For, plainly, not all the values and disvalues which come before us as overtones of acts, situations and objects can be accorded an unbracketed status, can be given as part of the world as it must appear to everyone, and not merely as part of the world as it in fact appears to a given individual. The problem of unbracketed objectivity among values is, however, simply the problem of necessary intersubjectivity. Those values can be put as part of the phenomena, and as to be recognized in the phenomena by 'right reason', which are also values that must tend to recommend themselves to all such as aspire to rise above the contingencies of personal interest and of partiality towards particular persons and their interests. Such values as those of bridge-playing, fishing or consorting with courtesans plainly do not fall into this inescapable, intersubjective class—even those of eating and drinking do not, since we can imagine circumstances in which we should not care for either—whereas others, such as those of happiness, freedom, justice, etc., plainly do. What has to be done is to furnish a 'deduction' of the same powerful though not emptily cogent sort furnished by Kant at many points in his transcendental philosophy, which will show that an endeavour towards certain highly general objectives and an avoidance of other opposed objectives, is part and parcel of the very idea of a rational, of an intersubjectively discussable valuation. Kant deduced various demands regarding generalizability of volition and respect for rational agents from the notion of the sort of will that can claim to be rational: what is desired is that the deduction should be extended to cover many of the countless other things—happiness, cultivation, mutual help, self-preservation, aesthetic pleasure, etc.—to which Kant in fact accords, even if left-handedly and grudgingly, a rationally justified status at definite points in his treatment. All these objects can be shown to fall into a totally different class from bridge-playing and consorting with courtesans; it is not absurd to say that one does not care for the activities just mentioned, but it is deeply absurd to say that one does not care for happiness or for beauty or for fair treatment or for the freedom to get what one wants, or to put forward, as a matter for common consideration and discussion, that these things are only important as enjoyed by this or that particular person.

The deduction to be attempted is, as we have said, not a formal derivation from premisses whose sense is clear, and the coverage of whose conclusion is no more than a more worked out or differently slanted version of the coverage of its premisses. It is a deduction in which there is a genuine pushing beyond both the sense and coverage of the premisses, in which there is a significant inferential move or step, precisely because there is a risk of the premises being true and the conclusion quite false, and in which there is no certainty of this not being so whether in the case before us or 'in the long run'. It must be a deduction which is reasonable precisely because it is not certain, and can never be forced into any specially guarded mould of certainty. That such deductions are of supreme importance in philosophy can only be shown by trying them out and by seeing to what they lead. We may note, further, that the sort of deduction to be attempted only enjoys a marginal position in the actual phenomenology of the unbracketed value-judgment. To recognize freedom as a value is in fact to respond with a segment of one's nature that transcends contingency and partiality, but it by no means involves being clear as to the transcendence of contingency and partiality involved. In the same way, merely to *hold* that freedom is an object of necessary love on the part of all truly detached, disinterested persons is not necessarily to see it as a value nor to love it thus disinterestedly. Metaphysical naturalism as it occurs in Kant's transcendental treatments is rightly ruled out as an analysis of what we understand by the absolutely right or good: it is not ruled out as a transcendental illumination of how the absolutely right and good come to be constituted as objects, come to be 'there' for us.

Into this transcendental constitution we now enter sketchily and tentatively, since we cannot hope to be more than this in the compass of a single lecture. What are essentially contingent in human interest are the objects of what Butler called the particular passions, or rather perhaps what is particular and special in them: particular forms of replenishment, occupations, companions, objects of contemplation, etc. There is necessarily something in personal interest which is entirely and essentially personal, which has no necessary tendency to recommend itself to anyone else: personal interest would not be fully concrete without it. Though one hesitates to give examples of it, and it is not plain that it can be isolated from elements that possess some universal recommendation, it is of the idea of personal interest that it should exist or be capable of existing. But it is also of the essence of personal interest that it should be capable of rising to objects of higher order, which presuppose the concrete filling of contingent personal liking and are impossible without it, and yet make no stipulations regarding the precise character of that filling, which are satisfied with *any* personal contingent filling, no matter what this may be. There are in short, and must be, interests of higher order which rise above, while they also presuppose, contingent interest of the first order, and which are such that any interested person is intrinsically capable of sharing them. And it is further correct to argue that these intrinsically shareable interests are also intrinsically such that they tend to be interests *for* as well as interests *of* everyone: the higher-order objects which everyone must tend to value, are also objects that everyone must tend to value for everyone. (Nothing of course precludes the possibility of having other interests which resist the trends just mentioned.) We have inserted words like 'capable' and 'tend', as well as words like 'intrinsic' and 'necessary', to indicate that it is in fact possible for interest *not* to develop in the directions indicated, but also that it is not accidental, not a mere matter of empirical encounter, that interest does develop on the lines suggested. To consider what it is to be a conscious person having conscious drifts in various directions is to see the deep 'naturalness', the nigh inevitability of the higher-order drifts in question. Their possibility is in fact implied in the power of overlooking and detaching oneself from anything and everything, which a conscious person, as opposed to a mere dispersed 'thing' in the natural world, cannot be without. It may be hard to see all these obscure, imperfectly binding exigencies, and to express them in relatively clear language, and much easier to deal with sharply definite facts and mere logical possibilities. But the phenomena of the world lose themselves in transcendental mists and the philosopher and his language have to pursue them there.

We must, however, attempt to bring into better focus the somewhat misty matters before us. Plainly, in the first place, it is natural and nigh inevitable, for a man reflecting more or less disengagedly on the objects of his various parcelled interests to acquire a second-order zest for the interesting as such and for any and every interest: it is natural, in short, for him to rise to the level of the cool self-love or the prudence whose remarkable element of creative novelty has seldom been sufficiently recognized. That we should, in a new, higher-order way, continue to be interested in things, while detaching ourselves from them individually and specifically, is as strange a fact as that we should be able to understand what only sense-experience can bring before us in states of mind into which sense-experience, or anything like it, does not enter, and the fact that either development is deeply understandable does not mean that it is in any sense simply contained in what precedes it. The rise to self-love is in fact a matter so strange that the further spread to rational benevolence is trivial by comparison: having come to be interested in, e.g., the provision of food at a time when I am not hungry, it is no great wonder that I am rationally moved by another's real or imagined need for food as much as by my own. A second-order interest in the interesting as such enables us to co-ordinate our own interest prudentially: it also by a relatively slight extension enables us to co-ordinate the interests of a number of persons. And, by an extension natural to it, once its ampliative zeal has got under way, it tends to extend itself to an interest in what is interesting to anyone or everyone, and to develop a defensive dislike of whatever sets bounds to its natural expansiveness. The Japanese goddess Kwannon, flailing out her myriad arms in untold exercises of benevolence, and gratifying the most humdrum as well as the most transcendental needs, is perhaps a better expression of this inescapable, basic utilitarianism than our own crabbed Jeremy Bentham and his Victorian followers. Satisfaction and the satisfactory, what people like or want, are as such objects of disengaged, second-order prescription and approval, and their recognized value is a phenomenon for everyone, and not merely for this or that person.

The passage to this higher Benthamite level is of course surrounded by countless perverse side-paths which relativistic theorists will be very ready to exploit. There is the disinterest which stops short at the individual person, or which perhaps pushes beyond him only to hold that *everyone* should pursue and value that which is to his own best interest. In this latter development the spirit of self-transcendence quarrels absurdly with the content given to it: selfishness is unselfishly recommended to everyone. A worse strain of perversity enters into a cult of misery, whether for others, oneself or everyone. The higher-order interest in interest has a bland, detached spirit which quarrels with aversion and objects of aversion: impartially to seek to frustrate one's own first-order wishes or those of others, though a perfectly possible and sometimes actual attitude of mind, represents a refusal of attitudes of the second order to accept their natural material, the corresponding first-order attitudes. That disinterested malignity can, from a purely formal standpoint, be quite as consistent an example of disinterestedness as disinterested benignity, only shows how little formal logic is qualified to deal with the possible, the acceptable or the reasonable.

Satisfaction and the satisfactory therefore rank as the lowest and plainest of intersubjective values: none can doubt their power to recommend themselves to everyone. Not far removed in plainness are such values as those of the free and the powerful, for the second-order desire that everyone should have what he desires dictates as a natural extension that everyone should have the freedom and the power to obtain and enjoy what he desires (other things of course being equal). And only a little less plain is the value of the fair and the just: an attitude concerned to consider the interest of *everyone*, tends by a natural extension to quarrel with arrangements and attitudes that arbitrarily promote the interest of some at the expense of others. It is only a small step further to the second-order interest in the love or affection which bridges the gulf between persons and which renders the other's interests as intimate as one's own: though partial and pathological, it has a kinship of spirit with the impartial pursuit of everyone's interest that necessarily approves itself to the latter. And it is likewise only a small step further from the second-order interest in the just satisfaction of everyone's interest, to the second-order interest in the practical zeal which pursues this latter objective and which makes sacrifices for it. Here we have not so much a case of one spirit approving a kindred spirit, as of one spirit approving a more dynamic, devoted form of itself.

The firmament of value therefore begins to reveal constellated segments corresponding to the traditional divisions of happiness, freedom, justice, love and virtue. The case of the unquestioned, classical values of knowledge and beauty presents more difficulty. Here we can again best cope with our deductive problem by making use in yet wider fashion of the conception of community or kinship of spirit. The realm of aesthetic appreciation has, as Kant emphasized, a profound vein of analogy with our ethical valuations and imperatives: there is an aesthetic disinterest, indifferent to all material exhibited, and interested only in the harmonious play of imagination and conception, which is quite akin to moral disinterest, where everyone is alike a member and a legislator in the kingdom of ends. What is well imagined as little panders to the specificity or the partiality of personal interest as impartial moral

legislation does so. Though one's conceptions of the aesthetic and
the moral may not at all points tally with Kant's, one may borrow
from him the doctrine that the moral approval of aesthetic objects
and activities rests on the fact that the latter are in a sense *mono-
grams* of morality: the integrity, purity and harmony of great art,
especially when dealing with debased, discordant material, is a
true analogue of its moral counterpart. And the same may be said,
mutatis mutandis, of intellectual endeavour and its products: this
has a disinterestedness in the face of contingent content which is
wholly analogous, in its own different manner and medium, to
axiological or ethical disinterest. It may further be argued that the
interest in sheer character which underlies aesthetic interest, as
well as the interest in sheer fact which underlies intellectual interest, are higher-order interests so fundamental to conscious life,
so constitutive of consciousness itself, as to fill a secure place in the
firmament of our valuations. It is not suggested that the deduction
here given is more than a rudiment. I have carried it very much
further in my book *Values and Intentions* to which I must here
simply refer you.

Value-phenomena exhibit further differences which are of great
fascination and complexity. There is the basic difference in our
dynamic life in virtue of which our conscious drifts sometimes
appear in an urgent, sometimes in a quiescent form, largely according as the situation towards which they press is judged actual and
existent, and as not readily to be rendered non-actual, or the
reverse. We acquiesce with satisfaction in the actuality of something towards which a conscious drift presses, and the verbal expression 'Let this thing be' is rather a plea for its continuance than
for its being here and now: we experience a positive urge towards
the actuality of something desired which is still bracketed as
unrealized, imagined or ideal, and the expression 'Let this thing be'
has here an urgent, imperative force. In the same fashion we experience undynamic pain and grief towards what our conscious
drifts veer away from, but what we judge hopeless to avoid or
remove, but we experience dynamic destructive or remotive urges
in the contrary case. In conformity with all these possibilities,
states of affairs come before us in a variety of lights, as more or less
imperatively or urgently to be realized or removed from existence,
or as merely being as they should be or as they should not be.
Every value or disvalue can come before us in an urgent as in a

more or less tranquilly contemplative form. It comes before us, also as making a 'demand' on the world to realize it or to remove it from reality, and this, in a limited range of cases, is a demand that *we* should do what we can to bring it about or to see that it does not come about. These demands have a phenomenological variety which traditional ethical theory has been far from recognizing. There are the demands which are mainly negative, prohibitive, and the axiological items with which they are connected are mainly evils, disvalues: there are the opposed demands which are mainly positive, hortatory, suasive, and the axiological items with which they are connected are primarily values proper. It is important to stress the total disparity and asymmetry of these types of demand, there being no substance to the view that a positive, suasive claim necessarily corresponds or ought to correspond to a balancing prohibitive claim warning us from the non-realization of the item in question, nor to the view that a prohibitive claim necessarily corresponds to a balancing suasive claim urging us on towards a correlated absence or freedom. It is an accepted and an acceptable principle that the absence of great evils is not necessarily a great good, and that the absence of great goods is not necessarily a great evil, and that altogether good and evil cannot easily be summed up in assessing an actual situation.

All the claims set up by the various values and disvalues, and in particular those realizable or avoidable in a given situation, converge in the single synthetic claim which is a man's personal duty at a given moment. Of this duty it is not the place to speak here. I have said what I have to say of it in my book *Values and Intentions*. All that I need here remark is that it is the least clear concept in axiology, and the most entangled with individual choice and contingency, and hence the least promising base for ethical analysis and theory. For the claims made on us by different values and disvalues are arguably quite disparate and incommensurable—there is no way of balancing the claims of truth against the claims of justice and so on—and the practical decision to give some of them a priority over others necessarily has an element of the purely arbitrary. An element of free decision, of simply opting for one set of values or avoidances of disvalues above many alternatives, cannot be evaded. This element of free decision has been absurdly erected into the sole basis of values in certain existentialist theories, an exaggeration which has at least this justification: that there is a profound connection between the sort of freedom expressed in arbitrary decision and the other sort of freedom, the Kantian autonomy, which underlies the constitution of the realm of values. Arbitrary decision involves a relation of cool distance from a number of favourable and unfavourable considerations which are seen and compared in that second-order manner which transcends the urgency of primary interest. When primary interest makes its agonizing entrance, pure arbitrariness vanishes. The constitution of the realm of values and disvalues similarly involves a detachment from primary interest: the values and disvalues in question are little more than varied ways of being detached, with, however, a retained foothold in, and presupposition of, primary interest. But there is a necessity, an ineluctability, in what appears at the higher levels of interest as valuable and disvaluable, which is quite antithetical to the arbitrary. The detached person *cannot help* discerning or feeling the permissible forms of his own detachment, and can only be arbitrary in his willingness to live according to them or not to live according to them, or to live according to them in one way or another. That there is an ultimate category of the purely arbitrary, and that it is one of the fundamental forms of conscious causality, is certainly vouched for by the immediate phenomena, there being countless cases where it seems primarily *we*, with our power of freely coming down on *either* side of a disjunction, that are truly responsible for coming down on a *given* side. We have argued further, in the first series of the present lecures and in *Values and Intentions*, that deeper scrutiny of the phenomena affords no ground to question this immediate view but rather to question, as confused, the deterministic obsessions which make it seem questionable. However this may be, it seems clear that the freedom of pure arbitrariness, if it exists, is quite distinct from the freedom from fear and favour, which is involved in the setting up of the realm of values and disvalues. These we do not and cannot choose, but we can and must make choices in their framework and in their light, even if, in the limiting, absurd case, these are deliberate choices of what runs counter to them or violates their appointed order.

My aim in this lecture was not, however, to dwell on the foundations of practice, but to sketch the firmament of values as a fixed, as in fact the most fixed furnishing in the human cave. Like the stars, values are occluded by many mists and are invisible from many latitudes, and are often inconsiderable in magnitude, yet they outlast the gross objects on which their remote illumination falls. Despite all that modern philosophers have thought and said, values and disvalues are the least banishable data in the human cave. And they not only illuminate all furnishings of the cave, they also, on the view taken at our present level of discussion, make us understand what the cave is for. It is there precisely to educe that kind of intersubjective, rational life, where the arbitrary and personal is subordinated to the ineluctable and impersonal, of which the values in question are differing specifications. The untoward, the irrational, the merely personal, have the teleological role of providing the necessary incitement and raw material for the rational, common, self-conscious result, and so all phenomenal existence can be brought under the sway of values, and something like the dominion of Good taught in the *Phaedo* proven true. But what we are holding is only a stage in the argument to which we have been driven by the absurdities shown up in previous stages: similar absurdities may again crop up and drive us on to further solutions.

RELIGION AND ITS OBJECTS

We have, in the last three lectures, viewed the human cave as dominated by a teleology of reason, as conducing in all its arrangements, whether toward or untoward, gross or subtle, to the release and development of a rational mind that can disengage itself from the immediacies and contingencies of personal and environmental existence, and can achieve stances and points of view and modes of activity that are essentially those of everyone, everywhere and at all times. Among the most important creations of this rational mind—if 'creations' they may be called when they exist only in and for the intentions that constitute them—are the varied family of abstracta, of entities of reason—characters, sets, logical forms, propositions, facts, intentional directednesses, truth-values, senses, meanings, etc.—which a quasi-scientific devotion to economy has delighted to decimate, fortunately quite in vain, since they so obviously have a clearer meaning for us than their murky substitutes, and are in fact the very prototypes of the unambiguous and the clear. Through these entities of reason, and through the logical principles that connect them, and the logical values that inspire these principles—principles not merely permitting us to educe the same truth-coverage from the same, but to adventure dangerously but reasonably beyond our starting-points—the whole realm of concrete particularities is taken up into the heaven of discourse and science, and is made over into that pure 'gist' that can be ruminated over and communicated.

This creation or constitution leads up, however, to a still more eminent creation or constitution, that of the values and disvalues, which are nothing but the new, mandatory objects of interest which arise when we seek to rise above the non-mandatory contingencies of first-order interest, and which are tailored to meet the aspirations of those who, by a strange but deeply rational transformation, no longer wish to act *as* anyone in particular or *for* anyone in particular. This creation is so imprecise in its contours, and so dappled over with varied iridescence, that it readily becomes suspect to the too simple intelligence. It is, however, despite its mistiness and its flashing variety, the most invariant of the cosmic fixtures, without which, in fact, we should have no stable co-ordinates in any field whatsoever. Now, however, we plan to rise to a yet higher reach of the cave's upper regions, to a point in fact which represents its zenith or crown or apex: if values are the stars of our speluncar underworld, what we are now to ascend to is its sun. This, unlike the Platonic sun, still firmly falls within the cave.

The apical phenomenon we are now to consider is none other than the *id quo maius cogitari nequit* of Anselm or the *ens realissimum* of Kant, to which noble creatures of rational theology we turn with some relief after the malformed spawnings of much modern obscurantism or ill-directed mysticism. It is also, to go beyond our tradition, the One without a Second, the Bright Golden Person beyond the Darkness of the *Upanishats* or the self-sufficing, omnipresent, infinite, all-begetting emptiness to which Lao-tzu could only give the name of Tao. It is an intentional object unique among cave-objects in that it brings into one focus all recognized values and leaves no room for an alternative synthesis beside it: it is also unique among cave-objects since it cannot be thought of in full seriousness except as existing, and as existing with necessity. It is an absolute since it is given as being, and given as being what it is, entirely *a se*, in and through itself, and not in virtue of anything that is not itself, and it is a religious absolute, since it is the one thing wholly fitted to satisfy the attitude of worship, of complete, unconditional self-dedication, in which religion consists. Religious awe is not, as it is often deemed to be, a contingent human development, an attitude that we encounter among other attitudes in ourselves and others, and that might very well have been absent from ourselves and from the world. It is not, as it has often been held to be, the mere product of man's original need, helplessness and ignorance which will 'wither away' in a well-appointed Marxist society or in a civilization built on science. None of the fundamental emotional attitudes of men and animals—those picked out by such salient names as 'fear', 'anger', 'hatred', 'disgust', 'admiration', emulation', etc.—are mere facts of nature. All have not only a definite 'constitution', in which their various traits hang together in a necessary or near-necessary manner, but there is also something inevitable about their emergence in a living and conscious being. They are all attitudes involving a definite 'policy', a definite way of conducting oneself, which is part and parcel of the 'being-in-the-world' of a living and conscious creature, one of the ways in which it expresses what it is—thus fear in principle avoids, anger in principle smashes, etc., etc.—as well as having a characteristic or normal object in response to whose judged or imagined presence the attitude in question arises. Thus fear avoids what gravely menaces or threatens the main activities and being of the creature, anger what obstructs it but is given as less grave, etc. So far are these attitudes from being mere contingent existences that they all have inbuilt norms as part of their consti-tution, norms which in part regulate their development, but which, to the extent that they do not so regulate it, offer an internal point of view from which the attitudes in question can be critically judged. Thus it is plain that fear when of something weak, in-offensive, perhaps beneficent, and known to be such, is an un-justifiable, abnormal or deviant attitude, one which certainly may exist, but which also has some tendency to eliminate itself as in-sight is strengthened. The continuance of fear in the face of known harmlessness requires explanation, but not so its speedy reduction or elimination. This necessary and normative structure of our emotions, this internal logic, if one may so call it, can of course be given a linguistic illumination in terms of the way in which the words 'fear', 'anger', 'rivalry' function in our speech, an explanation which appeals to the ultimate mere facts of human affectivity and of human usage. The connections we postulate obtain since they are part of the use of our words, and they are part of the use of our words since they are part of what happens in fact. This linguistic illumination is correct, but quite topsy-turvy, since it is plain connections of essence, imperfectly illustrated in experience, that justify linguistic rulings and not *vice versa*. It is when we see and understand fear in all the misleading pantomine in which it sometimes shows itself—in, e.g., Cleopatra's sublime moments of poetry and courage at the end of Shakespeare's tragedy—that we recognize its policy, its object and its intrinsic norms, which all go quite beyond what stands palpably before us. We may, however, be glad that the logic of the emotions, like so much other essential but not formal logic, should have entered modern philosophy through the back door of language rather than have been passed over altogether. We may likewise be glad that, at an earlier period, it entered empirical science through the portal of a doctrine of 'instincts', before extreme empiricism, smelling out its *a priori* character, found sufficient grounds for banishing it altogether. A good demonstration of the thorough-going apriorism of the emotions is to be found in the third book of Spinoza's *Ethics*. The possibility that such a book should have been written, and should illuminate our emotional life so profoundly, is sufficient proof that emotions are structures whose internal and external relations are at all points governed by real (and not merely definitory) necessities.

The attitudes characteristic of religion involve then a characteristic policy of deference, of humble self-surrender before what appears very much greater, stronger and more admirable than ourselves. It is no doubt the case that they were first evoked by untamed natural displays, by eerie and unaccountable manifestations, by acts of great kindness from remarkable individuals, by human need in the face of certain calamities, etc., etc. But the attitudes in question are part of the necessary range of performance of our creaturely being-in-the-world, and are, from their birth, stamped by inbuilt norms which to some extent govern their development. One can worship wood and stone, but only because one endows them with marvellous, unmanifest properties of various sorts: to recognize them as mere wood and stone is to tend towards the end of one's worship. One can likewise reverence an utter rogue as a saint, but to recognize him as an utter rogue, who has done things one abhors and despises in others, is to tend to be shaken in such reverence. Slowly and ineluctably, in deference to their inbuilt norms of appropriateness, our attitudes of worship tend to converge on an intentional object in which all the demands of reflective valuation are satisfied together. The adequate object of religious deference must not merely be valuable in this or that limited fashion: it must incarnate *all* the values that we recognize, and particularly all those that we recognize as mandatory upon everyone and not merely on ourselves, and it must incarnate all these values in an incomparable, unsurpassable manner: there must not merely be nothing better than it, it must be impossible that anything should surpass it. It must also be entirely unique and single, not set side by side with another case of the same recognized excellences, and all inferior cases of what is good must derive their goodness from it, and be incapable of making one independent step towards such goodness. And it must, in the last place, be a true absolute, one that is an ineliminable, necessary foundation for whatever is thought to be: its being must be demanded by its essence however strange and paradoxical such a demand may be, and it cannot be conceived with complete understanding if not also believed to be certainly and necessarily real. It is not, we may note, plain that the adequate object of worship must be a God after the Hebrew-Christian tradition: it is in fact arguable that a God who to some extent stands aloof from his imperfect world is less satisfactory and less adequate as an object of worship than one which conforms to the 'acosmism' of Spinoza and certain other philosophers, and who gives to the world and its contents no shadow of independence and otherness from itself. It is not plain, either, that we should confine the adequate object of religion to the category of thinghood or substance: it is arguable that it should be placed among characters, relations or essences or transcendentals, that it should be regarded as a state, a way, a core of personal being or a goal of the world, or something that combines and transcends all these, even as a deific absence of anything in any way definite. We are not at present deciding in favour of one type of religious absolute as against another, though there are and must be reasons for considering some of these absolutes more satisfactory than others, and though no more than one of them can be ultimately satisfactory. We are not even holding that all of them may not be infected with absurdity: objects of worship may be phenomena genuinely given to us in certain sorts of mental intention or attitude, which none the less, together with the attitudes that set them before us, cannot survive the most profound searching and scrutiny. There remains, however, for all of us, in certain moods properly called 'ecstatic' or 'exalted', an approach to something that can only be called the apical phenomenon in our world, nebulous perhaps, and changing with our cognitive and value-experience, but not nebulous in the extremity of its pretensions: it is as much central to the cosmic picture, to the world in which we all find ourselves, as the navel is central to the human body. A phenomenology of the first blush must sketch the profile of such a religious object, or of varied types of such religious object with their varying adequacies and inadequacies. A phenomenology of

F

the second blush must make use of the criteria of adequacy inherent in such appearances and in other appearances as well, to see whether such a religious orientation is an expression of *Vernunft*, of right reason, or whether it must dissolve and be discarded as we deepen our immersion in the essences of things. But in either case we are not shaping our notions in the arbitrary manner characteristic of much science, mathematical logic and analytic philosophy. For us the initiative lies with the object: we are trying to let the matters before us shape and reshape themselves in a manner suitable and inevitable to them

We may begin, then, by considering the character of *aseity*, of necessary and ineliminable being which is part of the constitution of many objects of religion—they are eternal, primordial, undecaying, deathless, etc.—and which tends to become more emphatic as religion develops, even reaching assertions of a nobly empty ontological type ('I am that I am', etc.). The negative characterization of the religious object in terms of emptiness and non-being, as in Taoism and certain forms of Buddhism, is not as different from its characterization in terms of being as it would seem to be, nonbeing or emptiness being thought of as rich in dissolved alternatives and as even harder to eradicate than what is called 'being'. Aseity or absolute being is a notion found difficult by philosophers, combining as it does the two utterly elementary notions of being and necessity, and rendered obscure by this utter elementariness. Philosophers find it hard to see what can be conveyed by saying that anything is or has being, since if it hadn't being it wouldn't really be anything—they forget that it could still perfectly well be thought of and even shown or seen—and harder still to see what can be conveyed by saying that something necessarily is, since this means that there is no conceivable state of things with which its being there can be contrasted, and these difficulties lead to attempts to construe these notions in ways which depart far from our ordinary use and understanding of them, and which create as many difficulties as they resolve. But being presents no particular problem to ordinary thought, having as its contrast the perfectly understood bracketed status of merely intentional objects, whether thought of or seen, as well as the utterly specific, even perfectly individual shadows which their believed or conceived absence is felt to cast, or to be ready to cast, on our believed or conceived world. That this, which I see before me, might not have been, nay

more that it is not even when or while I see it—I beg forgiveness
for such archaic English—are suppositions unintelligible to no one
but a philosopher. Necessity of being and necessity of being the
case have their contrast similarly with what freely permits of a more
or less serious bracketing; what necessarily is makes itself evident
in the fact that we cannot in full seriousness and absorption in our
subject-matter bracket it or imagine it absent from the world. As
Kant showed in the *Transcendental Aesthetic*, space and time in
their all-inclusiveness, boundlessness and seamless wholeness are,
for ordinary conceivers, perfect cases of such aseity: we may not be
able to form images of them, but the sense of their absoluteness
enters into the unfettered use of our imaginative schematism, or,
as we ourselves should put it, we feel it in our bones that they are
there and could not but be there. Matter or stuff is a less plausible
candidate for aseity, but it is given at least as having the relative
aseity that, once there, it seems to require nothing additional to
preserve it in being: it is part of its idea, only shaken by serious
criticism, to go on in its being and in its occupancy of space. The
aseity of 'consciousness' or of the conscious subject is a notion
which, though open to rapid sapping, certainly recommends
itself to ordinary thought, particularly in those intimations of
immortality which it requires much argument to reason down: we
receive with blank incredulity the information of our elders that
there were times when we were not, and it is likewise not at all easy
to believe that there will be times when we shall not be there. The
immortality of the soul may or may not ultimately recommend
itself to right reason, but the first-blush phenomena have as little
place for our own origin or demise as they have for a beginning of
space or time. Ordinary thought also quite readily performs
a Platonic inversion and discovers aseity, absolute being, in abstract
directions: philosophers may have difficulty with the notion of
self-subsistent truths or self-subsistent moral rules but they often
occur in the gnomic reflections of a Greek tragedy.

When religion enters the scene, aseity soon becomes explicit.
Though some religious objects and figures may be infected with
remarkable contingencies, with the matings and killings, e.g., of
a polytheistic mythology, there is a plain tendency, hastened on by
prophets and philosophers, for these to become mere surface
embroideries upon what is eternal, unique, selfsame and necessarily there. There is little doubt that even the God of Judaism and

Christianity, who is credited with so large an overlay of arbitrariness, the choice, e.g., of the Jews, the speaking by the prophets, the non-despising of a certain virgin's womb, etc., etc., is never thought to have a limited, local or temporary sovereignty, and never by implication one that might have accrued to another being or to no being at all. Barth and others have rightly seen in the God of Anselm's Ontological Argument the God of Christianity and Judaism, the God whose misleadingly styled 'jealousy' is no more than his unique ontological necessity. And if we turn from religion to philosophy, there certainly seems to be a game played with the notion of necessary being. This is of course true of the extracosmic God of Anselm and Aquinas, of the acosmic God of Spinoza, of the Absolutes of Fichte, Hegel, Bosanquet, Bradley and so on: none of these existences could, for their believers, have been replaced by non-existence. But what is remarkable is that this is also true of philosophers who have tried to make contingency part of the notion of existence and fact. Thus the systems of Russell and the early Wittgenstein are, in aspiration at least, systems in which nothing exists necessarily. Russell, e.g., explicitly says that it is a defect of a logical system if it has to affirm the existence of something in one or other of its axioms or theorems. Yet in *Principia Mathematica* (*22.351) we learn that the world contains at least one individual of unspecified character, a necessary consequence of Russell's refusal to distinguish between the necessity that something (*if* there is something) should be either ϕ or not-ϕ, and the necessity that there should *be* something that is either ϕ or not-ϕ. Wittgenstein likewise builds his world out of *Sachverhalte* or atomic facts regarding which he affirms that each of them can be or not be the case, while everything else remains the same. This seems to imply that there might happen to be no atomic facts at all, but this does not seem to be a possibility that Wittgenstein ever seriously entertained. The fact that two philosophers so opposed to anything Anselmian as Russell and Wittgenstein should none the less have followed a line so thoroughly ontological, suggests that some sort of a necessity of existence is in fact unavoidable.

It would appear then that religious and other persons handle the notion of aseity, of necessary existence, without any particular embarrassment: it is notorious, however, that many philosophers have found it gravely absurd. And the absurdity has sometimes turned on the Kantian point that all significant necessity is necessity *ex hypothesi*, necessity either that something *would* be the case if something else *were* the case, or necessity that something *is* the case *because* something else is the case. The necessary existence of a religious absolute is, however, a necessity not subject to any supposed or actual condition, and this is a necessity of which no sense can be made. To this general difficulty a more specific difficulty relating to 'existence' is added: this is the famous contention that existence is not to be regarded as a predicate or an attribute or a perfection of anything, that it cannot enter into or enrich anything's character or essence or notion, but that it involves rather a relation of characters or essences or concepts to what lies essentially outside of them, the realm of concrete individuality that we encounter only through sense-perception or some other form of *Anschauung*. This relation is by its nature one of which it is absurd to predicate necessity, except in an *ex hypothesi* sense with a non-necessary protasis. To form the notion of something that exists of necessity is therefore to form the notion of something which has an attribute which is no attribute, and this is either pure nonsense or self-contradictory. Kant's conclusion ought now to be that, since the notion of a God who exists of necessity involves one or other of these illegitimacies, it is itself a wholly illegitimate notion, one that we can know has no instance whether in the world of phenomena or the world of noumena. Whereas what Kant in fact holds is that the idea of God, necessary existence included, is a flawless transcendental ideal in whose noumenal reality we can have good practical grounds to believe.

Modern treatments of necessity and existence in the Russellian-Wittgensteinian vein have left matters much as they were in Kant's time except that now necessity is thought to rest on the rules of our language rather than the relations of our concepts. Existence, once again, has sense only when general descriptions have an extra-linguistic application: to say things exist is a roundabout way of saying that their descriptions apply. And the further rider is added that, *if* we could give sense to the necessary existence of anything, we should at once make anything we said of that thing empty and unmeaning. For the nature of necessary truths is that they hold whatever the non-necessary circumstances may be, and this means that there could be no saving or redemptive or consoling implications in the necessary existence of a religious absolute. On all counts then the implications of modern linguistic philosophy as of

Kantianism are that religious absolutes are not things that possibly may not exist: they are things or putative things which certainly do not exist, since reference to them involves either a violation of the forms or the rules of logic. We should not be agnostics or sceptics regarding God, Tao, Brahman, etc.: we should be flat rejecters of them. These implications were worked out by myself in an article published in 1948 which I intended to call 'Disproof of the Existence of God' but which out of deference to possible suscepti-bilities I renamed 'Can God's Existence be Disproved?' My article shows that, if necessity and existence are interpreted as much modern philosophy interprets them, the existence of a religious absolute is logically impossible: if a religious absolute is a necessary existent, and there can be no such thing as a necessity of existence, then there can be no religious absolutes. I still think this article is perfectly correct as far as it goes, and it shows Anselm as paradoxically refuting the existence of his creator in the very attempt to demonstrate that existence.

I shall now suggest that it is no true role of philosophy, and above all of a philosophy that claims to be 'phenomenological', to revise its account of phenomena, of the experienced world, and of our major enterprises in it, in a manner so radical that those major enterprises lose their sense. We may follow the methodological principle (which has its roots in Moore) that philosophical argu-ments and principles and methods that end by undermining too much of what we feel with our bones regarding the world and our tasks in it, end by undermining themselves. It is they, rather than our bones, that suffer. Revision there must be—the phenomena may in fact be said to revise themselves under scrutiny—but if, e.g., in some revisionary perspective, science comes to seem mere unprincipled guesswork, and values and moral precepts matters for quite arbitrary choice, then it is *such* revisionary perspectives, rather than the views that they subvert, that really require recon-sideration. This holds, though perhaps more shakily, of the ordinary, the philosophical and the religious notion of necessary existence. The notion that there are some facts of existence that cannot be thought away reveals no intrinsic absurdity: the alter-native to it is the supposition that there might very well have been nothing, which does not seem to be a deeply illuminating supposi-tion. Certain eastern sages have simply opined that before there was anything there was nothing, and that all there is came out of this nothing: whatever can be said of this opinion, it cannot be said to fill the mind with a flood of light. In dealing with each object in the world we certainly proceed as if matters that are accidental in regard to them arise in a framework of what they essentially and necessarily are, and all science is directed to discovering what that core of necessity or essence really is. (We do not in ordinary thought know how to operate with the Wittgensteinian notion of things that have no intrinsic character other than the power to be combined with other intrinsically characterless things.) This necessity of essential character depends, however, on there *being* things of the essential character in question which in most cases there very well might not be. Nothing, however, precludes the possibility that contingencies of existence, which may or may not be actual, point back to an existential framework which cannot be varied, such as in fact, space, time, matter, consciousness, the Ego, God, absolute truth, etc., are by many thinkers supposed to be. It is arguable that our inability to talk about the total absence of anything is merely a speaker-centric predicament, since there are always at least ourselves, our speech and the presuppositions of our speaking, but it is equally possible to regard *this* as an unwarrantable dogma. Nothing prohibits us from recasting the logic of existence and modality so that a necessity of existence has a place in its definitions, axioms or theorems, and while we cannot in such a logic hope to derive existential theorems from premisses which do not affirm at least the possibility of necessary existents, one may very well make it include principles which affirm just such a possibility in certain privileged cases.

Naturally the acceptance of such principles in a formal system will considerably alter the meaning of both 'existence' and 'necessity' in such a system. 'Existence' will no longer be the sort of Russellian notion that concerns only the application of general descriptions to unspecified cases: it will be capable of use in the case even of named and shown individuals. We shall be able to acknowledge or not to acknowledge the existence of *this* object standing before us in perception, and to regard the existence of things of the sort in question as depending on the existence of shown individuals and not *vice versa*. We shall be able to say, as ordinary speakers are able to say. 'This might not have existed' and even utter the more daring statement 'This thing before me *does* not exist'. The verb to exist will not, however, be confined in its use to cases where we thus encounter extraneous phenomena and fit some notion to them. It may sometimes be used in cases where we have tried *not* to fit some notion, e.g. occupancy of space, presence to consciousness, to at least one thing that we can imagine, and have found ourselves unable to do so. The objects of religion may evince their being not so much by astonishing empirical incursions as by their sheer inescapability: if we take the wings of the morning, we shall not successfully evade them. They may in fact involve concepts in whose case the more fully we approach the understanding of what they involve the more certain we become that they must apply, in whose case content and application are in the limiting view inseparable. This does not mean that from the *mere* idea of something we can progress to knowing that it applies, but that, except superficially and un-reflectively, it is not possible to have a mere idea of certain things. These ideas will, of course, forbid us to hold any merely empty, verbal doctrine of necessity, nor is there any reason, other than sheer epistemological dogma, why we should accept such a doctrine. Necessity is necessity, it involves a marriage of conceptual content and coverage with conceptual content and coverage, and there is no reason why it should not at times qualify a marriage of conceptual content with inevitable application. Such necessities need not be elucidated in terms of anything simpler, even if in some cases this may be appropriate. And we discover such necessities by an ever deepened, reflective boring beneath the surface of symbolism, of abstract manipulation, of licentious imagination. Such necessity once laid bare can, of course, be made a merely analytic matter and ought for mechanical purposes to be made so: it is more convenient to make axioms and premisses and rules do the work that must otherwise be done by direct, difficult intuition. But the prime cases of necessity can be held to be the synthetic, not the analytic cases, and the latter to be merely a limiting trivialization of the former.

I now turn to consider a remarkable circumstance that goes far towards justifying Anselm in his two proofs of the divine existence, the first where he argues merely to God's *existence* from his superlative perfection, and the second where he argues to God's *necessary existence* from the same superlative perfection. These proofs can be so read as to be plainly illegitimate: from the mere fact that existence or necessary existence enters into the intentional constitution of some object we have before us, it does not follow that anything can be said of such an object outside of such intentional brackets. We can say only what it is thought of as being and not what it is nor that it is. We can only say that if it exists it exists, and exists of necessity and not contingently. If we rule that nothing exists necessarily, or can exist necessarily, then it follows that our protasis is invalidated: a perfect being does not exist, and it is impossible that it should exist. This is the purport of my before-mentioned article. What I did not perceive when I wrote this article is that one can work its argument in reverse. If, instead of holding a necessity of existence to be impossible, one holds it to be conceivable, possible, then one is at once able to conclude that it is actual and necessary. It is clear in fact that a being having aseity cannot exist contingently or be contingently non-existent: this certainty violates its very idea. It can only exist necessarily if it exists at all, and if it does not exist necessarily then its existence is quite impossible. This means by a simple case of the *modus tollendo tollens*, that if we hold its existence to be possible it will also exist necessarily. An absolute being, one that has aseity, is therefore in the unique position that its necessary existence, and so also its mere existence, follows from its mere possibility. The only way it can *avoid* existence is in fact by being at some point internally inconsistent or otherwise impossible. If Anselm's notion of *id quo maius cogitari nequit* is really a 'flawless ideal of thought', as Kant said it was, then the existence of *id quo maius cogitari nequit* does follow from its mere possiblity, its consistent idea, exactly as Anselm conceived it. Only if the idea involves some hidden inconsistency or absurdity, as Gaunilo's notion of a most perfect island plainly does involve one, can it evade the toils of existence. One of these hidden inconsistencies will, however, be the having of viable alternatives, for what exists of necessity has no viable alternatives.

The argument just put has been symbolically set forth in ten elaborate steps by Professor Charles Hartshorne in his *Logic of Perfection*, and will carry conviction to many who find me unconvincingly terse. But Professor Hartshorne, like myself, must appeal to an 'intuitive postulate' to the effect that perfection, which entails necessary existence, is not impossible, and this is the Achilles heel of the whole reasoning: those who think necessary existence inconceivable can still circumvent Anselm and Professor

Hartshorne, and they might very well argue that the fact that the acceptance of the possibility in question leads preposterously to the acceptance of its truth and its necessity, shows that it ought to to be rejected. The argument has at least shown that, if one's ideas of the possible are not unclear and muddled (as they always to some extent must be), one cannot merely be dubious about a necessary being: one must either reject or accept it outright. And, in the context of the present argument, our attitude is one of tentative acceptance. Necessary existence seems to be part of any fully developed ideal of cognitive explanation, as it is part of any fully developed synthesis of values such as our religious and mystical experiences point to: there is, *prima facie*, the possibility that the notion can be developed in a viable and not absurd fashion, and the obligation to try to do so. And if we can construct a viable notion of a necessary being—and there can be only *one* such viable notion if there is one at all—and if our understanding of this notion is not merely muddled, then it follows at once that there is and must be such a being.

It will not be possible in the present lecture to work out a full theory of an absolute being, much less that of a religious absolute which incorporates and synthesizes all values, in whom in fact necessity of being is only one among many perfections. It will only be possible to explore a number of alternatives—alternatives, that is, at the present stage of our insight—and see which accords best with the position that we now have reached. A more adequate theology will perhaps shape itself towards the close of these lectures when we have boldly exceeded the limits of our present world and life. What we may, however, lay down is that a religious absolute, one that embodies all values, can obviously not embody these values accidentally: it cannot merely happen to embody the wise, the just, the beautiful, the compassionate and to be in other ways maximally excellent. So much is clear, not only because what accidentally possessed these perfections could conceivably not have possessed them, and could then have been surpassed by some other thing that did possess them, and so prove an inadequate religious object, but also because, secondly, the precise and specific ways of being excellent do not seem to admit of a complete, joint realization, but lie to an indefinite extent in different and incompatible directions, and also because, thirdly, even when such incompatibility does *not* confront us, it remains meaningless to conceive of a *highest* realization of such excellences. The realm of values sketched in the last chapter is antinomic and without a clear maximum: the value, e.g., of innocence and simplicity quarrels with the value of being widely experienced and knowing, the value of accommodating kindness with the value of stern self-consistency and fairness, etc., and even when there are not such practical conflicts, it makes no sense to conceive of any precise arrangement or disposition than which no better can be conceived. *Id quo maius cogitari nequit* fails of necessary existence not because necessary existence is an absurd conception, but because the notion of an exhaustive synthesis of all excellence involves contradiction and is also a plain case of an illegitimate totality. These antinomic and maximization difficulties do not, of course, diminish if the object of religion is thought to possess all its perfections essentially and necessarily, if it not only essentially exists but is also essentially omni-excellent. The only difference is that then paradox and antinomy enter the inmost essence of the object of religion, and impart a resounding hollowness to all its crowning claims.

The only way out of these quandaries seems to lie in the difficult direction of trying to transcend certain normal distinctions of categories: we cannot in the case of an absolute, an entity that has aseity and embodies all values, draw any clear distinction between species and specimen, or between the sort of thing it is, its essence, characters, structure, essential mode of operation, etc., and *that* it is. Following a mediaeval lead, we cannot distinguish deity from God as we can distinguish humanity from men: we have not, in such a case, anything like a mere form or nature which requires some other individuating principle to turn it into a full-fledged existent. The same would be true of non-religious absolutes: the character or essence that renders them absolute is one with the absolute entity that shows it forth. Thus for all those who, like Kant and ordinary people, regard space as something absolute, it is not really possible to draw a clear distinction between spatiality and space: spatiality is, if one likes, the individuality of space regionally, morphically, qualitatively and otherwise specified, while space is no more than the differentiations and possibilities that it admits. Hence the perennial disputes between those who espouse a substantival and those who espouse an adjectival view of space. Hence also the necessary uniqueness of space: it is a complete systematic character which is at one with what, by analogy, one is tempted to call its only possible instance.

These things which hold regarding space and spatiality hold *a fortiori* when we turn to religious absolutes. In their case it is quite destructive to conceive of a generic form of perfection which they humbly exemplify. Not only must we say with the schoolmen that a religious absolute *is* its being, its goodness, its power, its insight and its other excellences: we must also say that it in some way eminently is the being, goodness, power, insight, etc., of anything whatsoever. This is of course what all religious people feel when they say, deeply driven, such strange things as that God is Love, God is Truth, God is not good but Goodness itself or the Good itself, etc. The Platonism which makes an ideal form a more real and precious thing than its instances is a one-sided form of this tendency. For obviously we should not have an adequate religious object if it were merely an unsurpassed *instance* of certain valuable properties of which there were other inferior instances. There must be no manifestation of value *anywhere* which owes an alien allegiance; all must be its own, must in fact be itself. This is why religious people naturally regard all valuable attributes as gifts and graces from the Father of Lights, as in fact simply *being* the Father of Lights in action. It is the limiting coincidence of character with individual being which alone guarantees the absolute's uniqueness: if it is not a case of certain excellences so much as those excellences themselves, it will not permit of the numerical diversity proper to mere cases. And it is this limiting coincidence which alone, likewise, guarantees unsurpassability, to which it gives a new, 'eminent' meaning. Each case of some value or form of excellence may be capable of being surpassed by some other case, but something which is *not* a case of this value or form of excellence, but this very value or form of excellence itself, can very well be said to 'surpass' all its cases, inasmuch as it is the general possibility and foundation of them all. (All this, as we have said, was well understood by Plato, and much misunderstood by his critics.) It surpasses them much as $\aleph_0$, the number of the finite inductive cardinals, surpasses all those finite inductive cardinals, among which it is not to be found, but *of* which it is none the less the number. And it is this limiting coincidence which alone will guarantee the compatibility of the excellences which in their instances are plainly incompatible. To be a case of one sort of excellence is often necessarily *not* to be a case of another sort of excellence, but to be the *principle* of the one sort of excellence is not necessarily not to be the principle of the other. If we make our absolute a 'mind' it will in fact be precisely tailor-made to reconcile and to incorporate in unity and joint pursuit all the forms of excellence that it is logically impossible should ever be completely and jointly realized in their instances, a mind being, as Aristotle says, a place of forms, in which without matter we none the less have something not fitly called abstract but concrete.

Many will of course be revolted by the talk I have just permitted myself, which does not accord that absolute priority accorded to instances that has become mandatory in modern philosophy; it will be objected that to make God Love, etc., is like making an absolute of the number system. This objection is, however, invalid, since an absolute is, in intention at least, not the sort of thing that admits of abstract treatment, nor which can be divorced from full reality, whereas a number system may very well lack instances of its higher members, and so have the imperfection which has plagued modern mathematical theory. An absolute is, in intention at least, a real transcendental overleaping the distinction of case and attribute, of sort and instance, whereas an abstract number-system merely side-steps or ignores it. The whole notion of such an overleaping of categories of course raises immense difficulties, and it is not clear, as will be argued in the next lecture, that such an overleaping will not take us beyond the limits of the human cave. In the present context, however, we shall not dwell on these difficulties; we shall still consider that we have not reached nonsense in the notion of a being that exists of necessity, and that synthetizes all values not so much by having as by being them all.

If our theology has so far been fairly orthodox, it now takes a wild leap into unorthodoxy: we feel forced to hold of a religious absolute as of any other absolute that it cannot solely have or be a set of essential features or perfections, but that it must also have many contingent features. It must have, to modify certain notions of Spinoza's, a natured as well as a naturing nature, or, to follow Whitehead, a consequent as well as a primordial nature. What this means is that an absolute must always be the possibility of countless things as well as the actuality of some of them, its absoluteness of course consisting in the fact that it is the ineliminable framework of whatever is actual, while whatever is actual is simply the fulfilment of one or other of its essential possibilities. Potentiality is in fact as inseparable from the notion of a viable absolute as actuality, and the doctrine of the absolute as pure act, if seriously entertained by those who profess it, is also a case of pure absurdity. Space, for instance, whatever its ultimate tenability as a self-existent being, certainly has contingent as well as necessary features: we may go so far as to say that its necessary features *consist* in the contingencies that it permits. (Cf. Wittgenstein's view in the *Tractatus* that the 'form' of an object consists in all its possibilities of combination with other objects.) Thus space permits innumerable types of occupancy and motion which will diversify it in countless fashions: each such diversification is contingent, and might not have been realized, but it is the essence of space that it permits such diversifications, and that it permits them all. Even wholly empty space has a contingent nature, since to be void of occupants is as much *one* of space's possibilities as any case of occupancy. The same holds, *mutatis mutandis*, of a religious absolute whose necessary being sums up all values: its being is always the possibility of countless cases of such values, as well as the limiting possibility of there being no such cases at all. There is a logical dependence of a perfection, even if regarded as something which a thing *is* rather than has, on possible cases or exemplifications, and this is so even if the latter likewise depend on it, and are necessarily imperfect in their representation of it. This logical dependence also remains when there are no cases of the perfection in question: this perfection is always essentially something of which there *might* be imperfect instantiations.

The development of a theory of religious absolutes would be a long, interesting affair at the end of which, after considering and rejecting many alternatives, one would arrive at a viable religious absolute which could without absurdity be conceived as existing necessarily and as being in some sense the principle of all values. Here we can only suggest, in the light of the dialectical work previously done, that such an absolute would have to be far more inclusive and explanatory of contingent, imperfect, creaturely being than the aloof views of the religious absolute we owe to Aristotle and the schoolmen. It is tempting to place the finite creaturely world more or less outside one's religious absolute, as an inconsiderable, unnecessary appendage to its sequestered perfections, but in doing so, one really (as Hegel points out) renders one's absolute finite and imperfect, since one places many good things outside of it, and things good in a struggling, passionate, earnest, real manner that *must* be expressions of one's absolute if the latter is not to be desperately impoverished. One may even go so far as to say that there is an axiological as well as a logical dependence of a religious absolute on possible exemplifications, in the sense that it would be a defect if it remained shut up in itself, cloistered, not communicating to anything the excellence it possessed or was. This is the principle stated in the Platonic doctrine of the unenviousness of God, as well as in the Neoplatonic doctrine of emanation, and, though it may not be official school dogma, there is no doubt that it enters deeply into Christianity, for which the creation of a world is no gratuitous exercise or trivial divine sport, but a deeply serious, perilous venture, and glorious because it is serious and perilous. If Christian theology does not normally reach as far as saying that God 'would give up the ghost' had he no finite creatures to redeem and love, it certainly comes close, in its less guarded exponents, to saying and feeling just this.

As opposed to all this, we have not only the doctrines which make creation gratuitous, but the parallel doctrines which make evil negative, not in the sense of positively striving against and rejecting the absolute good, but merely in the sense of falling short of it or exhibiting it defectively. This notion of evil as mere defect is infinitely impoverishing to a religious absolute, and the parallel Vedantist doctrines of ignorance and illusion have the same impoverishing effect. Spinoza's doctrine of 'mutilation' in the finite modes, has likewise the effect of trivializing the human struggle, and thereby also the being and thought of the One Substance in which all mutilated views merely lose themselves. Here we may only say, in keeping with the stage so far reached in our whole phenomenological and dialectical examination, that a viable absolute, one not internally discrepant and so not incapable of existence, must be one which not only embraces all contributions of contingent creatureliness, but to which the existence of such creaturely being, together with its grave possibilities of evil and disorder, is both essential and necessary. The precise form taken by such creatureliness is of course by definition contingent, but that there should be *some* such creaturely contingency is not contingent but necessary, if the religious absolute is to achieve the plenitude of value which its conception involves. And with the existence of creaturely being go indefinite possibilities of real evil, for to every value there is a disvalue which not only falls short of it but actively tends against it, and whose parasitic contrast is moreover essential to the value in question. It must be in the great work of releasing all this contingency and evil and also, as far as possible, transforming and redeeming it, that a viable religious absolute not only reveals its perfection but also has or is it. Such at least is the doctrine of the Germanic theology hinted at by several mediaeval German mystics but which may be said to reach its highest peak in the Hegelian philosophy of religion. It is arguable that, so far from being anti-Christian, as it is from many Kierkegaardian perspectives, it can perhaps claim to be the best philosophical restatement of 'the meaning of the cross'. The themes we have touched upon will, however, concern us in our next lecture, when we shall also find ourselves increasingly dissatisfied with any merely this-world view of a religious absolute.

THE COLLAPSE OF THE REALM
OF REASON AND SPIRIT

————————

In the last four lectures we have been studying the appearances of the upper regions of the human cave, not merely in their immediate and uncriticized, but in their more fully reflected, revised forms and semblances. We saw that, suspended above the first-order existences of the bodily realm, and the second-order existences of the realm of mind whose primary concern is these first-order existences, is a realm of intellectual values and ideals, and of abstract objects cut and trimmed to match them, which gather together and arrange and simplify all that is to be found in the lower spheres in question. There are values and ideals of the selectively simple and the endlessly enriched, of the limiting and pointed and the embracing and comprehensive, of what is true to the detail of empirical encounter and of what is loyal only to the distinctive and significant and so forth, and in obedience to such values and ideals minds retract themselves to various thin-edged abstractions or spread and blur themselves in various rough, open-textured notions. All these intellectual ideals specify a basic endeavour or *nisus* to rise above the contingencies of individual encounter and personal perspective, to approach things in manners which pertain to mind, reason, intelligence as such rather than to minds, reasoners or intelligences. They also express a deep-set preference for consciously constructed, deliberately sealed-off intentional objects as against those merely culled from experience, thereby achieving that mastery over the empirical and the existent which is only open to those who are not too considerate of the latter.

Similar to the values just mentioned are the wider realm of values and disvalues which preside over all towards which we feel emotions or experience practical urges, whether positive or negative, values and disvalues which all exhibit, Humean

G

prohibitions notwithstanding, a firm logical marriage between descriptive content and emotive and prescriptive force, and which are in fact merely the correlated goals of variously specified forms of impersonal-mindedness. Here we have the comprehensive value of satisfaction or happiness, which is a necessary object of endeavour to all impersonally minded persons for all persons whatever, no matter what the contingent content of that satisfaction or happiness may be for anyone. Here too we have the values of freedom and fairness and reciprocal affection and of endeavour directed to the other values just distinguished, as also the more puzzling, outlying, analogically justifiable types of impersonality, the scientifically explanatory and the aesthetically perspicuous. And we saw, further, that it is of the nature of these varied values to culminate in a single, unique intentional object to which devotion, worship, unconditional self-dedication are the only appropriate attitude. In this intentional object *all* values are given as present in what we say, without knowing quite what we mean, is their fullest, most perfect, most original form, which is in fact not so much an instance of these values, as the united presence and being of these values themselves, and the source from which all valuable things derive them. This union is not to be thought of as abstract, because it does not so much sidestep as transcend the distinction between type and case, in doing which it is equally thought of as rising above the difficulty of reconciling the values which cannot be combined in the individual case.

With the removal of the distinction between type and instance goes the removal of the distinction between nature and existence: the object we are conceiving is not one in regard to which we can raise the question as to whether it is exemplified or not exemplified, or in which we can only raise it in a quite transformed sense. It is, if we like, an object whose being is not so much evident in any remarkable encounter, but in the sheer impossibility of getting away from it no matter how hard we try, but which is none the less not an abstraction since there are and can be no instances of it from which one might abstract. It is, in short, an object unique in category and in its overriding of categories, to which aseity or necessary being must be attributed. The logical objections to this type of object we saw to be question-begging. But we held, further, that it is an object to which the contingent cannot in any degree or instance be thought of as external; it is in fact necessary for the object in question to exhibit contingent characters, without which it could be not said to be fully real at all, though the precise form of these contingencies is of course by definition non-necessary. What must be the case only has significance as delimiting what may be the case, as setting bounds within which what may be the case will fall, and to know necessity or the complete round of alternative contingencies is to know the same thing from a different point of view. Even *not* to have any positive contingent manifestations is a limiting, purely negative case of contingency. We may hold further that the power and perfection of the object in question will be greatest—that it will be most truly the object it is—to the extent that its limiting necessities run far enough into the depths and differences of contingent detail, rather than emptily contain and permit them, to the extent, that is, that there are vastly many special necessities limiting every contingent instantial sphere rather than a few wholly general necessities bounding them all. The detail in the world must, in short, be deeply rather than superficially understandable, and relatively much, rather than relatively little, of its pattern must be such that, instrinsically or *ex hypothesi*, it could not be otherwise. It must represent, in some sense, the inevitable self-manifestation of the absolute being, though there will necessarily be some part of that expression which is purely contingent.

The logical position of an object conceived in this fashion we saw to be unique and exciting: if it is really a well-formed and consistent object, capable of a thorough working out in thought at a sufficiently engaged and not merely formal level, then it is also an existent and necessarily existent being. It is not conceivable except as existing. But if, however, we can discover in it flaws of categorial make-up or internal inconsistency, then it is not merely an object whose existence is doubtful, but one which can be shown up as impossible. The misconceived, quasi-empirical problem of the existence of a transcendent religious object there-fore transforms itself into the question of its real conceivability: if the notion of a necessary, all-perfect being makes sense at all, then there certainly is a necessary, all-perfect being, but does it after all make sense to speak of such a thing? And the whole thesis of the intrinsic conceivability and real significance of a being which unites all values and which exists of necessity, remains as open to controversion as any issue of common-or-garden existence. That we have found a place for a religious object as the crowning phenomenon in the cave, does not mean that a deeper look at the phenomena may not encase it in intentional brackets as a mere regulative ideal, a transcendental idea, which, whatever its inspirational importance, still does not permit a complete working and thinking out.

In our own actual casting-about for an object that might fulfil all these transcendent requirements, we have had recourse to the Hegelian idea of rational self-conscious Spirit, the suprapersonal life in which we all, in our attempts to rise above the contingencies of our individual approaches, in some measure participate. This common rational life is responsible for the whole crop of proliferating meanings and values that we have been studying, and it is responsible for their culminating fruit, the intentional object of religion, in which necessary existence and an embracing synthesis of values are combined. What more natural step than to hold that this common rational life is itself the reality which fulfils its own transcendent demands, and that, in painting the portrait of what is perfect and exists of necessity, it is really painting a *Selbstbildnis*, and not the vain likeness of an empty ideal? This is in fact the step taken by the Germanic theology of which the philosophy of Hegel is the most interesting and complete expression. It has of course to face the objection that there is an infinite and necessary gulf between the *ideals* which direct conscious rational life and that conscious rational life itself, and that any identification of the former with the latter must be absurd. It is, we may say, of the essence of conscious rational life to strive for a consummation *beyond* itself. To this it is the Hegelian answer that a gulf necessary to the being of what lies on either side of that gulf, is not really a gulf, but a piece of dummy scenery. Conscious rational life must indeed *first* envisage itself as engaged in an infinite task of overcoming the brute unintelligibility of sensation, the blindness of personal passion, the sheer recalcitrance of material instruments and media, the endless abrasion of personal interest on personal interest, and all the other untowardnesses of this life, in order *then* to rise to the higher-order insight that these untowardnesses are really part of the rational game, that their necessity as spurs to rational effort makes them really not untowardnesses at all, that this imperfect life of struggle is in truth the one kind of victory and triumph that can be rationally desired. When one is young, Hegel tells us, one sees this world as sunken in wickedness and as calling for endless reform; when one is old, one sees this world in all its wickedness and fruitful reformability, as essentially ruled by providence, as being in all its arrangements just as it should be. It is not, and should not be, a place for insipid edification or recumbent ease, but for unending, absolute actuosity, for insight that is always penetrating frontiers, for love that is always abolishing barriers, and for endeavours that always end in further tasks: only in its opposed tensions can it achieve quiescence and harmony. This vision of Hegel, this incredible move into moonlit, classical peace from what is essentially Fichte's Germanic vision of an endless Valhalla of moral heroism is, as we have held, the supreme philosophical and religious illumination of our post-Renaissance world. Arguably it explains and justifies our intellectual, aesthetic and moral efforts, it gives philosophical expression to our deepest mystical and religious sentiments and those in particular that are inspired by Christianity. From our own point of view it has the supreme merit of alone promising to dissipate or mitigate the many thorny puzzles and discrepancies which make us feel this life to be a cave. All the surface indifference and opposition and deeper collusion among phenomena, of bodies with bodies and of bodies with space and time, of what is here and now with what is there and then, of bodies with minds, and minds with minds, and minds with bodies, of knowledge with real being, of values with knowledge, of religious ideals with their worthless worshippers, and so on, here have their explanation and their organic unity: these oppositions and indifferences exist for the sake of the rational activities they render possible, and in this new context they lose their original character of opposition and indifference. The unity of the whole arrangement of factors is teleological, but its teleology hangs, as it were, in the air and is the work of no special agent: it is itself the absolute rather than its offshoot or manifestation. The absolute being, that which cannot be removed from being, and which incarnates all excellence, and which lends necessity to the main lines of the world while justifying the contingency of its detail, is none other than our own rational, self-transcendent, thinking being, for the sake of whose emergence and development all things are as they are. It is a being which in an extraordinary manner reconciles the transcendent perfection of our rational ideals, supremely gathered together in the notion of a religious absolute, with the ignorance, confusion, misunderstanding and even perverse wickedness of our present condition. Our present condition properly seen *is* the absolute perfection that seems to hover so unattainably beyond it. If these sayings are hard, the discrepancies that have prompted them are harder yet.

Our task in the present lectures is not, however, to carry further the teleological construction on which we have been labouring, but to show that, despite its freedom from the absurdities that assailed simpler minded views, and that were set forth in previous lectures, it still has subtler absurdities of its own. Our aim is therefore to bring to ruin the whole teleological fabric we have been rearing, and particularly its crowning religious manifestations. All these must be shown to involve tensions which pull in opposed directions, and that admit of no lasting accommodation. The cave, however understood or interpreted, remains a cave, with all the bat-infested, mouldering darkness that our fitfully spluttering intellectual torches only serve to intensify. It can then be argued that it is only by going resolutely beyond towards states and conditions of some deeply different sort, that the cave-like character of our existence can be finally transmuted.

The main uneasiness that affects the teleological picture we have drawn can be quite readily stated: it lies in its imposed, arbitrary, somewhat wilful character. We are within our rights to see phenomena in what light we will, and to bring them under what general forms or categories align them best. To see bodies, and space, and time, and minds, and abstracta, and values, and religious objects, all as bearing on the emergence and development of what we have called rational mind—the thought and desire common to us all which is likewise inspired by the desire to achieve such commonness—is a legitimate way of viewing the phenomena in question. Our common rational life has the most intimate and necessary relations to our dealings with bodies and with our fellows, and evolves its characteristic products in this context: if it is correct and inevitable to see our common rational life in its connection with them all, it is correct and permissible to see them all in their connection with it. The world of bodies and the social world of interacting persons do provide the pabulum, the resistances, the framework, the subject-matter for our higher spiritual activities, and are in fact their necessary presuppositions. It is legitimate for us to view them entirely in this bearing. There are here no crude issues of observational observability, no bow to be made in the direction of the method-mad epigoni of the metaphysical scientists of the past. We are not going beyond the experienced data in viewing them in one framework of relations, and that supreme in significance for feeling and practice, and not in another. But the data, though permissive of endless variations of stress and angle, none the less differ in their reception of these: an irrefutable way of viewing the world may none the less seem forced, wanton, *voulu*, not according easily with the material on hand. In the phenomenology of formal arrangements or *Gestalten*, it is well known that some formal arrangements more readily make themselves manifest than others: it is easier to see normally placed than inverted, pendent staircases, or thin columns widely spaced than thick columns close together. (These principles have, of course, much more than a merely *de facto*, empirical validity.) In the same manner, in the more fundamental phenomenology of cave-furnishing, there are some formal arrangements that only make themselves manifest with strain and effort, and maintain themselves with difficulty, whereas others come natural and easy. To view all phenomena in a special teleological relation to our rational selves may be forced on us by the pressure of the conflicts considered in our first series of lectures, but it remains a difficult, unstable way of viewing things which, like some strange effort of stereoscopy, is ready at any moment to switch back again to the deeply unsatisfactory, but more stable ways of viewing things out of which it arose. There is something forced, unnatural about it: it readily comes before us as febrile and insincere in character. All excessively idealistic ways of looking things have this forced character. They force on the data a slant that does not accord well with them even if they do not positively reject it.

We have put the point in an exceedingly abstract way. It can be given a more specific, quantitative slant. We are inclined to say that it is abitrary to view the *whole, vast* world of phenomena in its bearing upon a *single* phenomenon in it, however interesting and distinctive this last may be in its higher-order subtlety and complexity. The stars may be, as Hegel said, a mere light-rash upon the sky, infinitely insignificant beside the simplest human thought or emotion. But is there not something very wanton in seeing the whole meaning of the former, in all their immensity of spatial and temporal extent, in their role as a mere background or presupposition of the latter? Is there not likewise something wanton in regarding the whole series of world-stages which led up to conscious rational life, in their vast range of forms and phases, as a mere preparation for the latter, much as the prophets, sibyls and heathen poets and philosophers were seen as mere prefigurers of the coming of Christ? Why should they all be regarded in this single perspective rather than in the many perspectives that their structure and character permits and suggests, and which may have nothing to do with teleology at all? Why, we are tempted to ask further, should not any existence, however trivial, stake a similar claim to embodying the 'sense' and the 'truth' of the world, the goal towards which all its stages and arrangements tended? There seems a violation of simple justice in seeing so many and such various things in the light of one only among them, particularly when this exploits the biased appeal of ourselves and our kind. I am, in other words, revoicing the Renaissance protest against the Platonic-Aristotelian-Scriptural teleology from which protest modern science took its rise. To return to an anthropocentric, teleological way of viewing the world, however much based on the philosophical infirmity of our concepts, is like reverting to the stuffy devotions of a pitch-pine conventicle after sampling choral worship under some nobly rounded Renaissance dome. What we have said has been deliberately phrased in terms of logical values, of the ethics of conception and utterance, rather than in supposedly objective terms which merely mask the basically evaluative issues.

It is particularly when we consider such factors as the extent of space, now yawning ever more vacuously as planet after planet reveals itself bare of its imagined population, that a teleological absolutism à la Hegel seems more and more frivolous. Gibes as to the pointlessness of mere quantity, its vacant repetitiousness, lose their force: from the standpoint of interest, of value, quantity may be nugatory, but from the standpoint of theory, of unbiased vision, it weighs against the significant and the extraordinary, and may very well outweigh it. More terrible still is the contemplation of the long probable period when there *was*, and worse still, when there *will be* no rational life in the cosmos, when, e.g., the 'heat death' of the world or some similar consummation will have put an end to things. If anything is definite, it is that rational, spiritual life demands to have the 'last word' in a cosmic dialectic, and that its primacy will be utterly refuted if this demand cannot be met. Such prospects may be powerless to modify or destroy our values, but are not powerless to destroy teleological world-views shaped in terms of them, and it is hollow sophistry to pretend otherwise. There is, further, a senselessness and an inconsequence in the distribution of great evils in the world which makes it shallow and heartless to regard them as a mere shadow of the good things they set off and help to stimulate, and whose possibility certainly presupposes their possibility. Only if the world necessarily tended to ever better conditions, as the idealistic or liberal or evolutionary or Marxist views of the last century all too readily supposed, could a teleological view be more than forced and idle, a deliberate, interested bolstering up of one side of the phenomena at the expense of others. Possibly, as traditional religion and these lectures have repeatedly suggested, the solution of this world's absurdities lies in another dimension and another life altogether. Only this, it may be argued, would suffice to fix the wavering teleological perspective which this world's phenomena do all too little to justify.

There is violence, further, in the whole attempt to make of our shared rational life the religious absolute that we have attempted to make of it. An absolute exists of necessity, and our shared rational life is given as being the most delicate and precariously poised of products, and the most readily disturbed and disrupted. Though it may flower with more than empirical inevitability in the right conditions, there is no inevitability in the presence or duration of such conditions. It is only by a teleological *tour de force* that our shared rational life can be seen as extending its presence to the vast tracts of space and history in which it is not overtly there, by being held to be there in germ or in consequence or in silent presupposition. In the same way, a religious absolute involves a synthesis of the highest values, and this not merely instantially, but in some difficult sense essentially and in principle. Plainly again it is only by a dialectical *tour de force* that this can be held to be involved in our wretched, confused, heartless, piecemeal living, however much it may blessedly apply to us in our more lucid and generous moments. A religious absolute so put together will not readily hold together: it will break up into a necessarily non-existent ideal, on the one hand, and a poor thinking existence that humbly intends it on the other.

It is plain, further, that the requirements of a religious absolute, though not involving the logical absurdity with which question-begging arguments have credited it, are none the less far beyond anything that can be encountered or envisaged in the human cave. A necessity of existence may not involve the monstrous confusions with which Kantian and linguistic critics have saddled it, it may even have a putative fulfilment in what we feel in our bones to be true, e.g. of space, but can it be said to appear luminously in the centre of our experience, rather than tantalizingly and mistily at its apex? In the same manner, a joint presence of all values in a single principle, overriding the plain impossibility of their joint realization in a single this-world instance, and which is not properly a case of instantiation at all, is no more than an outline, a ghostly transcendental requirement, to which we can give no precise filling 'down here'. That the cave should involve such a glorious phantom at its apex is no doubt an important fact about it, but it does not make it less of a cave nor the glorious phantom less of a phantom. Aquinas may have worked out in exhaustive detail the sorts of things that we feel in our bones should be true of a supreme something that holds all life and being together, but in doing so he has used a language whose precise semantics could be clear only to the angels. Used by ourselves and in this life, it represents rather a groping after significance than the utterance of anything intelligible, and positivistic and linguistic criticism is to this extent wholly justified.

We face, in fact, the unpalatable truth that, though the objects of religion may be the supreme occupants of the human cave, which promise most in the way of explanation and justification, they are also plainly the most blemished by antinomy and obscurity of any cave-phenomenon. And, from being sublime inspirers, they are, by their nature, ready to swing over into being the most dangerous confusers and corrupters that the whole cave harbours. Subtle philosophical syntheses like the Idea of Hegel or the learned ignorance of Cusanus or the higher flights of St Thomas are powerless to hold their components together except under unusual and strong pressures: they are always ready to dissolve into a simpler vision in which one side only receives full emphasis, and perhaps becomes dangerously unbalanced through absorbing and swallowing the virtues of the other. What arise are not so much specifications of the absolute religious object as perversions and distortions of it, and these unhappily would seem to be the main religious population of the cave. It is on this interesting pathology of religion that I shall for the rest of this lecture concentrate.

There are three main directions in which the distortion of the apical religious object can most naturally be carried. There is, first, a direction towards sheer emptiness and featurelessness, towards a washing out of contingencies in a being so pure that it is, as Hegel pointed out, indistinguishable from nothing at all. This is the celebrated negative way, conspicuous in Hinduism and Buddhism and pervading the whole life and culture of Japan, where no tea-house is complete without some symbol for that transcendental nothingness which tea-drinking, like every other positive manifestation and activity, merely serves to diversify. This negative way is, of course, also to be found in Plato and Plotinus, as in much Christian mystical theology, even in the Thomist doctrine of the profound simplicity of God. There is, secondly, a direction towards pure abstraction, towards religious objects, usually multiplied, which do little more than give mythic concreteness to various one-sided facets of value, whether centred in what is immediate and ordinary, as in the household pieties of the Romans, or in transcendental, mystical perfections as in the aeons of Valentinus, the multiplied hypostases of Mahayana Buddhism or the more nebulous abstractions of emancipated theologies from Schleiermacher to Paul Tillich. There is, lastly, a direction towards full-blooded, concrete contingency and existence, a direction mainly characteristic of our own Semitic tradition and its later Arab offshoots. This, though in some ways the most rich and splendid of religious traditions, is also the richest in its antinomies, and in its odd, jarring descents from the magnificent to the squalid and even the monstrous.

The negative theology that I am first to consider may be a sophisticated rather than a popular way of picturing the apical object of religion, but it none the less has its roots in the logical process—whether one regards it as a 'proof' or a construction—which we studied in the last lecture. Values point beyond themselves to a supreme synthesis, an *id quo melius cogitari nequit*, and in this notion is included the demand that the object projected should in some sense *be* all the values it sums up, and not merely *have* them or be a contingent instance of them, that it should be them all together and of necessity, and that it should further embody the supremely explanatory logical value of necessary existence, of not

being the sort of thing that could not have been, and of being
further the sort of thing on which all contingent existences directly
or indirectly depend, and without which nothing that does not, like
the object itself, exist of necessity, could conceivably be. The
demands we have uttered strain syntax to the utmost, but it cannot
be doubted that they follow the trend of rising above one-sidedness
and personal arbitrariness on which all value is founded, even if
they may have followed it into the absurd. The strain of trying to
go beyond the limits of plain sense leads, however, to a lapse into
the opposed direction of simplification: we drop the difficult
demand that our absolute should embody all the specific values
which obviously quarrel in their instances and admit of no
accommodation, we place contingency entirely outside of it rather
than make of it its necessary filling and complement, and it readily
becomes the irremoveable blank background, the void logical
space, of everything and anything, rather than the embracing
entity which its inherent logic would make of it. We now have the
characterless Brahman of Vedantist theology, the unqualified
voidness or Shunyata of Nagarjuna's interpretation of Buddhism,
the featureless One of the first hypothesis of Plato's *Parmenides*,
the first Hypostasis of Plotinus, the 'Nothingness' of Erigena, of
Jakob Boehme and many others, as well as other absolutes less
austerely and purely negative. It is of course easy to see the defects
of this particular perversion of religion, that with its elimination of
contingency and finitude it also eliminates reality and every conceivable form of value. A love, e.g., merely in principle, which is
not a love of anyone or anything, but only, with senseless circularity, of itself or of some emptily distinct shadow of itself, is not
only an *Unding*, a mere truncated intentional phantasm, but it is
also, in this abstract truncation, devoid of all goodness or value,
which is inseparable from the notion of unbracketed, not merely
intended objectivity. The case is even worse if the specificity of
characters like love, beauty, etc., is disdained, and the absolute good
is not thought of as being absolutely good in *any* specific manner.
And the defect is at once felt by many negative theologians who
like Plato in the *Parmenides* swing over from the first featureless
One to a One as richly diversified and as contradictious as the first
One was seamless and austere, or who like Plotinus turn the lack
of a need for anything into a source of endless emanation, or who,
like those who profess the 'Germanic theology', think that the

absolute being, or nothing, must necessarily declare itself in its creative Logos and in the creaturely being which, in so far as it has solid substance, is essentially an offshoot or 'spark' of the absolute itself. Nothing and nothingness may, as intentional objects, not deserve the abuse which analytic enlightenment has heaped upon them: they do not spring from a mere misunderstanding of syntax but represent a limiting possibility that, at certain levels of abstraction, we can and must conceive. Whatever decision we come to in regard to necessary being, we can only come to it by first trying to conceive, and thus, at one level of abstraction, actually conceiving, that there should be nothing, and directing our thought to an all-embracing class that is void of all members. That our thought of this class exists, and that the class itself has a sort of higher-order being, can be kept from view or regarded as irrelevant. But, even in this artificial context, it is clear that nothingness as an intentional object cannot be separated from the other possibilities that give it sense, and that it in fact is merely one of those possibilities. For there to be no A, no B, no C, and no D, for something not to be A, not B, not C, and not D, are merely limiting permutations of a set involving the four members A, B, C and D, and having no special position among them. We may say in fact that for there to be no world at all is merely one way of there being a world, and that the elimination of all positive contingencies is only a limiting contingency which takes us no way towards the necessary and absolute. And negations only have value in relation to what they are the negations of. If a room is cluttered with in-numerable knick-knacks and gewgaws, it will gain beauty and dignity as they are stripped off one by one, but if all are removed and the room itself demolished, beauty and dignity will have vanished too. These are reflections which might well be pondered by those intent on losing themselves in some inadequately conceived, merely negative samadhi or Nirvana. The negative theology has its in-defeasible position in religion, as negation has in all spheres of valuation, but even its vacuity abhors a total vacuum.

From the one-sidedness of a pure necessity of properties, we proceed to the one-sidedness which makes the religious absolute no more than an intentional object, either covertly, by identifying it with a truncated abstractum or set of truncated abstracta, more or less clothed in imagery, which one tailors to suit one's own needs, or overtly, as in modern times, by characterizing it exclusively in terms of some human attitude or relation or experience, whether as that on which we have an ultimate relation of dependence, or as that with which we have an ultimate concern, or as the appropriate object of worship or unconditional self-dedication or religious experience. The Mahayana's evasion of the early Buddhist atheism by multiplying nebulous shapes corresponding to the Buddha's various perfections of wisdom, compassion, etc., even to the abstract Dhamma or doctrine which he said would guide his disciples when he was gone, is an example of the first more covert type of construction, whereas the modern exclusively idealistic or phenomenological or 'existential' study of the object of religion belongs to the second, overt type. In all these treatments the object of religion is bracketed in a manner which, while it makes construction an easy matter of running up fronts or façades without elaborate buttressing or foundations, and while it removes the penalties of imperfect coherence and even formal contradiction, still fails to give the religious object the full solidity which is the reverse side of the totally committed *seriousness* of authentic religion. Such phenomenological treatment is what we ourselves have practised in our lecture on religion, and what acknowledged masters like Otto and Scheler have practised more adeptly: it is the proper introduction to a true philosophy of religion. The phenomena must, however, be studied, not merely in their first piecemeal abstraction, but in their revised integrity and complete mutual accommodation, and to *keep* characters so difficult as necessary existence and a non-instantial synthesis of values in intentional brackets, is in a sense to dissolve them altogether. A religious object that in any sense *might* not be is, as we have seen, an object that *could* not be at all: in the same way, a religious object whose existence we merely dally with or entertain, without unconditionally committing ourselves to belief in it, is in a sense not really conceived of at all. The unique, limiting position of a necessary existent has consequences not only for ontology but for epistemology: what such an existent may be can be clear only to those who fully believe in it. Argument about it can never serve to add something extra to its mere notion: it can only show up the absurdity of trying to treat it as a mere notion, and not as the irremoveable background that all mere notions presuppose. It is clear, further, that the relaxation of philosophical tensions which we have hoped for from a religious object, as the summit of the realm of reason, is not to be had from it as long as it remains merely an intentional object. All that we then have is the infinite aspiration and concern of man, seeking against all reason for something that will bring health and sweetness into the singular mixture of collusion and discrepancy, of profound fit and misfit, in which all cave-life consists. This disastrous, poisonous mixture is not rendered more drinkable by our mere hope of replacing it with some more palatable prescription.

We may now turn, in the third place, to what I may call our Semitic way of existence, in which we are not afraid to impute contingencies of manifestation to our religious absolute, to make it manifest itself in one excellent fashion rather than another equally possible one, to make it elect to manifest itself positively rather than, what is equally possible, not to manifest itself positively at all, to associate it in varying degrees of intimacy with various contingent existences, some being its directly chosen channels, some only things for which it is remotely and intermediately responsible, while some represent an extension or direct embodiment of itself. We are not, in short, afraid to credit it with something like the capacity of turning a disjunctive possibility into a categorial actuality which we feel to be of the essence of human will or choice. Our God, if he be a god, must be a living God: he must operate freely in creation and history, there must be an element of the beneficently arbitrary and wilful in what he achieves or elects not to achieve. We shall not here be concerned with the overtly perverse forms of this view in which arbitrariness and contingency cover the *whole* field of the religious object's activity, in which this is deemed responsible not only for fulfilling and following, but also for arbitrarily instituting all logical and axiological norms and proprieties. Nor shall we be concerned with views in which the range of the absolute being's activity extends to what is as such evil, and not merely to what is incidentally or instrumentally or permissively such. Religious objects framed on either pattern violate the principles of their construction: they have nothing that would deserve the self-dedication even of our humble worship. The notion of an absolute that is quite arbitrary, whose dispositions at all times range over all formally possible alternatives, is not perhaps so absurd a notion as some have found it, and has even a certain one sided-dignity. Possibly the amoral Brahman of the *Upanishats*, whose decision to be many has a childish straightforwardness of purpose, is arbitrary in this manner, but even here its choice seems channeled between the elementary values of unity and rest, on the one hand, and of richness and movement, on the other. The proposition that *quicquid appetitur appetitur sub ratione boni* may not be a self-evident truth, since the primary ends set before us by engaged, single-minded appetite precede the second-order rational ends or values which involve detachment and impersonality, but it seems evident that arbitrariness, too, is a higher-order phenomenon which operates only in a pre-existent framework of ends set either by mere appetite or by the higher-order, impersonal interests which found themselves upon it. In any case, whatever the ontological conceivability of a being of quite unfettered arbitrariness, it fails to achieve the synthesis of values which is essential to an adequate religious object. Its egoism need not, e.g., include that necessary and passionate love for all egos, that burning repudiation of repudiation and that exclusion of exclusiveness which is inseparable from the developed idea of deity. In its unlimited self-will, the absolute would in fact come close to the pure Satanism which, whether actual among men or among beings higher than men, certainly represents a necessarily possible declension from the idea of deity.

The kind of religious object that we have to consider, and that the higher types of Semitic thought certainly tried to frame, is one in which the arbitrary falls within and fills in the necessary, the necessary consisting of the metaphysical values of simplicity, unity, self-existence and power, together with all the other moral and non-moral values of justice, mercy, truth, beauty, etc. God or the religious absolute cannot fail to will these values because, in a manner which defies ordinary grammar, he not only has them but is them, but within the bounds set by these basic forms of excellence what corresponds to a will in the religious absolute can and must determine itself quite freely. There is nothing in the idea of deity to exclude, e.g., the choice of one way of manifesting itself rather than another equally valuable or even more valuable way: all modes of self-manifestation or non-self-manifestation necessarily involve just this. Existence in the sense of instantiation necessarily involves a choice among contrary possibilities, and it is logically impossible to instantiate *all* good possibilities, whether in a single world or in many sequences of worlds. The best of all possible worlds is a logical absurdity which imposed amazingly on the acute mind of Leibniz, and the infinite perfection of deity consists in fact in the simple circumstance that it alone is best, and that it is logically impossible to carry out this 'bestness' in any set or series of instantial realizations. If deity is *id quo melius cogitari nequit* it is not this as being a case, or as producing cases, of every possible form or shape of goodness: it can only lie in its being them all in principle, or in being the root and source of them all. There is therefore no *a priori* reason why deity should not have operated more intensively through Abraham or Moses or Mohammed than through Socrates or Buddha, though the notion of deity induced by my *own* moral development makes it hard for me to think that it did so. And the notion of a supreme embodiment or incarnation of the Logos or contingent, creative side of deity, is one that is in no sense unacceptable or absurd in principle nor in any way at odds with the notion of deity, though its supremacy would necessarily be a contingent and not a necessary matter.

The difficulties of the Semitic way in religion lie not, however, in its principles, but in its necessary corruption by the circumstances of cave-life, in which alone we are considering it at present. The demands that the religious object should exist necessarily, and should have all its perfections necessarily, and should in fact rather *be* them than merely have them, are not such that that they can readily be given a fulfillable sense within the limits of the cave: we cannot fully understand what they involve, and we are inevitably driven away from them towards what we think we can more fully understand. What we are driven towards are contingencies decked out with all the glory and authority of what is inescapable and necessary, and monstrously lording it over other similar contingencies. We bow down to specificities and particularities whose only source of dignity and authority lies in the impersonal values they exemplify, and we give them all the dignity and authority of those values themselves, withdrawing deference from other specificities and particularities which, on the face of it, exemplify precisely the same values. Certain practices, certain subtle formulae, certain special groups, certain unique persons, etc., then become for us the sole channels through which contact with the ultimate principle of all value can be had, and alternative practices, formulae, groups, persons, etc., though not in general character different, are felt to be suspect, detrimental,

H

mysteriously corrupted and corrupting. And what then happens is that the unchangeable axiological bones of deity become confounded with its variable, contingent covering, and that, worse still, the latter acquire the absolute status of the former. The unsurpassability which necessarily lies in another dimension than that of instances, which is, if one likes, a 'spirit', a 'meaning', a pure universal incapable of full expression in any instantial set whatsoever, then becomes wedded and committed to a particular set of instantiations, than which no contradiction could be more gross or more glaring. To worship the contingencies in which deity becomes concrete is a part of piety: to obliterate the distinction between them and the necessary framework they fill in can only be called impious. It constitutes in fact the wickedness of idolatry, and it is a strange fact that the Semitic prophets and apostles who have been most deeply conscious of this possible transgression have also been the most often guilty of it. The heathen in his blindness may bow down to wood and stone, but he has seldom or never confused the contingent particularities of the poor object before him with the divinity which breathes in it, nor denied that others might find divinity in very different objects. It may not be wood or stone that attract our idolatrous devotions, but these have been given to historicistic, personal and doctrinal specificities whose subtlety renders them far more noxious. What is wrong in all these proceedings is not the reverence for the specific and particular which is part of any developed piety, but the exaltation of the instance into the role of its supra-instantial pattern. And that this leads, with an intrinsic probability, to various evil forms of persecution and discrimination is not anything I need stress or document: such have been the bane of our Semitic religious. The Nothingness of Nagarjuna or the abstract aeons of Valentinus are innocuous by comparison: no one has had to suffer for failing to see the merits of either. We may note further that the possibility of the religious object manifesting itself through certain unique objects is only a possibility. It is consistent with the essence that it should have countless graded 'theophanies' with none at all uniquely pre-eminent.

I may here say briefly why I consider the Messianic life and mission of Jesus as a shadow of the cave, and not as the unique incarnation of absolute deity that Christians suppose it to have been. My reasons for questioning the central dogma of Christianity are reasons of emphasis: that in the notion of the Messianic status of Jesus there is a stress on the contingent carrying-out as opposed to the essential core of deity which I cannot but see as unbalanced, and which leads, I think, to a large amount of essential emptiness and circularity. What I shall call the Messianic circle is the feature which above all stamps Christianity as a cult confined to that cosmic catacomb which I have called the cave. I can explain what I mean by considering the history of theology. In my youth I studied the even then old-fashioned writings of Harnack in which great stress was laid on a distinction between the gospel *of* Jesus, whose content was the new life about to open to truly repentant persons, and that life's revolutionary values, and the gospel *about* Jesus, mainly put about by Paul, whose content was the special, saving role of Jesus as displayed in the unique events of his life and death. Jesus was in this theology not supposed to have spoken much about his special, saving role, but, if anything, to have only shown it forth in the values he inculcated and himself exhibited. It was to other, later eyes that this role became emphatic, was connected closely with traditional prophecy and eschatology, and began to overshadow the original view of the coming Kingdom. Everyone will know that this view of Christian origins has long been burst asunder, though not all will be happy in the fact that this is so.

It is plain beyond doubt that the gospel *of* Jesus was, in the main, a gospel *about* Jesus, a doctrine about his own secret, unique Messianic status, and that the difference between his views of that status and those later held by the Church are of quite minor significance. Fundamentally the Church only worked out a clear theological statement of what Jesus in his claims regarding his unique position both thought and taught. The peculiar values exhibited and inculcated by Jesus are moreover all so closely tied up with his conception of his own Messianic status that they cannot without distortion be separated from it: even so cosmic a parable as that of the Prodigal Son has Messianic overtones, which is of course even more true of parables like that of the Wise and Foolish Virgins and of many others. The behaviour of Jesus is throughout that of a wholly special person: it is not, and has not been thought to be such that we should in all its details imitate it. All this is, of course, particularly true of the events and acts that surround the Passion. There all turns on Messianic status and nothing on any set of value and prescriptions that Jesus may have taught. Jesus was not put to death for any spiritual doctrine or way of life, but for claiming to have a status which to some seemed to involve blasphemy, while others thought it had dangerous political implications. The Passion was plainly a provoked death, in which all turned on what seems a deliberate revelation of Messianic status, and only a genuine Messiah could have had the right to provoke such a death. It was, we may say, a High Mass performed with a living victim for essentially ritual purposes, and so standing beyond all bounds of the morally meaningful and permissible. The anxieties of Gethsemane were likewise not anxieties regarding the world or the truth or even Jesus himself, but anxieties regarding the ability of Jesus to carry out the hard Messianic programme ahead of him and also regarding God's endorsement of his attempts and his claims. If one does not believe that Jesus was the Messiah, or is not clear what being a Messiah could mean, then there is nothing in the crucial acts of Jesus, nothing even in his crucial teachings, which would establish his divinity. And if one doubts whether divinity would or could behave in this essentially ritual manner, stressing the historical, personal and particular rather than the inescapable values behind them, then the strange events of the Passion serve to refute rather than prove the Incarnation. It might be thought to assimilate Jesus to God to maintain that his special relation to God, like the very being of God himself, is something that we cannot at all understand unless we also believe in it, that something of a circle is inevitable in its case. The position is not, however, analogous. For God is not thought of as a contingent, escapable being who might or might not have been there, but as the inescapable crowning synthesis of all values, whereas the Messianic status of Jesus and the circumstances of his ritual death might quite well have been otherwise. Buddha was plainly Buddha, the Enlightened One, in virtue of the surpassing excellence of his Dhamma and his person, but in the case of Jesus we have always to ask in virtue of what he was the Christ. And it is the presence of this circle which has been responsible for what we can only call the monstrous element in Christianity: the fanaticism, e.g., which made Augustine believe in the damnation of unbaptized infants, that led Kierkegaard into his strange gloating over Abraham's senseless attempted sacrifice, and which is evinced in the occasional exalted selfishness of some even of the

Christian mystics. We must regretfully say of many Christian saints what Augustine said of the pagans: that their virtues were at best splendid vices. All this of course need not take away from the complete personal faith and self-dedication of Jesus, who made of events and doctrines sorry and strange in themselves symbols of the redemptive love that Christians have always seen in them. Nor are we prevented from seeing in such events and doctrines a revelation of divinity in a state of kenosis and in servitude to unsatisfactory Jewish traditions.

What we conclude at this point is that we cannot sustain any purely this-world resolution of the tensions among phenomena in terms of a teleology leading always to the emergence and the ever richer development of interpersonal, rational life, that we cannot prevent such a picture from switching over into an opposed sinister version in which rational, interpersonal life remains a mere excrescence upon an order essentially purposeless or perhaps actively malign. We conclude also that the actual religions of the world, which all represent rational faith at its highest, are also all phenomena of the cave, which incorporate absurd, sinister and even monstrous elements, which most apologists have sought to minimize, but which some modern exponents have deliberately exaggerated.

OTHERWORLDLY GEOGRAPHY

———

I have been attempting in the first five lectures of the present series to reform the cave immanently, to remove its unbearable tensions by way of co-ordinating ideas or ways of looking at things without attempting to go beyond the cave and its varied phenomena. The conception with which I attempted to allay tension was a variety of religious absolute, one that was thought of both as a necessary existent, and the basis of all contingencies, something that could not be thought of as absent from reality however much its manifestations might vary, and something that in the second place was a principle of the higher values that emerge when we cease to be merely interested in this or that, and become interested in the interesting as such, and in the manner of its interestingness. The absolute we were working with was, however, essentially teleological in its explanatory role: it was the sense or goal or *raison d'être* or Hegelian 'truth' of the world, rather than anything that was thought of as underlying it or creating it. The world was as it was, with all its tangle of opposedly tending phenomena, in order that the rational, supra-personal, interpersonal life of man should emerge and develop, and should transform its natural and social environment to accord with its own rational patterns. And this teleological perspective meant that all things inert and sense-less, or even contrary to the rational *nisus* of man, were seen as the mere raw material or preparation for the latter, that without which rational interpersonal life would be impossible, and which, seen in this regard, loses everything that is untoward and un-suitable about it. The world's not being as it should be, comes to be seen as a higher-order case of its being as it should be, once it is seen as being a necessary condition of 'the one thing that counts', our rational, intersubjective, self-conscious being.

The objection to this deeply penetrating, transforming view of things lay, however, in its essentially arbitrary, somewhat feverish character: on reflection it readily seemed a forced gloss put on the immense indifferences and resistances of material being to the small-scale aspirations of man. To see all the inert, ugly, problematic things around us in this happy, resolving light, could readily seem an exercise in collective egoism and unwarranted morale-building, and, seen as such, it readily switches over into a sinister view—whatever the deep difficulties of the latter—in which man and his rational purposes are a mere momentary iridescence shed upon the inert, ugly, problematic things just mentioned.

There were also difficulties in the fact that the proposed religious absolute proved on examination to be a poor specimen of its kind. There is conceptual violence involved in treating what is, from many points of view, a highly dependent, readily disrupted phenomenon, as what gives sense to the vast complex web of phenomena on which it depends. There is even more conceptual violence in seeing its imperfections in the forced teleological perspective we impose upon them, not merely as instances of perfection, but as in some sense 'moments of the Idea', one with absolute perfection itself. Our conscious life certainly has an inherent *nisus* towards the rational idea of perfection, but this rational idea obstinately lies beyond it, and cannot without conceptual forcing be made part of it, at least not in the conditions of this earthly life. But, if we then look around, and study the immense luminous appearances which the rational idea of perfection casts on the cave-ceiling, the various objects of religion, they also reveal the antinomies and discrepancies which haunt all cave-phenomena. Necessary existence is nothing that can be clearly envisaged in the cave, and a joint embodiment of all values, which consists in being them rather than having them, and so avoiding their incompatible instantiation, is not anything we can reconcile with cave-limitation, and so necessarily deteriorates into one distressing distortion or another. We have, on the one hand, multiplied abstractions which never rise above being merely intentional objects, or exalted negations which never really establish their difference from the nothingness or the unconsciousness which is devoid of religious value: we have, on the other hand, the existences dignified with many adjectives expressive of omnitude which none the less do not escape the scandal of particularity and contingency. They are not, in fact, beings that embody *all* values, but arbitrarily exclude many. They are for the most part grandiose magnifications of human persons, with particular one-sided policies and tempers, and with much more sensitiveness to violations of their own *amour propre* than to those of the core of values which they embody. All rational life points towards a religious absolute, and yet it seems impossible to bring such an absolute into the circumstances of cave-life.

It is here that there will have to be a third turn of the wheel in our lectures, reminiscent of the three historical turns of the wheel of the Buddhist Dhamma in India. We shall embark on a radically new policy: we shall attempt to pass beyond the closely knit phenomena of this world to phenomena which, while never grossly disconnected from the things in this world, and diverging continuously from them, none the less end by differing from them so deeply as to deserve the title of 'otherworldly'. These otherworldly phenomena have an important role to play in what by contrast we call *this* world, and may, in virtue of this role, be said always to be *in* this world and to serve as its necessary background, to and from which our thought and experience normally shuttle back and forth. But, though thus involved in this-worldly dealings, otherworldly phenomena still are parted from the latter by a barrier, which gives them a distant, half-discerned, visionary character. They are *somewhere else*, quite out of the main nexus and traffic of cave-factors, and the transition to them necessarily involves an element of suddenness, which it is not unreasonable to connect with unusual experiences, as well as with the great, standard cruces of birth and death. What I shall be attempting to do in all this is neither to extend experience, in the sense of encounter with particulars, in some unusual, speculative fashion, much less to build on experiences of a unique, extraordinary or occult character; if I am right, experience in the sense of alien irruption will become blessedly less and less important as one rises in that upper world. It is in fact through philosophy, and philosophy alone, that we are drawn towards that upper world which supplements our own, and which is framed precisely on the recipe that, when seen in connection with this-world phenomena, it must iron out the conceptual wrinkles that we cannot otherwise get rid of. The problems and puzzles of philosophy, so far from being based on avoidable linguistic misunderstandings, will be guides towards a truly understanding use of language: they will function like the discontinuities and unevennesses in a woven fabric which point to explanatory continuities running on the other side.

We shall not in all this be attempting a Platonic flight from a half-intelligible world of shadowy opinion to an intelligible world of stable being, but from a world of experience which is only un-intelligible as long as it is seen without its necessary continuation and complement, to a fully continued version of the same. The other world, divorced from its function of illuminating and regu-lating what goes on in this one, will in fact be as essentially un-intelligible as this one is if correspondingly divorced. The other world is, in fact, not so much another world as another half of one world, which two halves only make full rounded sense when seen in their mutual relevance and interconnection, much as, at another level, we saw that the moulded, shaped space of the world could be nothing without the bodies that diversified it, and those bodies without their moulded, shaped space.

The accommodation that promised to remove the tensions in our world, was, we held, teleological: an inner purpose alone could explain that semblance of maladroit collusion that we could not help encountering everywhere. But this teleological accommoda-tion could not be maintained with phenomena limited to this world, but was always switching over into a non-teleological epiphenom-enalism. With the backing of the phenomena of another world such a switch-over may be avoided, the teleological accommodation maintained, and the phenomena 'saved' in the sense of being freed from the discrepancy and antinomy that would otherwise always haunt them. The move we are making is only a stage more complex than moves frequently made in the past. A 'future state' has often been brought in to make morality meaningful, or to justify us in following its dictates. We, however, are introducing a future state to make *all* our rational enterprises meaningful and justifiable, in-cluding our ordinary dealings with men and things as well as the more elaborate experimental dealings of science and technology. In doing this we are following Plato, who likewise founded the sciences and the higher flights of practice upon experiences had in another world. We are also, in a way, following Descartes and the seventeenth century rationalists, who brought in God as the supreme guarantor of our various forms of rational faith. We, however, are taking the unusual step of making Heaven, rather than God, the guarantor of our rational enterprises, God being conceived as what occupies the apex or zenith of this Heaven, rather than Heaven conceived as a place presided over by God. The objects of religion are for us the supreme pole of the other world and the antipodes of our own. The extraordinariness of all that we are premissing is perhaps mitigated by an injection of gradualness. The other world will only reach conditions unlike and opposed to our own after it has followed a course whose starting point is in fact in our own world and whose first stages very much resemble states in our own. This postulated gradualness contrasts, however, as said before, with a certain suddenness at the actual point of contact with our own world. Birth and death are acknowledged by all to be large changes, and so are any terrene ecstasies that might translate us to one or other of the doubtless numerous celestial zones. The speculative extension we are positing, though it postulates actual testing experiences, and is to that extent like science, is not like science in that the spur to all our speculative activity are not puzzles of detail such as the anomalous expansion of water or the Michelson-Morley experiment, but philosophical aches and tensions that affect the whole of experience, and are strongest at the meeting-points of different fundamental categories. Our basic conceptions also have 'affinities' like our most detailed empirical notions: they point to likely completions and continuations, and point away from unlikely, discrepant ones. Where scientific tensions only lead us to postulate new types of particle or modifications of fundamental scientific formulae, philosophical tensions lead us to complete our world with a whole new type or set of types of worlds. But, since such completion is speculative, it can never be stronger than its base, the philosophical tensions it is devised to allay or remove. But in the actual other life it will, of course, cease to be a speculative construction, and by a vision and experience we cannot hope for in science we may see the total system of phenomena as so dominated by a teleological order that any other way of seeing them becomes forced and artificial. This beatific vision, for beatific it will certainly be, cannot be superseded by a rival perspective: those who enjoy it, and who see things in its context, cannot but be clear that it sums up the sense and 'truth' of everything.

We may now introduce a geographical analogy which we shall follow throughout the ensuing lectures. This is the analogy of earthly geography in so far as this varies from latitude 0° at the equator to latitude 90° at the poles. Celestial phenomena as seen from the earth vary vastly according to latitude, and so do many climatic and other phenomena which relations to the main celestial bodies induce. There is, e.g., an extremely paradoxical contrast between the almost uniform sequences of days and nights at the equator and the vastly varying periods of day and night at the poles, but there is also a gradual transition from one to the other which does much to alleviate that paradox. Near latitude 0° there are likewise wider possibilities of movement in latitude which steadily contract as one moves towards the poles, until at the poles all lines of longitude come together and same-latitude movement freezes into immobility. At the poles too one has the paradoxical situation that all great-circle movement must be due north or due south, whereas at the equator there is great-circle-movement in every possible direction. The paradoxes are, of course, quite trivial once one understands them, as are the comparable para-doxes involved in the pushing on or back of the clock as one travels, or the perennial marvel of the day lost or gained as one crosses the Pacific. But the analogy is apt since I wish to suggest that otherworldly conditions have the same sort of wholly under-standable and therefore quite trivializable relation to this-worldly conditions that life in high latitudes has to life at the equator. Only, whereas the facts of this-world geography depend ultimately on contingencies such as the sphericity, rotation and revolution of the earth is a given cosmic position, and at given angles, velocities and directions, the facts of what we may call spiritual geography are, on the view suggested, all necessary facts of being, matters that could not conceivably have been different, and on which all con-tingencies depend for their very possibility. It may be possible to construct a formally consistent system which would take no account of them, but what is there set forth will only be abstractly possible: fully thought out and considered, no supposable system could be other than the system in question, and what runs contrary to it will deserve at a deep level to be ruled out as self-contradictory.

In the system we are considering there will be an 'equatorial' zone of maximum differentiation, whether of individuals, kinds or categories, and the closest possible approach to the exhaustively determined individuality and to the clear-cut identity and diversity that our formal systems normally postulate. But as we pass away from that zone, and go up steadily in latitude, there will be a steady vanishing of the harsh definiteness and distinctness of individuals, and a steady blurring or coming into coincidence of the divisions among kinds and categories, until in the end one approaches and perhaps at last reaches a paradoxical, unitary point of convergence, where the objects of religion may be thought to have their habitat. Alone these are as absurd in their coalescence as the dispersed matters at the equator are absurd in their dispersion, but together they make up a wholly intelligible system, and the only intelligible system that there ever could be. In our geography, also, as in earthly geography, the distinctions of the equator will always be retained in reduced or virtual form as one nears the pole—they will not be simply lost in a blurred outcome—just as the unity of the pole in a sense overarches the whole range of equatorial difference, the pole being always due north or due south of every equatorial point. What we have said involves an extremely questionable use of metaphors and pictures on which no possible weight can be laid: its value will depend entirely on what use we make of it. We shall now try to give a meaning to it all by asking ourselves: What happens when one moves up along a spiritual line of longitude, passing from ordinary physical life at the equator to the mystical conditions that prevail at the poles? How are our categories transformed and brought together in the process? And how does the whole journey up and the corresponding journey down illuminate the problems of life in the human cave?

It may first be held, in harmony with Platonic, Thomist, Hindu and Buddhist teaching, that movement away from the equator of dispersed physical existence to the mystical pole of the world involves a gradual attenuation of the sensuous element and a corresponding increase of the 'empty', the 'formless' (which for Thomism is the formal), the purely noetic type of experience. Sense has two distinct and independent cognitive features: it illustrates or carries out or fulfils a cognitive reference, and provides it with its element of *Anschauung*, of intuitive contact: it also obtrudes, irrupts, does violence to us in highly characteristic fashion. Sense-awareness may be said to be a case of compulsive illustration. The former trait, that of being illustrative, it shares with imagery: imaging something may have all the manifested, illustrated character of sense-encounter. The latter trait it shares with many experiences, emptily cognitive or emotional and conative. Much that, as we say, we feel with our bones, e.g. the infinity of space, is phenomenologically compulsive, and so are many accesses of emotion and many odd practical impulses. In sense, however, both traits are united, and it is in sense that we most frequently feel the compulsive causality of independently existent body, an indubitable phenomenological fact out of which many philosophers have manufactured highly objectionable theories. The intrusive, pictorial character of experience, and the empiricistic methods that assort with it, are what is characteristic of low-latitude spiritual existence, and what some expect to find in high-latitude states as well: it is, however, precisely what must fade out as we progress to higher spheres until, in the end, at some Arctic circle of spirituality, it vanishes altogether. All this is doubtless painful and meaningless in an era of scientific thought which turned away from the experimental findings of the Würzburg psychologists in the present century, as from the earlier findings of James and Stout, let alone from those of Aristotle and the school-men who preceded these, a wilful ignorance that has been vastly extended by Wittgenstein's random broodings on the subject. Anyone who has done even rudimentary introspection knows how full and rich are our awarenesses of complex situations and possibilities—this is particularly true of dreams—which are only illustrated in the most vestigial manner, if they are illustrated at all. To read Titchener's unsurpassed analyses of the purely sensuous element in many of our complex awarenesses, is almost inevitably to be converted to the Würzburg doctrine of imageless thinking, which Titchener above all desired to discredit.

Leaving aside as a mere mistake the belief that cognitive experience is necessarily sensuous, or consists in a manipulation of sensuous elements, or in anything but an intention of the mind to what it is actually concerned with, we may yet point out that empty noetic experience is in no sense devoid of an analogue of sensory content: everything illustrated in sense is also capable of existing in and for the intellect (though the converse should, on our view, be rejected as untenable). The precise pattern of an odd face, or the turns and twists of a melody, or anything else however dependent on sense for its full presentation, may live on intact as 'an abiding mood in the soul' (to use Lotze's telling phrase) long after its sensed or imagined presence has vanished. And there is, further, a necessary logical relation of sensuous to noetic presentation in the case of all things capable of being sensorily given at all: they could not be noetically given, if they were not also capable of being sensuously given, and we may add, *vice versa*. Applied, however, to the special issue on hand, the life beyond body must display the same sort of fading away of the sensory element that we experience in our thinking. The lower regions of this life may well be a rupa-loka or form-world where there is much that has the hard definiteness and observability of the things of sense, and alleged communications from these regions—for which we do not vouch in the least—would seem to confirm. But as one rose in this world compulsiveness and illustration would abate, everything would become more dream-like (though not necessarily confused as in dreams) until in the end we entered an arupa-loka or formless zone—the Thomistic realm of pure form is, despite terminology, no different—where nothing at all was sensuously or imaginally given. Here the most diverse characters—even such as are necessarily disjoined in their instances—could be given together without clashing, and even combined in interesting, empty patterns *incapable* of sensuous realization. Used with an intention towards sensous fulfilment, such patterns might provide standard examples of contradiction, thoughts necessary to the realization of their own contradictoriness and also serving certain propaedeutic and analogical purposes. But such patterns would permit also of another use: to bring before us that subjective life of thought which, though entirely actual and non-contradictory itself, none the less has it as its chief glory that it can be *of*, directed *to* the non-actual and the self-contradictory, and so by contrast can grasp the categorial import of what is real, consistent and absolutely necessary. And such patterns also will permit us to form a conception of the life of a God, whose peculiarity it is to contain in a real, consistent, intellectual embrace the whole round of possibilities whose complete instantiation would (in virtue of their incompatibility and higher-order inexhaustibility) be a logical impossibility. In the higher latitudes of the world, experience, in the sense of crude, pictorial irruption from without, would cease to afflict us, though we should still be in touch with the most detailed elaboration of every notional possibility in all its implications and contrasts, and this would be richer rather than poorer than such experience. And everything that was carried out at lower levels might likewise reappear in purely notional form much as the raw observations of the scientist, gained with such labour 'in the field', reappear on the well-lit, well-ordered shelves of some great library.

Having made myself somewhat ridiculous by these descriptions —which at least do not purport to set forth Swedenborgian travels—I shall go on to say that progress from low latitudes to the mystical pole of the world must also necessarily involve the steady liquidation of corporeality. This must be held, not on account of any mere liking for τὸ ασωματόν, but on account of the intolerable tensions in the notion of body, its precise adjustment to a cognitive apparatus to which it professes to be indifferent, its inseparability from a sensitivity from which it professes independence, its inability to explain its solid occupancy of space, its reference back of its character and behaviour to those of its parts while demanding that it should not lose all that character and behaviour in the dark slide of an infinite regress, etc., etc. Idealism or spiritualism will establish itself, but not by any sudden act of argumentative legerdemain, nor without maintaining matter at lower levels, and leaving it to form the disciplinary walls of our cave. What I understand by body will be clear from what I held in my previous phenomenological study of the bodily world: bodies come before us as impinging actively on our senses, as themselves causing us to take note of their existence and properties, as affecting others as they do ourselves, as having great solidity, constancy and inertia, as appearing variously but as always being much simpler than their varied appearances would suggest, as occupying space in some very exclusive manner, as being there regardless of anyone's perception or non-perception, and as being modifiable only by changes which are themselves bodily. These traits give bodies their primacy in the bodily world and also their surd character, since they afford no true anchorage for the subtle life by which they are understood and manipulated. As one leaves the zero of bodily existence, the bodily will no doubt still be evident in experience, but its power to regiment that experience will gradually diminish. The bodies in higher spheres will not affect all who see them in precisely the same manner, they will have some but not all the malleability of imagery, the laws that govern their changes will be, in part, the subtle associative laws that obtain (we may believe) in the brain rather than the rigid laws that govern inorganic substances, and will show a sensitiveness to significance, purpose, relevance, appropriateness, logical connection and so forth which is not conspicuous in matter down here. The indifference of bodies to perception will likewise be mitigated, and the spectators and auditors will to some extent

determine, not the mere nuances of bodily appearance and interpretation, but the actual bodies that are there. Bodies will in fact
fulfil the function of enabling conscious persons to have common
themes of reference and communication without oppressively
forcing on them in and out of season what they do not care to see
and know. Life will be lived in what will have many features of an
imaginary environment except that some definite degree of solidity
and collectivity will still be present as they are not in pure imagination and dreams. As one moves upwards towards the mystical
pole, this bodily scenery will become much eroded, though its
thematic content will still afford common reference-points to
communicating intelligences together with many much more
abstract contents, not very differently from the manner in which
the episodes and landscapes of some past vacation are revived and
talked over by those who have been through them together.
Possibly too, at very high levels, a mayavic, purely posited and
imagined character in our present sense-world may become
apparent. What is more or less an unacceptable philosophical
myth in Kant and Fichte may become a living experience: we may
be able to go behind the scenes and see how our present stage has
been set up and rigged. We may share, in other words, in the work
of a productive imagination instead of merely reading about it in
some of the most obscure pages in the history of philosophy.
However this may be, bodies as we know them in ordinary sense-
encounters will be but limiting cases of the more pliable, vanishing
bodies of higher spheres, and, seen in this context, we can grasp
many of their most paradoxical features without difficulty, and can
also grasp the disciplinary role they fulfil in the cosmos, as being
the perfect exemplars of hard objectivity. We can see how the more
fluid, higher-latitude bodies would be impossible without such
hard, wholly objective ones: the latter alone are fully corporeal,
and the bodies in higher states batten on the memory of such full
bodiliness. On the other hand, all the adaptive, accommodating
features of earthly bodies, their congruity with perception, their
subjection to vital and conscious control, etc., spring from the
derivation from the bodies in higher spheres. Bodies, earthly and
heavenly, can well be said to be parasitic upon one another.

If movement from our this-world equator to its otherworldly
pole involves an attenuation of corporeality, it will also obviously
involve an attenuation of the spatiality which serves as a foil and a

substratum to corporeality. This attenuation does not, of course, mean that there will not always be, at any level, something which answers to the continuous, duly arranged, appropriately distanced side-by-sideness of whatever appears or has being, so that whatever exists also coexists, and is a node or phase in a cosmos or world. Only superficial thought can conceive that there could be a plurality of interconnected items without something like a common medium which is the pre-existent possibility of their conjoint, un-confounded, duly ordered being, and the sensuous space of sight and touch merely carries the sundering role of such a medium rather far, and brings it to such clearness that many have indeed forgotten the unbroken, endless continuity which is equally of the essence of space. Hearing, bodily feeling, various qualitative orders, as well as such intellectual orders as those of probability or spatialized chronology, involve spaces in which the items are much less clearly set apart, and it is to be expected that as one rises in spiritual lati-tude spatial order will tend to be more and more of this interpene-trating than of a strictly sundered type. The spatiality of higher spheres may, further, be credited with a variability which will put the most irregular, non-Euclidean versions of this-world spatiality utterly in the shade. It will be a spatiality in which the remote can suddenly become near or the near remote, or in which journeys can be protracted or shortened as in dreams. It is also not unplau-sible to suppose that the higgledy-piggledy distribution of contents characteristic of this-world spatiality will be remedied: things will be drawn close or set apart with some regard to their mutual affinity and relevance. The sort of tidiness that thought imports into its materials will become more and more evident, and there is little danger, we may suggest, of some shocked fundamentalist straying into the wrong set of post-mortem scenery. It will further be a spatiality which goes further and further away from the sheer numerical diversity which only seems to characterize space at our level, and which gives rise to so many worries concerning indis-cernible diversities in symmetrical universes. As we rise in latitude, simple location will vanish: everything will be predominantly somewhere, but more distantly present everywhere else, and all journeys will therefore have the Plotinian property of in some degree taking their starting-points with them. This means that nothing will have any graspable individuality that is independent of character and general context, and the flowers in an endless wall-

I

paper will merely be a curious diplopic manifestation of an identical flower. The attenuation of spatiality at higher levels will also enable us to grasp phenomena that are strange at our own: the field-phenomena and *actio in distans* which are seen throughout nature, the relevance of space to bodies and of bodies to space, the quasi-intentionality of the brain and other organs, their response to remote realities rather than the influences which immediately impinge on them, and above all the curious behaviour of specimens of the same natural kind which keep in step with one another no matter how widely they may be distributed. If our loosely assembled Newtonian world stems from a much more tightly engaged Plotinian one, we can better understand many of its Neoplatonic features.

Next in order, obviously, to an attenuation of spatiality is an attenuation of temporality, a subject fraught with many pitfalls. That progress along a line from zero latitude to the pole is progress from the most parcelled, piecemeal, blatantly successive form of time to the most undivided or 'eternal' form accords well with mystical feeling, and accords also with our profound sense of the intimately discrepant nature of time, its basic ambiguity among priorities, it being unclear whether the spread-out, ordered temporality which appears frozen in the past (and some say in the future as well) is a mere projection of the impassioned, changing life which rushes unceasingly through the focus of the present, or whether the latter gains all its sense and content from the former. This quarrel of essence is mitigated if what we experience here is a limiting case of an experiential series in which the pinched focus of the present steadily expands till it achieves the embracing momentariness, the *punctum stans*, often spoken of by the schoolmen. This embracing momentariness is often conceived as an immense or infinite acceleration of experience, so that a whole world-period or the whole of time is telescoped into an experienced instant: it could be more fitly conceived as an immense slowing down of experience, so that a single pulse of experience covers the whole vast or infinite stretch in question. What we must at all costs avoid is that assimilation of the future to the past which blurs what we have held to be a fundamental categorial difference, and, in so doing, turns time into something that is not time at all. It is part of what we mean by the future tense that what we say in it may be, in part at least, irremediably disjunctive, inclusive of alternatives between which there is not, though there will be, a categorical settlement. The Law of Excluded Middle prescribes that there will be a sea-fight tomorrow or that it is not the case that there will be one, but it does not prescribe the quite different disjunction that there will be a sea-fight tomorrow or that there will be no sea-fight tomorrow. These categorial trivialities must be true for experiences and phenomena at any level, even degenerately in their last, limiting reduction at the mystical pole. The future is only settled there because in the infinite slowing-up there achieved all happenings are held in a single drop of realization. This does not mean that an attenuation of temporal order, with all its internal indecisions and stresses, is not present at that level, much as it is present in our vision of the past. Nor does it mean that we can steal a march on the future by some ecstatic rise to that level: ecstasy, as we shall argue, moves along its own separate life-line, and it is an ecstasy for this or that being at one point of time, with all his one-sidednesses and limitations, not an ecstasy for everyone or for all times. Prophecy only is possible inasmuch as countless alternative futures may well be displayed at higher levels, and may at times teach us what will almost certainly happen, or what will happen if we take no counter-measures, etc. By and large, however, the gradual transcendence of temporality as we go upwards enables us to understand the real encapsulation of the past in the present, and the settled character of the past's content, which is otherwise so extraordinarily puzzling. History can be reconstructed, and the future more or less reliably projected, because at a higher level, which is for us unreachable, they are all actually there. Our own true and useful language of tenses will of course not be useful at that limit, except in bracketed fashion, as applying *within* the stages it summarizes. It is doubtless an aspiration towards that mystical limiting stage that has led so many modern logicians and analytic philosophers to prefer tenseless to tensed forms of symbolism and expression.

If spatiality and temporality become condensed and transformed on the journey towards the mystical pole, the same will apply to the individuality with which they are bound up. Individuality at any level is a thing demanded and postulated rather than a thing actually given, which is why Plato believed individuals and their properties to be objects of opinion, not knowledge. What we have before us in sense-perception, etc., is what we try to pin down as a 'this' but what proves on examination to be merely a something, in which there is nothing to grasp but a wholly general characterization. The 'this', the paradigm of individuality, is, as Hegel held, perennially elusive. Relatively, however, individuals can be pinned down at the ordinary this-world level, identified and reidentified on many occasions, and made the standard subjects of ordinary this-world discourse. They are not then the same, in their numerical multiplicity, with any species they may embody. At the higher levels of being, however, individuality will become more and more indistinguishable from the species it embodies, and there will not even *appear* to be numerically distinct things to which general characterizations are applicable. All this seems wholly meaningless to modern reflection to which numerically distinct individuals, directly encountered in sense-experience are the sheet-anchor of absolute faith, all else being an empty hypostatization of an abstraction. For us, however, the highly specific, illustrated somethings one encounters in sense-perception do not differ wholly or in principle from the less specific, more general somethings that one encounters in thought. It would, however, be misleading to say that at higher levels one moves in a world of mere species: better to say that at higher levels the distinction between species and specimen becomes idle and inoperative. One *has* individuality there in the sense of complete, self-sufficient being, but it is a being where one can no longer distinguish between the mere instance, which lower-world spatiality and temporality seemed to offer us in endless multiplicity and the sort it exemplifies. With this goes a gradual vanishing, as held before, of the puzzles connected with the identity of indiscernibles, or with the inductive importance of natural kinds. The kind dominates the individual at our level because at higher levels, the kind or the species *is* the individual. And obviously we have gone some way towards understanding the theological mysteries according to which our religious absolute is not merely wise, just, beautiful, etc., but rather wisdom, justice, beauty, etc., themselves. The analogy with dreams and dream-like creative writing is also evident: in a dream the figure before one is generic or specific rather than pin-pointedly individual, and one shifts from one vague identification to another without loss or difficulty. All this does not mean, as said before, that this higher level attenuation of a distinction does not point to its more fully fledged presence at lower levels. The generic or specific being of higher spheres would be quite void of sense of dignity were there not also the would-be merely numerical individuality that we encounter down here. Equally, however, there is nothing uniquely paradigmatic about individuality down here: it too shifts, spreads and eludes and is unintelligible apart from the yet more dissolved individuality yonder.

So far we have limited ourselves to the impersonal aspects of phenomena: we may now consider their personal, conscious features. These too must be gradually set aside or profoundly modified as we journey upwards, if the notional uneasinesses they occasion are to be genuinely resolved at all. Bodies and the bodily we saw must be gradually resolved with all their air of proud indifference to conscious experients: if this is so, the organized bodies in which minds or egos are embodied must likewise be set aside. Their curious necessity for the continuity and full expression of conscious egos and for their communication with other egos, while yet maintaining an essence alien to all consciousness, their remarkable vergence towards memory and understanding in the brain and elsewhere, while yet proclaiming their incapacity for such performances, their dominance by mechanical laws which permit none but a miraculous entry for the causality of freedom: all these are features of organized bodies which are only tolerable if seen as odd, limiting cases of features better shown at higher levels. At such higher levels there will still be organized bodies, some of which may be more or less permanent and glorious integuments of conscious egos, but they will differ in many respects from our natural bodies. Expression, which is here so much hampered by lamenesses, stiffnesses, deformities, maimings of countless sorts, will there be infinitely freer, limited only in fact by the resources of the expressive person. And we need not doubt that, at higher levels, changes of shape such as are related in legends, may well be as easy as changes of clothes are down here. Expression will further be aided by the less clear distinction between private images and public percepts, and a person's silent meditations may well inscribe themselves on the environment, at least at will. Wittgenstein often derided the comic-strip mode of representing a man's thoughts by a captive print-filled or picture-filled cloud floating above him, but what he found so categorially absurd may well be an everyday fact in higher spheres. Ultimately, perhaps, at the formless levels of being, we may cease to need even glorified bodies of bliss. Bodies and the bodily will, however survive in notional attenuations, and Socrates will doubtless be as irremediably snub-nosed and short of stature there as here.

I now come to features of extreme importance and difficulty on which it is easy to fall into error: these are the features of mental separateness and ego-distinctness which normally go together in this life, and about which so many insoluble difficulties congregate. Our references to foreign interior states are as confident as they are unillustrable and unfulfillable, and this constitutes a great surd of cave-existence, as is also occasioned by our deep sense of our own personal identity, which underlies rather than involves the use of any possible set of criteria or marks of identity. These surds will be rationalized if in the life to come persons somehow become less opaque to one another and are able in some manner to interpenetrate, as mystical feeling has always held that they can and will do, and as, in many states in this life, we feel momentarily that they *are* doing. It is here important that we should not merely regard mental separateness and ego-distinctness as a low-level phenomenon which will simply dissolve or prove illusory at higher levels, a single self emerging which will comprehensively recall, and attribute to its sole self, states which, when they occurred, did so in mutual ignorance and profound disconnection. This, though superficially consistent with the 'deep' character of the ego, which is such that, though intrinsically capable of declaring itself it is also intrinsically capable of existing undeclared, is inconsistent with the profound importance of personal separateness and its entwinement with all our higher values. Nor must we, on the other hand, conceive of the separateness of persons as maintained in all its present sharpness at higher levels, and merely mitigated by new modes of direct cognition, so that soul speaks directly to soul. Telepathic experiences or experiences of spiritual communion are not in principle different from ordinary modes of communication through bodily behaviour on which, as we have seen, they are parasitic in this life, and which must exist yonder as much as here. If in another world, the priorities are reversed, and a telepathic hunch is more basic than an observed gesture, the profound absurdity of our understanding of others is not thereby alleviated. Obviously the distinction of persons must have the same sort of irremovable, categorial place in the world as distinctions of time and tense, and if either can be thought to 'vanish' in certain ultimate attenuations, this is a vanishing in which what vanishes must be retained *qua* vanished, and must be intrinsically capable of a full reappearance. Certainly there must be a profound identification yonder, to which it is however essential that it should be the point of convergence of distinct routes, which can again be followed, and which introduce multiplicity even into what is profoundly simple. Dear St Teresa in her accounts of her relations to her Divine Friend here obviously strikes the correct, the experienced note: their encounters were like a light temporarily losing itself in a larger light, and yet afterwards resuming its separateness, or like water in some vessel temporarily losing itself in a larger body of water from which it could again be taken. It would be a rash and superficial interpreter who would see anything really different in the *Tat tvam asi* of the *Upanishats*. The communication of egos at such higher latitudes are blessedly beyond the puzzlements of the Wittgensteinian *Blue Book*, but the puzzlements of that book would be impossible without the communication effected at that level, whose authenticity they in fact throughout presuppose.

Another distinction that we may suppose to be gradually attenuated as we progress towards the mystical pole is the difference between intentional conscious act, on the one hand, and intended object, on the other. This distinction, so much misunderstood in modern British philosophy, we have endeavoured to set forth in our first series of lectures, in all its categorial peculiarity, above all avoiding the confusion which turns an intentional object, something thought of *as* being such and such, into an object which really *is* such and such, and then, when this proves impossible, erecting it into some sort of intermediate object or replacing it by the assemblage of its elements, etc. The self-transcendence involved in intentionality is neither a real relation to what lies beyond the act nor a relation among real constituents in the act: it is in fact not properly regarded as a relation at all, though it may be consummated and validated by a relation. These categorial peculiarities are, however, deeply puzzling; there is deep difficulty in conceiving both X and an intention towards X as two independent existences, when there is also so deep, so wholly internal an affinity among them. This difficulty is, however, attenuated if at higher levels there are intentional objects which necessarily 'coincide' with objects that have being, and if such objects cannot fail to have the constitution they are thought of as having. But this is precisely what is possible when the objects of thinking are the truncated ideal objects of pure thinking, which are little beyond outward-turned forms of our own intentional approaches: to be triangle-wise in one's orientation to objects only differs by a shade from being abstractly oriented to triangularity as such. In purely ideal references conceiving and conceived have, we may say, merely a courtesy distinction, a point made by Aristotle when he held the mind to be a place of forms. In other words, the being of ideal entities is their being in and for minds, and the being of minds is perhaps no more than the being and use of such ideal entities, involving however a peculiar kind of personal multiplication covenanted in the make-up of the ideal entities themselves. It is, then, our profound sense of the virtual vanishing of intentionality at the highest level which both makes its presence puzzling at lower levels, and also serves in the end to remove that puzzlement. If we can understand intentional references and the transcendent realities which they may fit, as having, as it were, a common root in phenomena capable of being really given and experienced at higher levels, their puzzling character will be lessened. They will seem like two broken halves of the same coin which necessarily fit each other's cavities and bulges.

Finally we may opine, once more in accord with mystical feeling, that movement towards the mystical pole involves a steady attenuation of the tension between fact and value, in which superficial thought sees no problem, but in which deeper thought sees the gravest of problems. For plainly, despite Hume, we cannot but see profound absurdity either in the existence in ourselves of extraordinary aspirations toward world-transcending values, or in the almost total indifference of the world to such aspirations and their goals. The very notion of a value includes some tendency to compel acceptance on the part of all conscious beings, and even some tendency to exact conformity from unconscious things. Hence the extreme naturalness and credibility of miraculous violations of the bodily order: they involve the understandable intervention of another order. All these reflections gain strength when we reflect on the governing presence of good form, simplicity, unity and other logical values in the merely bodily world, which men of science utterly rely upon in their investigations, however much they may give positivistic 'justifications' of such reliance. But the falling apart of what is and what should be also has its intelligible possibility, an absorbed consideration of which readily blunts our sense of the opposed affinity. It is in the conditions beyond this world, as traditional religion has always maintained, that we have the firm warrant which gives rationality not only to our attempts to better ourselves and the world practically, but also to know it theoretically. The phenomena of this world alone give absolutely no firm warrant to either. All this does not mean that there may not be many shapes of evil in that other world, either as deviant or as interstitial phenomena necessarily given with the values they presuppose, or even as fully developed perversions backed with a far more horrible intelligence and energy than are ever encountered on this earth.

At the mystical pole of our whole geography we may place an object of infinite and no longer puzzling perfection, which we need no longer conceive as a mere supreme instance of incompatible values, but as the living principle of all those values themselves. With the removal of instantiation a necessity of existence is no longer the puzzling thing that it is at lower levels, and we dimly understand how such a being may be utterly self-existent, and how all other existences may depend on it for what they are. To this mystical pole of all being, all peripheral things will have their necessary life-lines, along which movement is possible in either direction, and their consequent relation to the mystical pole in question is as little to be regarded as one of sheer mutual exclusiveness as of sheer coincidence and identity. In a sense, the life of the mystical pole pulses out towards the remotest periphery, and the latter may be thought of as being as necessary to it as it is to the periphery. (I here follow Meister Eckhart, Hegel and the 'Germanic Theology'.) But it is spread out not only over all beings but also over all categories: it is not only the perfection of conscious personality, as envisaged in traditional theism, but also the perfection of blessedly unconscious thinghood, the perfection of pure adjectival being or character, the perfection of relational connection, the perfection of suffering, of truth, of loveliness, of social communion, even of that pure Nothingness which the

Chinese and Japanese have found so appealing. What we have asid is, however, merely the rhetorical recognition of a unique logical and ontological status to which we shall try to give more flesh and blood in a later lecture.

In ending this lecture on mystical geography I shall no doubt have disappointed many, who expect the sort of journey I have been describing to be rather like an ordinary excursion in latitude, a voyage of discovery to the Indies, in which many strange things would be reported, but strange things of the same sort as those of which one has had experience here. If reports are to be trusted, there are regions of the life beyond that might well satisfy a celestial tourist, armed with the right sort of Baedeker. In its upper reaches, however, the reticence of St Paul is more appropriate than the graphic eloquence of St John the Divine. Many feel the utterances of the higher mystics to be distressingly lacking in content, but what would they have? Detailed stories reminiscent of the social columnist? For these there could only be a marginal place in the limiting ecstasy. The sort of journey I have been describing is a journey *away* from contingent empirical diversity towards the necessary pole of unity in which all comes together. While it is not best understood as a journey towards emptiness and negation, it is idle to expect it to lead us to garish new things.

THE NOETIC COSMOS

We shall devote the present lecture to pondering over the putative structure and contents of what must be held to be a most important and central zone of the 'upper world' we are speculating about: the zone which corresponds to the noetic cosmos or intelligible world of Plato and Plotinus, and which seems not very different from the Dharmadhatu of Buddhism. This is a zone parallel to that of the floating meanings and notions which, as we saw, are constituted by our earthly thought in the upper regions of the cave. Only whereas we then were dealing with ectypal mental constructions, involving much that was arbitrary and correspondent only with human approaches, it is now our design to say something about the originals, the archetypes, which these intentional objects merely seek to copy. For us the two zones are necessarily distinct, since the archetypes in question are not mere patterns and ideals of cavethought, but are thought of as given in a real experience which is never adequately ours in this present life, and which is only by courtesy different from the archetypes it presents or contemplates. Things as abstractly seen by us in the cave may at times, we hope coincide with things as they really are 'yonder', but we must also allow the possibility of wide divergence and inadequacy. The relation is that which Aristotle has described as holding between the active intelligence which 'makes' all forms and the passive intelligence which merely receives them; it is a relation we all feel to exist when we struggle to give a true account of anything, to work out its deeper implications, to penetrate to its essence, to see it in a manner in which it not only becomes clear but also beautiful. It is, we feel, because there is a real eidetic order guiding our feeble adumbrations, that our logical, mathematical, scientific axiological and aesthetic inquiries are at all possible.

The noetic cosmos that we are attempting to sketch can be held to be a high, but not the highest zone in our upper world. It is not the mystical pole of the world where all things come together in unity, but the world's first declension into diversity, a sort of Arctic circle which we may, for the purposes of our treatment, place in the beams of an unsetting midsummer sun. At this level we are beyond sense and its compulsive illustration: all is defined, graspable character or essence with no surd substrate beyond it requiring endless elucidation or analysis. At this level, too, we are beyond instantiation and its repetitious inanity, though we are not beyond any degree of specificity of character or relative position or of spatial and temporal order and pattern. What we have is a world of εἴδη, of good forms, which is not to say that the distorted and the deviant will not have an interstitial place among them. At this level, also, we are beyond all opaque separateness of conscious individuality and reference: what we have is an improved version of what Leibniz spoke of in his monadology, mind as such with a single set of universalized contents specified in a set of mutually perspicuous, complementary standpoints, each embodying its own idiosyncratic emphasis. What we have, moreover, is a world where the splintered separateness of different intended contents is overcome in the unity of intending mind, mind being precisely the medium in which what conflicts or falls apart in the instance can be reconciled in the thought. Our world is, further, a world where the distinction between intending reference and intended object, while not done away with, has lost the gulf-like connotations which transcendent instances promote: it has become like an exteriorization and an interiorization of the same phenomenon, a case of the concave and convex so often spoken of by Aristotle. What we have said, however, requires careful point-by-point treatment, as it is only too easy to be expansively empty in discoursing on such themes.

The points we are about to consider were to some extent thrashed out in the Platonic Academy which first hazarded the great inversion, looking for what absolutely is, not in the dark depths of a particularity which we opine rather than see, but in the complete perspicuity of definite characters which are, despite modern objection, the very paradigm of the graspable and the clear, and which seemed to be moving from that inversion towards a further theory of a mind, which, as real or more real than defined characters, was able to unite and make fruitful use of them all. Echoes of that great discussion are to be found in Aristotle's supremely interesting accounts of Platonism in the *Metaphysics*

and in the statements of commentators on these accounts: they
are less clearly present in what may quite properly be called the
exoteric dialogues, to which modern Platonic scholarship has increasingly confined itself, while it may also be said to have misunderstood much of their drift. Even the most sympathetic modern
accounts of the world of forms see little more in it that the varied
abstractions conjured up by thought and science rather than the
basic blue-print of the empirical world.

We may here take a lead from the Platonic Academy and make
the prime inhabitants, the ground-level content of the noetic
cosmos, the patterns of *things that exist by nature* rather than by
art, defect, choice, chance, accident, mixture or any other distortion of 'nature', however much it may afterwards be necessary to
find a place for the latter *somewhere* in the intelligible world. What
primarily are there for noetic experience will not be bloodless
categories or discarnate variables, but the 'natural kinds' truly
representing the structures of our material particles (of which
Plato and Pythagoras and modern physics have alike given geometrical accounts, going on from thence to their various compounds
and complex admixtures, proceeding to unitary organisms of
various sorts and ending up with such living things as exercise the
higher cogitative functions, including some which perhaps have
much more remote presiding connections with the realm of bodies,
than we have, and ending up with the communities, the ideal
'republics', which such beings may form. There seems no reason to
depart from this basic Platonic position: the pattern of the well-
formed unit, the well-rounded self-sufficient thing is obviously the
Alpha of the intelligible, however little it may deserve to be its
Omega. We first understand events, acts, virtues, defects, relations,
assemblages, intentions, categories in terms of it, but not it in terms
of the infinitely fine ontological dust that it raises. If it is possible
to reverse this priority at higher levels of reflection this can only
be if we sublimate the original priority at such levels. Logical
atomism, the process-philosophy, associationistic psychology, the
sense-datum epistemology, etc., all prefer to winnow this interstitial dust and are in the end stifled by it. True or metaphysical
science always wins through the dust to those clear, simple, invariant patterns in which there is no reason to believe except that
they specify reason itself.

It is important that we should here stress the element of sheer contingency, of sublimated fact, that we must think of as present in the noetic cosmos, and which is analogous to the contingency down here in the region of individual encounter. That there should be such a pattern as that of the kangaroo as such or the kangaroo itself is as uncovenanted and surprising a fact about the ideal world as that there should have been those reduplicated individual kangaroos which astonished Captain Cook when he first saw them hopping around in Australia. The kangaroo as such, we may hazard, is quite different from the griffin as such, to which we can only accord a highly secondary, derivative status, poised some-where between the real possibilities which the genus Animal covers and the additions which exist only for mythological fancy. Such characters as colours, odours, etc., have likewise an obviously contingent status: their relations among each other are all necessary and essential, but the characters themselves have no aseity. It is not necessary, we may say, that there should have been such characters at all. In this respect what we say about the prime forms in our noetic cosmos contrasts strongly with what we say about the more ultimate categories that they specify. The patterns studied in abstract arithmetic and sufficiently abstract geometry are patterns which it probably would not make sense to suppose absent from the noetic cosmos. All this will of course be wholly meaningless to modern linguistic analysis according to which it is sheerly arbitrary to attribute, or not to attribute, being to 'entities of reason', natural of factitious, and which would find it highly artificial to attribute ideal being to *some* such abstracta and not to others. The procedure of science, however, argues otherwise. Though there are now no dodos, being a dodo is felt to be a real pattern of organic being, whereas being a griffin is not: notes too high for anyone's hearing are likewise genuine, well-formed characters, whereas colours lying outside of the colour-pyramid are not. It will be argued that the 'existence' I here attribute to forms or patterns is a mere generalized reflection of the existence of actual instances of such forms, and that our knowledge of the former depends wholly on our knowledge of the latter. But there are collocations due to choice or chance which, however much repeated, as in the case of manufactured articles or lucky throws with unbiased dice, do not point to a genuine pattern lying behind them, and it is clear, further, that our knowledge of forms involves many elements of what some would call an 'intuitive hunch', whereas others would speak of 'noetic insight', but which in any case goes far beyond what experience lays before us. Our noetic insight is indeed valued for its use in predicting and controlling such individualities as we encounter down here, and these too have an all-important role in testing its genuineness. But that they are thus important, does not mean that prediction, control or testing make any sense without invoking matters far beyond their purview.

The ideal contingency we have been considering also goes far towards explaining the *de facto* necessity of natural laws which would otherwise be extremely puzzling. Natural laws, the main object of physical research, are given as applying to possibles as well as actuals, and as excluding all but a definite range from the former, but they are also given as principles that might have been otherwise, as necessities, therefore, whose necessity is not necessary but contingent. The difficulty is resolved if we revert from the crabbed modern notion of law to the old notion of the kind or species: laws are necessary as expressing how instances of certain natural species will behave, in virtue of the essence or nature of such species. The existence of the instances, and even more fundamentally of the species behind the instances, is, however, in the last resort a contingent matter: there need not in fact have been such a prototype or species.

We may here deal with another view much canvassed in the Platonic Academy and descended from earlier Pythagorean speculation: the view which saw in the objects of the noetic cosmos the product of two factors, of a dark principle of indefinite, flowing quantity, on the one hand, capable of increase and diminution without limit, and having varieties equal in number to the dimensions of space and time and perhaps some others, and a principle of unity or limit, on the other hand, through which indefinite quantity was variously bounded, thereby giving rise to all forms or ideal patterns. The metaphor of genesis involved in this account is confusing and unfortunate, and means no more than that every form or species can be regarded as involving a limitation of one or more types of flowing quantity. To these types of flowing quantity we are told that Plato gave the names of 'the many and few', obviously the purely arithmetical dimension, the long and short, obviously the dimension of linearity, the broad and narrow, i.e. the continuum of surface-magnitudes, and the deep and shallow, obviously the continuum of surface magnitudes. If we cast our glance over a wide range of Platonic writings—and the Pythagorean doctrinal framework must have served as a thought-background to Plato's notions throughout his life—we find the *Republic* adding the swift and the slow to give an account of the movement of solid bodies (time, as in the *Timaeus*, being inseparable from regular movement), while in the *Philebus* many species of indefinite flowing quantity, e.g. the hot and the cold, are recognized, all of which are counted by the basic principle of limit. To all the species of flowing quantity Plato gives the embracing name of the Great and Small, signifying by this queer term, not two things as Aristotle confusedly supposed, but simply the basic property of continuous quantity that it can be added to or extended on the one hand, or reduced and divided on the other, without let or hindrance. And while this indefinite, flowing principle is more unrestrainedly evident in the world of instances than in the world of pure natures, the genius of Plato saw it as existing in a tamed, overcome form in the latter. In all this construction Plato is propounding a philosophy of mathematics as interesting as that of Frege and Russell. Only, whereas they start with finite magnitudes and assemblages, and can never convincingly rise above them, Plato starts with the infinite or indefinite as a first principle, and by repeatedly limiting it tries to reach all finite numbers and magnitudes. (Though the precise detail of this construction was, of course, fantastic and even more fantastically garbled in our sources.)

What is, however, extremely fascinating and illuminating is Plato's view that all natures of natural kinds and their basic excellences, can be given an analysis in terms of the two factors thus involved, that they all can be reduced to 'numbers', not in one or other of the perverse senses given to this procedure by Aristotle, but in the sense in which a reduction to numbers is a reduction to a set of precise proportions or numerical relations (an interpretation considered by Aristotle in, e.g., *Met.* A 991b, 1092b), a sort of reduction of which Plato gives examples in the structures of the elementary particles of fire, earth, air and water in the *Timaeus*, in all of which, as in many other instances, there is a 'schematization by forms and numbers' (*Tim.* 536) which reflects a more ultimate schematization in the forms themselves.

It is clear, even at the ordinary level of phenomenal givenness, that nothing is more deeply characteristic of or essential to a natural species, e.g. an animal or a plant, than the characteristic proportions of its various parts and organs, the characteristic rhythms of its responses, and so on. Alter any of these continuously, and 'quantity' soon changes into 'quality': one is confronted by quite a different sort of thing. And such proportionate structure applies to all the characteristic expressions of individual personality in physique, gait, speech, writing, facial expression, etc. The form of the individual, his 'soul', if one likes, certainly consists in 'numbers' or numerical harmonies, which would not prove its mortality, as strangely argued in the *Phaedo*, but rather its permanent significance or immortality. The only question that arises is whether the quality of things can be reduced without remainder to proportionate features of the kind indicated. As we saw in our first series of lectures, this is one of the most difficult cruces in the phenomenology of body. We are both tempted to frame such a reduction, and yet feel that all would vanish in emptiness were it carried through. (This is in fact Aristotle's objection to the whole analysis: that proportions are necessarily proportions of something to something.) The crux in question is best dealt with by holding that, while there is an intimate relation of essence between quantitative relations and qualities permitting of quantification or arising out of quantification—a relation which inspires all theories of primary and secondary qualities—neither can without absurdity be reduced to the other, but exists 'in and for the other'. The forms in the ideal cosmos will not, therefore, have the purely numerical constitution which Plato thought they must have, but will also embrace much splendour of quality.

Here too we may borrow one of Plotinus's happy emendations of Platonism, and place in the realm of forms what are practically forms of individuals. The ideal world will have to have the violence done it of containing the same generic pattern many times over, but only in so far as such a generic pattern appears variously specified or unspecified or set in different ideal contexts. We shall not have the artificial Aristotelian situation in which we acknowledge forms only of a certain degree of specificity, e.g. Man, but not anything more highly generic or specific, e.g. Animal or Caucasian Man. We shall be allowed on this proposed construction to acknowledge an ideal pattern of Man in General but also to acknowledge ideal patterns of many sub-varieties of humanity, such as are in fact acknowledged in valuable ethnological or psychological

K

classifications. There is, further, no reason why we should not acknowledge ideal patterns which incorporate factors due to choice and chance: the contingently existent has an ideal status when considered as *one* of the ways in which an ideal genus can be specified or circumstanced, and even considered as *the* way or as *a* way in which it has in fact been specified or circumstanced. Everything, even the merely factual, has an ideal status, only a duly placed, relegated one; an exemplified character is, *qua* character, different from an unexemplified one, even if the difference is rightly seen as peripheral. There is, further, no reason against, and strong reason for, postulating an essence or ideal pattern for certain individual beings, an essence representing a peculiar sort of being which the being in question alone instantiates, which perhaps cannot be instantiated by another individual, but which need not extend to *all* that it has, is, does, or undergoes. Leibniz, as is well known, framed a notion of individual essence covering every circumstance, however trivial, in an individual's actual history, or setting, so that none could be thought different without substituting another individual for the one is question. This Leibnizian concept, though legitimate, is not what we here intend. We are endeavouring to frame a notion of an individual which permits us to imagine him or it differently qualified, placed in differing situations and reacting differently to them, perhaps faced by the free choice of others and reacting freely to them. Such a notion or εἶδος will involve a distinction between features which are intrinsic to it and features which accrue to it externally, which fill in the gaps it leaves open but which might have been differently filled. It is this conception of ideal individuality that, following suggestions of Plotinus, we should be advised to frame, and to locate among the prime furnishings of the ideal world. The more inclusive individuality of Leibniz could be given the same interstitial status that we accord to other contingent specifications. We are, here, however, faced by the interesting question whether *all* individual specimens of *all* kinds shall be held to have peculiar individual patterns, or whether this is true only of *some* individual specimens of *some* kinds. One is moved to take some view of the latter kind. The nature of certain individuals, whether human or animal, is felt to involve something so enormously distinctive and such a close mutual 'belongingness' among its central traits, as to qualify for genuine *sui generis* status, whereas other individuals seem only contingently to specify or individuate possibilities characteristic of some more general essence or kind. Socraticity, we feel, was something *sui generis*, but not so the habit of being this individual earwig. Possibly men and some higher animals are unique in achieving this *sui generis* individuality. The sort of point now under discussion is of course quite beneath discussion from the standpoint of modern analysis: *we* alone, as linguistic arbiters, can decide whether being Socrates constitutes being a peculiar sort of thing whereas being this earwig does not. But the fact that we do feel the issue to be discussable and even momentous does tend to show that it objectively is so, and that for a suitable otherworldly, noetic vision, some *soi-disant* essences may well count as ultimate articulations of the noetic cosmos whereas others do not so qualify. Spinoza, in his theory of survival *sub specie aeternitatis*, has said much on these lines.

We are here led on to another major Platonic issue, the relation of the forms or essences to goodness or value. The *Republic* teaches that it is the form of goodness or value which gives being to all the forms and also illuminates minds and makes them mindful of the forms in question: it has, however, itself a dignity beyond that of the forms and their being, and presumably also, since it gives cognizability to the forms while it is itself the source of all cognizability, it is not known as the forms are known. This doctrine plainly implies that the forms are particular specifications of goodness or value, 'values' in the sense in which we used the plural in a previous lecture, marrying together indissolubly what modern philosophers prize apart as descriptive and evaluative meaning, while goodness itself is neither a form nor known as forms are known, only because it is (we may say) what it is to be a form and what it is to be knowable itself. There can be little doubt that, from its first inception, the axiological and mathematical sides of the Platonic view of the forms were firmly married, as for the Pythagoreans, and the good was always a mathematical as much as a value-concept, being in fact probably identified with the Pythagorean principle of Limit, which Plato, possibly out of deference to the Eleatics, renamed 'the One'. What the *Philebus* states explicitly, all earlier dialogues imply, the *Republic* in particular by the close unity it institutes between mathematical and moral education, that goodness consists always in some sort of 'governance by numbers', by precisely proportional measures, and by numbers peculiar to the thing or enterprise on hand. What we have now ourselves to enquire is the extent to which we can endorse the construction of an ideal world in which descriptive content is thus closely wedded to value, and in which both have a close connection with the Greek idea of a logos *qua* quantitative ratio.

We said in a previous lecture that the whole field of human abstraction is presided over by certain fundamental logical values, which some, whose conception of the 'logical' is narrow, would possibly call 'aesthetic'. We do not frame any and every abstract conception, but only such as have clear and unchanging outlines, or great unity and simplicity which also stretches to cover extreme diversity, or deep 'truth' to the rich detail of instantiated fact, etc., etc. (There are also logical values lying in opposed directions, and not to be confused with mere fallings-short of the above excellences, which in some contexts, e.g. those of poetry or mysticism or philosophy, have unusual importance.) What we are now maintaining is that the ideal world we are constructing should have as its prime members types which exemplify high logical values, and this is in fact exactly how we do want to build it up. The forms which are thought to underlie natural kinds, or to set patterns of law for the whole universe, or the individualities which we think really distinctive, are all characterized by an aesthetic salience and a fruitful simplicity as well as by deep relevance to changing instantial detail. The only difference in our attitude is that, in our previous treatment, we were treating the values which guide our abstractions merely as high-level needs of the thinking person, which shape the objects of *his* intentions, whereas now we are seeing them as the governing principles of a world which underlies and determines the multiplied instantial world of our sensuous encounters. We are holding, in short, that the same noetic cosmos which affects us with a desire or need for certain conceptions, also affects the instantial world and makes it conform to this need, that the need and the material which meets the need have an affinity derived from this common source, and rendered understandable thereby. There are, of course, a vast family of non-logical values, aesthetic, moral, hedonic, energetic, etc., etc., and, these, it might seem, have no necessary relation to the values which make objects understandable, and give them a firm place in the noetic cosmos. But these other values all have profound analogies and affinities with the values we have called 'logical', and they all also represent the way in which our thinking being detaches itself from contingent goals towards goals ever more generalized and shareable. The same craving for universality and necessity, which leads us to build up a world of truth and logic by which all thinking persons will be bound, also leads us to build up the other impersonal goals in question. These other non-cognitive values therefore reflect trends essential to the understanding of thinking man, and therefore *have* logical or cognitive value as well as *being* peculiar types of excellence: it is impossible to understand what man is without seeing him in relation to the ordered family of transcendental ends that he cannot help setting himself, and which all deviations from such ends likewise presuppose. And it is reasonable to hold that no collective or individual human structure can be truly understood except in terms of the specific values it frames for itself, and which are its own collective or personal ideal. The good, therefore, presides not only over the whole noetic cosmos but also more specially over that part of this cosmos which embraces conscious purposiveness, whether animal or human.

Any *complete* endorsement of a view which makes goodness or value preside over the whole noetic cosmos will, however, involve the acceptance of a view like that of the *Phaedo*, according to which being good is somehow a good reason for being or for being so, with an added rider that it is ultimately the *only* reason for anything's being or being so, so that all cases of the indifferent and the bad will have somehow to be accorded an instrumental goodness, as being necessary conditions or inevitable consequences of what is *per se* good. This, rather than the totally unacceptable view that evil is a mere case of defect or negation, and so negligible, is what will require reflective endorsement. A full discussion of evil will occupy us in another lecture: here it will be enough to stress that it is not good enough to locate departures from perfection in the region of instances, and to explain their imperfection either by defects of instantiation as such or of some material involved in instantiation. This facile solution is inadmissible if only for the reason that an εἶδος, a general pattern, is inherently and not accidentally a possibility of instantiation, a point that Plato was coming more and more to see, and that it therefore requires the realm of instances as much as the latter requires it. This is particularly obvious if we adopt a view which connects εἴδη, general patterns, with values, for each value is inseparable from the demand that something should *be*, and *be* not merely in some unfulfilled, ideal sense, but in the sense of the most full-fledged instantiation. Instances may occupy a lowly place in the system of things, but this place is none the less indefeasible. Every deficiency and distortion, therefore, that can arise out of the instantiation of the prime members of the noetic cosmos, must be inherent in those members and discoverable in the structure of that cosmos: what is discordant, defective, distorted, hybrid must exist inter-stitially in the world of ideal patterns. This was perhaps obscurely seen by Plato when he drew back from a too confident exclusion of untoward and squalid elements from the dazzling realm yonder, and when he was not afraid to admit the presence of the Great and Small, the principle of unlimited quantity and to that extent of evil, into the realm of forms. The imposition of the Limit on the Unlimited, or, to quote from another context, of the Works of Mind on the Works of Necessity, may have seemed a somewhat sorry enterprise down here, but Plato must have seen it as mirror-ing a wholly successful enterprise yonder in which continuous quantity was quite dominated and therefore good. But whether or not Plato was thus fully percipient, or was merely the purblind logic-chopper he is currently thought to have been, it is plain that, since possibilities of instantiation lie in different directions, and conflict with one another in their realization, and so lead to ugly clashes, compromises, colourless intermediates or one-sided victories, there are boundless possibilities of evil in all instantia-tion, and, since the possibility of instantiation is inseparable from ideal being, in ideal being itself. Even the ordered world of numbers has and must have its interstitial surds, an evil well known to the Pythagoreans and also to Plato. We may add to this necessity of logical evil in the ideal cosmos, the necessity which rests on contrast, it being plain that the value and clearness of anything salient, harmonious and pure depends on contrast with what is none of these things. And we may add the necessity which rests on resistance, it being plain that all higher types of spiritual excellence involve the overcoming of opposed resistances, as also the necessity which rests on freedom, it being plain that the 'values of the will' are at their highest when choice is least trammelled, and when, *pace* Augustine and countless others, a contrary choice of evil is both logically and metaphysically possible. When all these necessities are considered, it seems plain that evil is in numerous distinct ways inwrought into the essential fabric of what is good, and hence must be present in the paradigmatic as much as in the instantial order. Only in the former the patterns of what is hybrid, confused, ill-fitting, deformed or perverse will have an essentially different rank and position from the primary patterns of generic and individual goodness: the distortions and defects in question have a place in that cosmos, but only *as* distortions and defects, which are as such wholly parasitic upon goodness, and so no more than its inevitable shadows. The whole noetic cosmos, and so indirectly the realm of its instances, can therefore without absurdity be brought under the sway of the good, what is edifying can also happily be recognized to be logically necessary, and the programme of the *Phaedo*, of finding the supreme explanation of everything in how it is good or best for things to be, can therefore be realized. As to the further connection of value or goodness with proportion, we may be indulgent to this characteristically Greek exaggeration. Quantitative considerations certainly enter into many of the least formula-bound cases of excellence, but we have learnt from our romantic, Gothic past to value the *other* element in the forms, the unmeasured, dark, Platonic Great and Small. What exceeds all bounds and evades all compass is intrinsically precious to us since it is part and parcel of all that is intelligible.

We may now hold that, just as the noetic cosmos includes innumerable legitimate and deviant specifications which descend indefinitely into detail, so it will also contain patterns of higher and higher generality, until we end up with those categorial patterns whose being has no element of contingency and whose relations *inter se* are all necessary or involve *a priori* probability. The *a priori* eidetic sciences, of which phenomenology is one, lie behind (we may say) the contingent eidetic sciences which provide the material for this actual nature. Generic forms are, of course, a different set of ideal entities from the sorts which specify them, or from the generic aspect of the latter: the former are given apart from their specifications, while the latter are absolutely one with them. This constant reduplication of ideal entities in differing contexts is what surprised Plato into his doctrine of mathematicals, but the possibility of having 'many-alike', though embedded in different ideal contexts, must be held to be characteristic of the world of forms. Everywhere one encounters a splintering which, though not the last word in the matter, is deeply characteristic of the ideal as opposed to the instantial world: there may be patterns which are in a sense complex, e.g. the higher integers, the forms of animals, etc., but they are in a sense *new* patterns of which what we are inclined to call the separated elements are not really elements at all. The number Five, being Five as such, is obviously no part of the number Ten, though logically presupposed by the latter, and the genus Animal, considered in its pure generality, is in no sense part of the species Kangaroo. Entities of different levels, just *because* they are so essential to one another, are for that reason set wholly apart. It is a well-known principle in class-logic that classes, just because they are no more than the *collection* of their members are *therefore* separated from the latter by a categorial gulf. It goes without saying that our noetic cosmos will include separated abstracta belonging to other categories than the individual or substantial, and that these abstracta too will be of varying degrees of generality or specificity, or of complexity or simplicity. They are the finely splintered interstitial dust necessarily generated by an original set of larger splinters, and they necessarily generate a finer and finer dust in their own interstices, in a manner that recalls the generation of various types of matter in Descartes' vortical physics. They contribute to the ideal cosmos by giving to each facet of everything, and to each facet of each facet, an independent ideal position, as by also giving an independent position to any and every case of union and connection that the cosmos embodies. The last point is of great importance. Though (from one point of view) essentially splintered, the ideal world contains patterns of every degree of internal complexity and coherence: it must contain detailed specifications of any and every complete world, of which our own world is (so far) only one among others. Here, however, we must guard against a profound mistake: the mistake of making the noetic cosmos a mere assemblage of possible worlds or Carnapian state-descriptions set side by side in some indifferent 'logical space'. In our world abstract possibilities of structure and arrangement are plainly parasitic upon the sorts of things and the sorts of arrangements that are there, and so too the infinite, merely possible worlds of Leibniz and Carnap must be given a peripheral place surrounding a single world-pattern which is also *the* world-pattern, the blue-print of our actual world. This unique actual world will have its unique model yonder, much as Plato placed a single ideal living creature behind the one world in which our lots are cast, and in fact derived the uniqueness of the latter from that of the former. Real being and truth make sense only where there is a single, all-embracing, content-informed, highly coherent system into which all specific and individual facts can be fitted, and this is as true of the ideal as of the actual world.

Our construction of the intelligible world has more and more assumed the character of the exploration of a mythical lumber-room, in which almost anything may be discovered, and where disorder rather than cosmos seems predominant. It is now time to lay greater stress upon the *experience*, the blessed conscious life, in which all this splendid variety is brought together, and which alone gives it an ultimate hold upon our credence. The great inversion of Platonism, whereby characters take ontological precedence over instances, has a deep and liberating hold upon our view of the world: it substitutes, as we saw, the lucid and the graspable for the everlastingly obscure and elusive. Individuals there well may be, and we may at times indicate them with our physical fingers or hold them in our physical hands, but all that our minds can lay hold of in them is irremediably characteristic and universal. The great inversion is, however, unacceptable unless we can carry it further, relating the characters thus distinguished to a mind that embraces them and unites them, and which employs its intentions, not so much to mediate transcendent references to instances, as to put before itself ideal objects which exactly correspond to the scope of its intentions. When I think abstractly of being such and such and no more, or of a such and such and no more, or of such and such's being the case and no more, I put before myself an object tailored to fit the approach, the conscious light, in which I might view an object, so that object and approach can without absurdity be said to be the same thing differently regarded (like the concave and convex previously mentioned) and so that the intention is wholly adequate to and exhaustive of the intended object. The essential ambiguity of the word 'concept' has been often noted, it being used to stand for the *manner* in which something is conceived by someone and also for a truncated something which precisely fits that manner. This ambiguity springs from the two-sided unity of pure thinking, in which it is not really possible to have the intended without the intention, nor vice versa. For ideal patterns, while perfectly intelligible as intentional objects, cannot be thought to have uninstantiated being except in and for certain intentions, and it is because of this profoundly intimate relation of intention and intended that our knowledge of the latter can be so completely luminous and adequate. Ultimately *all* instances, other than instances of mentality, may need to have this purely intentional status accorded to them, since they too never really have the completeness that their nature as individuals demands. This is, however, *a fortiori* true of the truncated universal objects of thought and perception which fall infinitely short of such completeness. The ideal world therefore points to a *mental* completion in which all its scattered objectivities, whether truncated and abstract, or 'open' and concrete, will be intended, and it is to such a view that we find Plato tending in his later dialogues, Aristotle having recourse in his view of a mind as a place of forms, while the whole notion becomes explicit in Plotinus's view of the Divine Mind as embracing and in a sense *being* the whole world of forms. Obviously no abstractum can be anything unless it illuminates, by contrast and in countless other ways, the systematic totality of other abstracta (and thereby indirectly the whole realm of instances), unless it forms part of a single grand total of discourse or dialectic, both points made in Plato's *Parmenides* and his *Sophist*. The need for mutual relevance is precisely the need for a single embracing mind, for it is only in such a mind that the essential splintering of abstract entities can be overcome. Mind is therefore no otiose, contemplative subjectivity, but the essential cement of the ideal world; it alone enables it to stand on its own legs, to be a cosmos, a unified world. We may note too, in passing, how by our passage to such a mind we begin to see the solution of the puzzle which has teased us so hopelessly thus far: the impossibility of achieving that exhaustive synthesis of possibilities or of 'values' in which the whole phenomenological cosmos was seen to culminate. The notion of such a complete synthesis is from the point of view of instantiation absurd: one cannot possibly realize the totality of possibilities, both because there is no upper limit to such a class, and also because there is no way of instantiating certain possibilities without excluding others. The independent subsistence of a set of abstracta, were it conceivable, might not involve a similar contradiction, but it would involve a splintered side-by-sideness (or not even that) which certainly yields no genuine synthetic unity. But the *thought* of all possibles, all values, or even the thought of the unrealizable synthesis of them all, has nothing impossible about *it*, and its perfection may even be said to consist in the sheer impossibility of carrying out its content instantially. It is, in fact, to use the language of religious paradox, the sheer contradictoriness of all that God intends (not of course of what God is) that places him infinitely above and beyond all of his creatures, who all represent one-sided essays in instantial consistency. It is because divinity cannot *make* divinity, that it *is* divinity. These readily misunderstood paradoxes apart, we are led to place in the intelligible world a mind that holds it all together and for whom all its splintered and coherent fragments, its realities and unrealities, alone form a unitary picture. This is not a new view, but we have tried to see it, not as arbitrary and edifying, but as categorial and necessary.

We must not, however, escape from one sort of instantialism only to fall a prey to another: the mind for which and in which all abstracta intentionally are must not be *this* mind or *that* mind, not even a supreme mind set high above all finite minds and imparting light to them all. Such a supreme mind would merely be one mind among others, however superior in origin and content, and its exclusion of other minds, even of their interesting one-sidedness, would deprive it of any absolute or paradigmatic status. The mind that furnishes the cement of the intelligible world can be no less than mind as such, an absolute that overlaps all distinctions of kind and instance, and so a mind *shared* in varying degrees by all instances of mentality, and ever more completely as they advance towards the mystical pole of all being. The conclusion to which we are irresistibly drawn has, however, its own deep difficulties. Does it not make the mind which, we say, illuminates the intelligible world, a mere limit to actual minds, an imaginary focus, moreover, where nothing actually is? And does it not make mind as such, like the varying abstracta it houses, a mere abstractum itself demanding incorporation in another mind by which it will be intended?

These difficulties must be embraced and turned into victories. It is a proper and happy truth that the mind which illuminates the intelligible world is nothing without the instantial minds that more or less adequately embody it, and that it requires as they require it. Some of these minds, seen from *our* elevation, are practically indistinguishable from it, as our minds may well seem indistinguishable from it from the lowly stance of domestic animals. And we may certainly hazard the suggestion that there is no degree of instantial approximation to it that is not somewhere or somewhen equalled or surpassed, even though the sum-total of all such approximations may represent an illegitimate notion. But the relation of this universal or absolute mind to instantial minds will not be that of a mere intentional object to which their thought tends, but of a goal towards which their being necessarily drifts: the peculiar intentionality involved in this case, as better philosophers have stated, is that of a *nisus*, a zeal, a burning love. And though the requirement is mutual, the Platonic inversion is still proper: it is better to see in mind as such the cause of the *nisus* which informs instantial minds, than to see instantial minds, in all their purblindness and weakness, as the celebrants of a strange theurgy or theogony, in which the absolute mind first comes to light. The intelligible world is therefore presided over by a mind which is not anyone's mind but to which all minds, set outside this world at varying distance in the sphere of instances, aspire, and by which they may be said to be inspired. Ultimate truth in this region seems as close to atheism as to theism (or vice versa), a fact evinced by the perennial wobble of enlightened opinion on the matter (meaning by 'enlightened' the view of Buddhas and Messiahs, not of what are generally called 'advanced thinkers').

The elevation to universal mind or to mind as such must not, however, be so interpreted as to remove from the noetic cosmos all shadow of personal emphasis or point of view. Nothing that exists anywhere in the realm of instances can fail to have its 'as such', its paradigm yonder, and so certainly also that strange multiplication of points of view, in a sense overlapping yet in a sense exclusive, which characterizes instantial mind. Mind as such does not merely have instances mutually indifferent, but instances given as in possible communication with one another, and this is as much 'of its essence' as any general feature of intentionality. The life of mind is always *of* objects, but it is also always lived *with* others, and the ideal cosmos must therefore preserve all real and thinkable differences of viewpoint, and its intentional structures will be in every way as interesting as are its animals or its atoms. But in the intelligible world no such standpoint will be privileged: each will be a centre of everything, much as in space every point is a centre for all space. Instantial minds as they ascend in latitude will therefore approximate more and more closely to the non-privilege or omni-privilege of mind as such: they will indeed see things from their own point of view, but will mirror all other points of view so sympathetically, that there will be less and less difference between the mirror-image and the reality. In the end it will represent a distinction without a difference whether we say that we have A sympathizing with B or have B sympathizing with A. This limit again exists only in approximation, and makes sense only as the goal of instantial minds, but this will not lessen the propriety of a Platonic inversion which treats it as much more authentic and more potent than the instantial minds which approach it.

Very similar things can be said if we consider the gradual vanishing of temporality which will obtain as we advance towards the limit constituted by the intelligible world and the mind that surveys it. Temporality can never vanish as long as there is instantial mind, for we cannot, as seen before, divorce awareness from an ever varied achievement of salience: a thing must appear *as* this or *as* that, and it must always appear as something different as long as we have it in mind. This does not, however, mean that, as mind rises in latitude, it may not more and more approach to a state indifferently describable as one of infinite acceleration or of ultimate arrest of experience. On either account succession draws ever closer to the *punctum stans* of eternity, in which succession is merely a courtesy order in what is experienced as a unity. But the actual experiences at upper points on a world-line will be aeonian rather than eternal: they will sum up vast periods in unity, but will still point beyond themselves to a past and a future. This again does not mean that there is something factitious about eternity: it can be thought of as more real and explanatory than the aeonian or non-aeonian experiences that approach or aspire to it. The aeonian character of high-level experience will, as said before, not involve any absurd decision of issues before they are decided, only what we may call a sublime rush in which it is impossible to postpone or await the future, a rush that from lower levels will always give the impression of a picture gradually enriched and augmented. And even in the sublime rush of aeonian experience there must, we feel, remain something of historicity. What must be supposed to be

condensed in its near-momentariness is the sort of deeply theo-
dicistic recasting of history towards which Hegel struggled, a recasting in which all successful achievements, as well as all failures, will
be seen as the necessary, or necessarily contingent, elements involved in the attempted instantiation of exhaustive perfection in a
necessarily imperfect, one-sided, transient, instantial world.

I shall conclude this lecture by reading you two passages which
portray the noetic cosmos: the first is a well-known one from
Plotinus's treatise *On Intelligible Beauty* (*Enn.* V, viii, 3, 4), while
the second is from an account given by Suzuki of certain untrans-
lated portions of the *Gandavyuha*, a portion of the *Avatamsaka-
sutra*, one of the great documents of Mahayana Buddhism. Both
are highly alike in their content because, doubtless, both express
precisely the same experience, the same vision, which may be said
to lie obscurely behind *all* human experience and endeavour.
Plotinus writes of the life yonder: 'For all there is heaven:
earth is heaven, and the sea is heaven, and so are animals and
plants and men, all heavenly things in that heaven. The
gods in that heaven do not think meanly of the men it it, or of
anything else, since all are of heaven, and they go through that
spacious land while remaining at rest. And life is easy yonder, and
truth is their parent and nurse, their substance and sustenance, and
they see all things, not such as are in flux, but as have true being,
and they see themselves in others. For all things are transparent,
and nothing is dark and resistant: everything is inwardly clear to
everything and in all respects, light being made manifest to light.
And each thing holds all within itself, and again sees all in each
other thing, so that everything is everywhere, and all is all, and
each all, and the glory infinite. Each of those things is great, since
even the small is great, and the sun yonder is all the stars and each
star the sun, and again all the stars. One thing stands forth in each
though it also displays all. . . . Each there walks, as it were, on no
alien earth, but is itself always its own place: its starting point
accompanies it as it hastens aloft, and it is not one thing and its
region another.'

I shall now read from Suzuki's account of certain passages in the
Gandavyuha, descriptive of the Dharmadhatu or region of essence.
I have sought in vain for a full translation of them. 'The Buddha of
the *Gandavyuha* lives in a spirit world which has its own rules. In
this spiritual world there are no time-divisions such as the past,

present and future; for they have contracted themselves into a single moment of the present where life quivers in its true sense. . . . The Buddha in the *Gandavyuha* thus knows no time-continuity; the past and the future are both rolled up in this present moment of illumination. . . . As with time, so with space. Space in the *Gandavyuha* is not an extension divided by mountains and forests, rivers and oceans, lights and shades, the visible and the invisible. Extension is here indeed, and there is no contraction of space into a single block of existence; but what we have here is an infinite mutual fusion or penetration of all things, each with its own individuality yet with something universal in it. . . .To illustrate this state of existence, the *Gandavyuha* makes everything transparent and luminous, for luminosity is the only possible earthly representation that conveys the idea of universal interpenetration, the ruling topic of the sutra. . . . With the annihilation of space and time, there evolves a realm of imagelessness or shadowlessness (*anabhasa*). . . . In the *Gandavyuha* there is no shadowiness; it is true there are rivers, flowers, trees, nets, banners, etc., in the land of purity, in the description of which the compiler taxes his human imagination to its utmost limits; but no shadows are visible here anywhere. The clouds themselves are luminous bodies inconceivable and inexpressible in number, hanging all over the Jetavana of the *Gandavyuha*. . . . This universe of luminosity, this scene of interpenetration, is known as the Dharmadhatu, in contrast to the Lokadhatu which is the world of particulars. . . . The Dharmadhatu is a real existence and not separated from the Lokadhatu, but it is not the same as the latter when we do not come up to the spiritual level where the Bodhisattvas are living.'[1]

As you listen to this remarkable account, you must reflect there is a temple in Japan, the Todaiji temple at Nara, dedicated to this amazing message of interpenetration. Unlike the dwellers in the upper world, you will, however, be becoming worn out with all this glory. In my next lecture I shall try to relate it to the life of the human soul, to the incarcerated and potentially free human person.

[1] D. T. Suzuki, *Essays in Zen Buddhism* (Third Series), London. Rider and Co. 1958, pp. 79–81. Quoted by permission of the publishers.

THE LIFE OF THE SOUL

In the last two lectures we first sketched the geography of a total world which stretches from the dispersed, peripheral realm that we call the human cave, to a mystical pole of unity where the life-lines stretching from this region have a common point of inter-section: we then sketched the special appearances of a high-latitude circle in this world, the circle we called that of the intel-ligible world or the noetic cosmos. Geography is for us, however, merely a preparation for ecology: the role of the world we have been constructing is to house the intelligent beings whose lot is cast in it, and to provide the background and points of encounter in which they may fulfil their destiny. Among those intelligent beings the most important for us is man, and we may therefore say that our whole cosmology, like the cosmos it sketches, is constructed for the sake of man. This teleology is not the absurd, ego-centred construction that it seems: we saw at the end of our first series of lectures that it was only in terms of some such teleology that the immense tensions and antinomies in the experienced world could conceivably be ironed out. It must be because they are all *needed* for the emergence of rational interpersonal life, and for the logical, aesthetic, practical, personal and other values that it embodies, that such surds are as they are. They are chasms which exist as necessary presuppositions of the rational bridges we build across them, and in building which we, as rational persons, in effect build ourselves as well.

The teleology to which we were committed by our first series of lectures was not, however, one that could be sustained in a merely this-world setting: to impose it on this world is to view the latter in a singularly forced, arbitrary way, that is moreover always breaking down into deeper despair. If such despair is to be kept at bay, we have need of the otherworld vistas we have been construc-ting, and that not merely as a self-saving, personal opiate, but as something which saves the phenomena, which redeems them from utter absurdity and logical collapse. The use of otherworldly perspectives to give sense to our moral endeavours has of course been common in popular religion and ethically inspired philosophies: the use of such perspectives to explain certain facts of knowledge is peculiar to Platonism. We alone seem to wish to use it to explain all human existence and its setting, including much that seems to have little to do with man at all.

The use of otherworldly states to illuminate this-world conditions must take account of the prime fact that they are deeply hidden from us, that we have nothing that counts as a certain encounter with them, not even much that counts as indirectly pointing to them, as being such that it could hardly have been as it is had our life not had an otherworldly background. The construction in question is no ordinary hypothesis, no extension of this-world pattern in an unfamiliar direction, which, though daring, is at once rewarded by a vast amount of this-world confirmation, which would not at all fit some slightly different extension. It is a construction in which we not only go in quest of new facts but of facts ordered by new, not wholly understandable categories, in which we grope in the dark, and in which our gropings have no clear link with what we have encountered or expect to encounter 'down here'. It is in fact a movement *away* from the plane of our normal exploration, based only on highly general characters of what we encounter here, and involving, moreover, not only a great turn in a new direction, but a great leap towards states which, though having affinities with this-world conditions, are always thought of as being 'deeply different' from them. It is, in short, a profoundly unjustified leap, if justification is measured by the strength of this-world indications and evidence, and for many it would also seem a leap of doubtful significance, since we do not profess to be able to point to instances which would illustrate what we mean. The full justification of truth and significance lie all in anticipation: *now* it is impossible to understand, explain and vouch for all that we say, but *then* all will be simple and clear. To some the whole venture is necessarily chimerical, one into which costly intellectual effort is being vainly diverted: our reply is that chimeras haunt all human undertakings, and are not less part of the scene because we turn our backs on them. The spectacles of another life may one day unroll themselves before us, but the

L

abstract constructions of mere positivism never did and never will. What we are, however, obliged to show is not merely the need of otherworldly construction for the solution of this-world difficulties: we are also obliged to show the need of otherworldly obscurity and uncertainty for the solution in question. An otherworldly background must in short not function in explanation except as a deeply, obscure, uncertain background: the waters of Lethe must lap it around, and a palimpsest of pure naturalism must overlay and blur the sense of its inscribed message. It is only as *not* seeming to be a likely continuation of this-world states that it can, from a higher point of view, really *be* their inevitable continuation, their explanatory completion. Our life, in short, is lived in a cave, and whatever surrounds and explains cave-life must seem sharply cut off from it, utterly separate from it, occurring in quite another territory or medium. The justification of this seeming discontinuity must lie in its utter necessity for the higher forms of spiritual life, a necessity that we at times deeply feel, but at other times find it very hard to argue for. What we must be able to show is that an astringent touch of despair is as necessary as a touch of hope to the carrying on of the higher spiritual enterprises, and that we can only win to regions where all will be gloriously bridged if we have also toiled at levels where the very possibility of such bridging seemed utterly in doubt. The difficult contentions we are hazarding will, however, only acquire full persuasiveness when we have carried the argument a little further.

The otherworldly continuation we are postulating is a continuation of the conscious thinking person, of the self-identifying person, and it must be a continuation in time, though at its extreme limits it may well do something that could be called 'passing out of time'. It must be the sort of continuance that a conscious person could say that *he* had or was about to have, and that he would not say that someone else, another person or ego, had or was going to have. Other types of queer continuance there well may be in which it might be reasonable to say that the acts and states of someone were continued in the acts and states of a number of distinct persons, or continued in the acts and states of someone who continued the acts and states of other persons as well, or continued in acts and states that would be said to belong to some other person. There may well be forms of individuality more fluid and shifting than those that men ordinarily ascribe to themselves, and the life of spirits or angels may well offer phenomena to which such terms as 'coalescence' and 'fission' have a profoundly justified, not lightly given application. Human individuality, with its seeming promise of indefinitely continued, separated duration, at least in principle, may be only one among several patterns of individuality which the cosmos provides, though it is hard to believe that it does not also enshrine the most valuable possibilities in that cosmos, a belief expressed in the doctrine that the Divine Word took on human and not angelic form, and that the human Buddha was the teacher of gods as well as men.

However this may be, the continuance we are considering, which is necessary to make the upper world play its full part in the whole spiritual economy, is one in which the individual conscious person can project his identity, in some deep sense, beyond the limits of his fleshly being, in which he can be, and feel himself to be, amphibious, capable of life in two media, much as even in this fleshly medium he can pass from the sphere of overt bodily response to that of internal spiritual adjustment and vice versa. This continued life in two media need not be thought to involve the full actuality of a memory spanning the whole period of continuance, though it does involve the real possibility of such a memory. Even in this life we all acknowledge the possibility that we may have done and undergone many things of which we now have no recollection, and that we may pass over into states in which we shall not remember what we are now doing or undergoing. Identity of self is a matter presupposed by memory and not constituted by it, and nothing is easier to conceive than that *we* shall be in states without remembering the state in which we now look forward to them. But to project our identity in this manner is also to expect that it will be capable of announcing itself in some manner, that such announcement, though not trivially necessary, is none the less inherently likely. There must therefore be states in which anything and everything in the past history of a personal self or ego is inherently likely to be given, if the notion of its separate continuance is not to be emptily formal. It goes without saying that personal continuance will be emptily formal if it does not further go with a deep heritage of character and personal traits which comes out more clearly the more we enter into the whole habit of the person concerned, and which alone could afford positive ground for speaking of such continuance. And just as there are principles of growth and senescence which enables us to detect the friend of our youth in the mature adult or withered elder before us, so there must be rules of transformation or transfiguration in virtue of which earthly persons are connected with their glorious or darkened shapes in another world. Those accustomed to directing intentions to the dead know how at times they make themselves known to our feeling in an extraordinary glorified manner, recognizably the same, yet all raised, as it were, to a higher degree or power of themselves.

It may here be held, further, that some attenuation of bodily continuance is part and parcel of personal continuance beyond the limits of this life. The distinctness and discreteness of persons, though not the same as spatial distinctness and discreteness, only becomes fully manifest and contentful through the latter just as the mutual self-revelation of persons to persons and all their mutual intercourse require the continuously graded distances and the limiting contacts of space. As we have held, the lower latitudes of the unseen world involve many approximations to bodily being, though with diminished persistence, resistance, inertia, publicity and other bodily traits. Personal continuance might at this level assume dispersed forms, such as widespread and intermittent appearances, all characterized by a style or a use of symbolic devices that connected them with a particular person. Cézanne might reveal his presence by a subtle look cast upon the landscape rather than by any particular bodily form. But the full exercise of personal being demands the use of many sensitive and active bodily channels, and could not be contentfully continued in a wholly dissimilar medium, any more than the pattern of a symphony could be continued in a series of smells. After-life continuance, while it may assume many vagrant and detached forms, as it does even now in letters, tape-recordings, etc., must in the main continue itself in something like a persistent body or set of bodies. In this life we are simply located, laboriously operative, slowly changing beings, with our heritage stored in our muscles and nerves, and our whole solidity and salience as spiritual beings depends on these facts. In the life to come we may change in these respects, but not quite beyond recognition, if our continued subsistence is to be a contentful matter. We are, moreover, beings whose prime way of showing ourselves to our fellows is more than a misty velleity just because it involves the solidities and publicities of the flesh, and, though this will certainly be attenuated as we rise in spiritual latitude, there is sound reason for holding that, even in such attenuation, we must retain some shadow of sensuous glory or inglory, something that could count as a spiritual or otherworldly body. If all this were utterly dispensed with, the distinction of persons would cease to be a contentful matter. Such a dispensing with personal distinctness may well be the rule at or near the mystical pole, but not at latitudes at which *we* can think or speak.

We now come to a great crux in our speculative construction, where religious tradition is almost equally divided. Shall we make personal continuance two-sided so that it extends before as well as after this present life, or shall we make it one-sided, so that it becomes entirely a matter of futurity? And, if we hold the former, shall we adopt the view of a rhythmic alternation of this-worldly and otherworldly states, of repeated incarnations with intermediate otherworldly periods, as in Hinduism or Buddhism, and as also taught by Pythagoras and Plato, and a vital part of the finest Platonic dialogues? It is not the policy of these lectures to take a firm stand on an issue so essentially obscure. We cannot, however, avoid saying that the Indo-Pythagorean-Platonic account forms a coherently thought-out cosmological picture, which also fits in better with the spiritual geography we have been constructing than the alternative Christian account, which seems in fact to be a strange compromise between an essentially this-world eschatology and a genuine otherworldly cosmology. The Jews, as we saw, let the *necessary* side of their religious absolute, its crown of ineffable excellences, incapable of realization in any set of existent instances, however prolonged or extensive, become lost in a contingent historical series, a divine act or programme, carried out on earth and ending in earth's transfiguration, which they rightly saw (we may say) to be the *other* side of a worthwhile religious absolute. To what we may call the contingent element in divinity, the element necessary in general but not in any precise form, they accorded the homage which only the necessary can deserve, and hence their God became a being in whom the exercise of magisterial decision became exalted over all other forms of excellence, while man's supreme virtue lay in unquestioning submission to that will. In this religion of magnificent arbitrariness, so satisfactory to a deep, though not to the deepest, segment in human nature, the violent and catastrophic everywhere took on the role of the adorably necessary, and what wonder that the

whole arbitrary drama should point to the unpredictable coming
of a divinely sponsored Messiah, to the uprising of the dead from
their graves, and to the inauguration of a kingdom where
righteousness and brotherhood and other absolute values should
be present in sensuous and highly personal form? In this scheme
violence dominates categories and values, and removes all philosophical tensions: there is no need of another world in which the
quarrel of categories and the quarrel of wills and values will be
gradually adjusted. Opacity and resistance yield to the touch of
God and of the appointed hour. When, however, it became clear,
in the disillusioned dawn of unfulfilled eschatology, that the
divine kingdom was not of this world in a sense different from that
intended by the heavenly Messiah, the need for otherworld
extensions began to be felt, and gave rise to all those hasty constructions, long hallowed by tradition, in which it is impossible
not to see a mixture of the improvised and the borrowed. In this
construction the soul's sudden origin at birth saddled the Creator
with a load of unsearchable arbitrariness which a responsible
theology should have sought to mitigate. The soul's asymmetrical
persistence seems paradoxical in this setting and serves little real
purpose, and we have, on the one hand, the unprofitable torturing
of those whose wills are irrevocably set in evil, and a purgation
whose result is foreseeable, on the other. On this other world
picture the old, this-world eschatology is still superimposed: at a
'last judgment' previous judgments will be recapitulated, and
bodies raised to give full concreteness to beings whose long
survival without them proves that they never really needed them.
What survives and tells in all this incongruity is simply the soul's
progress towards the mystical pole where all good and all being
are concentrated, the soul's necessary love for what is at this pole
and the love-like response which draws it beyond itself, the
necessary obstacles which choice and chance put in its path, and
the varied circumstances which form the setting of its progress,
and the continuation of that progress and its conditions beyond
the setting of this present life. All this and considerably more is to
be found in Plato's stress on the importance for our eternal well-
being of each trivial choice here and now. The Christian picture
has confused the Platonic otherworldly vision, without, however,
wholly destroying it. The consensus of the best spiritual opinion
and insight in regard to the life beyond is, in the view of the

present lecturer, to be found in the cosmic speculations of our
Aryan ancestors, whether Brahmanic, Buddhistic, Orphic,
Pythagorean, Platonic or Neoplatonic. To this the Jews added a
vision whose intense moral fervour provided the necessary complement to whatever is negative, inert and emptily transcendental in
the otherworld vision in question. We may be urged to be Jews in
regard to this world, and Brahmins or Neoplatonists in regard to
the next.

We may now hazard a view which applies alike to the Indo-
Pythagorean and the Christian view of the after-life: that the
after-life is in a sense parasitic upon the present one, and that its
task consists mainly in an assimilation, a spiritual digestion, of the
experiences and acts of this one, seeing them in wider and more
fluid contexts, comparing them with ideals and values of varying
sorts, consolidating their contributions into a new phase of
resolution and attitude, but not advancing effectively beyond them.
Whereas our this-world existence, with all its agony and blindness,
is the phase of our life where alone we confront serious problems
and resistances, where alone we enter into profound personal
commitments to others, and where alone we make firm resolves and
perform momentous and influential acts. In the essentially yielding
medium of the upper world, the events of earth-life can be relived
over and over, their import seen in most varied connections, their
lessons learnt and their outcome purified from whatever dross
clings to them but they cannot significantly be added to: that can
alone be done among the resistances and obscurities of earth-life,
in what we have called the cave. What we are professing is
unfashionably Victorian in spirit: that the highest of all values are
inseparable from earnest effort, that they require doubt, in-
security, temptation, suffering and profound difficulty, and that
only cave-life with its narrowed perspectives and mocking
antinomies will enable them to be realized. The life at the world's
mystical pole may be one of bliss and peace, but it is bliss and
peace springing from the intensest actuosity, and we can only
share in that bliss and peace by sharing also in that actuosity. It is
in the cave alone that such full sharing is possible for us, and the
life beyond is therefore essentially a lying back on our laurels, a
period of absorption and refreshment, or, in the unfavourable
case, of becoming really clear how lamentably we have performed.
This is of course in accord with Christian otherworldliness for

which the soul's destiny is always decided in this life, and often dramatically in our last moments, but in the Indo-Pythagorean scheme the intermediate discarnate state could also have the function of gathering together and consolidating the experiences and attitudes which will pervade the next life, and which will be real influences even though their precise source is forgotten. This suggested view might look at incarnate life in a manner different from the actual Indo-Pythagorean tradition, and might accord better in spirit with the Christian-Jewish valuation of transfigured earthliness, of bodily resurrection and of a God who did not despise the Virgin's womb. No explanation, in fact, seems required of the need for earthly existence whether on the part of a creative or a creaturely spirit: it is the need which drives us to produce works of art instead of meditating on absolute beauty, or which drives a seaman regularly to his confined, difficult life at sea in preference to an existence in which impact and action are alike muted and muffled. But we need to set aside this need for real engagement, which is the characteristic Jewish-Christian contribution, a need for disengagement and distance and self-collecting understanding which is inseparable from the former, and lives by negating it. This dual need is best served if the soul's life is a regular alternation between disengaged discarnate states, in which memory of previous states becomes fully actual, and engaged incarnate states in which the waters of Lethe remove all but the narrow view necessary for the living, practical issues on hand. It is not so well served by the Christian scheme of a brief incarnate phase followed by an endless discarnate one, but in that scheme too, though there may not be waters of Lethe, there is a corresponding obscurity regarding a future state, towards which nothing inclines us but philosophical and moral faith. In both schemes the other life sheds a precious illumination on this one, and reduces the sting of its problems.

It may now be held that the traditional view is correct in seeing in the other world a region where what is and what ought to be are gradually and often painfully brought together, as they need not be at all brought together in this present life. The other life is, in short, a zone of recompense and purgation, where spiritual beings at least tend to see and feel the error of their ways and, on the alternating assumption, to re-enter life repentant and with a new orientation to their problems. It is also a zone of spiritual refreshment where the values achieved in fleshly existence can be permitted to shine forth in their full glory. The progress of the soul in the other life is accordingly, plausibly, first through states in which, in the less resistant otherworldly medium, personal interests and passions can have the full scope denied them in this life, and can shape the environment much as they now run wild in our personal fantasies. The dreadful monotony of personal passion will be most profoundly felt where there are no restrictions upon its gratification and where all combines to pander to it. Sojourn in an otherworldly Venusberg can probably be relied on to produce satiety for the delights it offers much more readily than can many years spent in libertinage in an earthly city of pleasure. And the same would apply to the gratifications of personal passions like malice, cruelty, vainglorious ambition, etc.; give them full rein and their wanton one-sidedness would soon be felt as *ennui*. Only the most determined ingenuity could hold back this utter, final weariness, the fruit of all mere going against the grain of things.

The progress of the soul will further be aided by the increased translucence of personal relations: here in this life the bodily shells of things alone force themselves upon our notice, and then only when they are near at hand. The interior appearances and responses to things from other standpoints make no strong impact upon us and are readily disregarded. In the other world, however, these interior appearances will not be so readily evaded, and they will pierce to the very citadel of our self-feeling and of our comfort, so that we shall not be able to take up an attitude towards them without also fully living through their response to this attitude. Nothing better assists the development of an impersonal conscience than a change from the position where putting oneself into some-one else's shoes is a gratuitous imaginative exercise, quite optional in the case of animals, to one in which it is a haunting, solidly elaborated, infinitely vivid necessity at all times. Only the most determined wickedness could ride roughshod over a protest that the wicked person himself felt in all its intensity. Most human wickedness consists in an unjust overriding of the needs and claims of others, and such overriding will be cured, not by intrusive punishments inflicted by otherworldly jailers, but by a steady reduction of the gulf between ourselves and others. There is no reason why we should be mealy-mouthed about otherworld agonies. The unbaptized or the heretic may have nothing to fear, but the perpetrators of crimes like those of the grimmer Nazis will certainly require millennia to re-enact, to realize and to repent fully of what they have done. The punishment for wickedness must not be conceived legalistically: it is of course essentially self-administered. What we have called the impersonal segment in the human person, the segment concerned to rise above all contingency of content and person and to pursue only that which makes a necessary appeal to everyone and for everyone, is no accidental offshoot of human nature, coaxed into unnatural predominance by certain forms of social training: it is the necessary part of human nature, which will tend to emerge, as a phenomenon of higher order, upon *whatever* contingent set of personal interests may at first serve as its substructure, and which will tend further to be strengthened by so many forces pushing in one direction—all the forces pressing towards open universality which, we may say, represent the essential *nisus* of consciousness itself—that it can only with difficulty fail to achieve the centrality and authority which are part of its idea. In this life the immediacies of sense and of personal passion may combine to stave it off and keep it marginal, but in the freer medium of otherworld life it may open floodgates which will ensure its supreme sway. It will not suffer us to turn away from the terrible impact of the attitudes of others, but will open us up to their full penetration, and in so doing reconfirm its own authority over us. We shall ourselves voluntarily enter into the wrongs inflicted by ourselves on others, and shall continue to plumb them until we have absolutely foresworn them. That in some rare cases this might *never* happen is of course perfectly conceivable, since there is nothing mechanical about spiritual purgation, but to be thus obdurate must involve deep difficulty. To be wholly successful it must involve a profound deadening, warping and stultification of the spirit, the perverse negation of what it essentially is, a negation we cannot put beyond the bounds of possibility since it is involved in the higher possibility of negating such a negation and setting it utterly aside. On the basis of such perversity souls may indeed erect for themselves a cold realm of wickedness, a very Versailles of damnation, perhaps filled with aesthetic, intellectual and other amenities to which a perverse twist has been given. Such possibilities are, however, parasitic upon the normal developments from which they deviate, and which they so unhappily frustrate. What we are saying will not preclude the possibility of many beings who would play a part, as one might say, in the management of the hells and purgatories we have been outlining, but they cannot be the basic agents in such zones of concentration. It is the soul itself that by its own inner conflicts gravitates to the equilibrium or the disequilibrium of an appropriate hell or purgatory, and which must go to such dark places of torment or uneasy joy because, basically and secretly, it is inflamed with a necessary love for a necessarily existent, omni-excellent object, without whose crowning being it could neither deviate nor repent of its deviations. What is essential is to see the deep necessities, not unfitly to be called 'logical' or 'categorial', underlying what would otherwise be a not very edifying set of myths.

The higher levels of the world to come will be reached after the purgations of the lower regions have been gone through, and will, as we have said, represent a glorified version of all the achievements of the human person in earthly life: its hardest sacrifices for difficult impersonal ends, its deepest penetrations into the life and interest of others, its aesthetic visions of exhibited essence, its scientific illuminations, etc., etc. These experiences involved celestial overtones when they occurred on earth, and these overtones may vibrate for a period which to the celestial sense has every mark of being endless. As argued above, time becomes more and more arrested at higher spiritual latitudes, so that it will be more or less a matter of viewpoint whether we describe these heavenly conditions as lasting for aeons or as compressed into a moment. What will be characteristic of such heavenly conditions will be moreover a full consciousness of the context of our earthly achievement. We shall see them in the full setting of our own achievement in former existences, if such there were, and also in the full setting of all human achievement and possibility, in the full superabundance, that is, of the noetic cosmos and its infinite riches. And we shall see them at a level where the schism between being and value has been healed, where all is above all secure, and where the anxiety which affects lower levels of being has been wholly exorcized. From such a vision it is quite possible that we shall return, and shall want to return, with renewed energy to the encounters and decisions of earthly existence, as long as these have relevance for our spiritual progress. We may here again grant the possibility of a heavenly administration responsible for many of the details of celestial existence. Quite possibly numerous exalted beings have elaborated their own 'pure lands' where the higher forms of spiritual refreshment will be available to many. As before, it will be the soul itself that gravitates to its appropriate 'pure land', dedicated to the flowering of its own brand of spirituality.

We here come up against a difference of opinion between the Christian and Indian point of view which requires careful consideration. The Christian view, with its stress on ultimate arbitrariness, readily makes the purgative, penal and compensatory arrangements of an other life arbitrary arrangements: they are what the supreme Will allots to those who have obeyed or disobeyed its decrees. The Indian view has in the main held to a curious semi-mechanistic view of *Karma* or Action, doubly curious in a system like that of early Buddhism where impersonal causal connection, rather than personal agency, alone links the various momentary phases of conscious and unconscious existence. *Karma* or Action is in part an ethical concept in that it involves, among other things, that evil deeds promote misery in this or another life, whereas good deeds create happiness or at least alleviate misery, but it conceives the moral order it postulates in quantitative and mechanical terms. A certain amount of ill desert hangs like a cloud, as it were, over an evil-doer, until it discharges itself in an appropriate amount of suffering. *Karma* or Action is also, less questionably, a theory of attachment, which explains why personal life continues in the courses to which it has committed itself, and necessarily undergoes the full working out of its own attitudes, but this profound view is not, as such, necessarily moral. In a value-free order such as early Buddhism postulated there is no clear reason why some cases of attachment, i.e. those involving recognized forms of immorality, should bring more misery than others, i.e. those involving obedience to established precepts. The ordinary virtues are, in fact, only loosely connected with a pure emancipation-philosophy, as indeed became evident in the last tantric phase of Buddhism when the violation of ordinary moral precepts became a sure sign of the higher emancipation. The notion of *Karma* or Action would in fact seem to be a thoroughly confused concept, a genuine case of the naturalistic fallacy, i.e. it covertly brings in issues of moral value while professing to offer us only a pure naturalism. What it requires to work satisfactorily is a deep-set teleology such as we have unabashedly postulated, an equation of the highest values with the objects of necessary and ultimate tendency and desire. It is possible to have an abstract notion of things as they are, into which value-considerations do not intrude, and it is possible to have abstracted understandings of value from which considerations of fact are excluded, but deeper insight into either shows them to be securely married: the one is given as endowed with an inherent *nisus* to pass over into the other. If this be admitted, *Karma* or Action will work, but it will be transformed out of all recognition, since it will no longer merely be our past evil or good deeds that will produce present misery or happiness, but our past commitments in their conflict with our own inescapable commitment to certain supreme perfections, which either underlie all life and being or lie wholly beyond it. And once *Karma* or Action is given such a twist, it will also lose its mechanical character: there is no precise measure of ill-desert and no precise equation of it with degree of misery. The misery which compensates and duly punishes an offence is the misery necessary to make us fully aware of its enormity, through every fibre of our practical being, and the amount and character of misery required will differ according to the person and the circumstances. Suffering as such, not bound up with any realization of ill-desert, has no purgative or other value, and merely adds to the evil of the universe.

The notion of *Karma* or Action is further absurd as applied within the limits of our present life, where it implies a denial of the indifference of inorganic bodily masses to value-considerations, and of the freedom of human agents to neglect value-considerations or to trespass against them. Alternatively it presupposes some sort of unintelligible pre-established harmony between freedom and chance, on the one hand, and spiritual teleology, on the other. Obviously an avalanche must be able to overwhelm me, or a wicked man to waylay and rob and murder me, whether or not this fate is written into my *Karma*, and whether or not it is a fate that I deserve to undergo. The precise difference between the cave, where mass-effects satisfy nobody and everything is at cross-purposes with everything, and the upper world where there is an ever increasing accommodation of value and being, would be quite set aside by such a gross intrusion of values into the sphere of this earthly life. What we have therefore, whether in our earthly or our upper world, is an order, neither mechanical nor arbitrarily personal, which gradually brings the extremes of fact and value out of an apartness which is necessary to their being truly brought together. This deep *nisus*, operating through and overcoming mechanism, is not really distinct from our religious absolute itself. For the mystical pole of the universe is not merely a geographical but a magnetic pole, which inevitably, though not mechanically, draws things towards itself.

We may now attempt, with extreme tentativeness, to sketch a typical biography of the conscious human spirit, both in this earthly life and in other worlds. On the one-life scheme this history will have a somewhat arbitrary, hidebound pattern: personal development will start at various points according to the natural endowment of particular infants and the particular cultural and personal circle into which they are born. Earthly life will develop both the personal and the supra-personal, absolute interests of the man in question, and in the life to come there will be, in the favourable case, a gradual purification of the personal side of the man's nature, and its transfiguration into such glorified impersonal values and merits as it is able to show forth. But on any many-life scheme there will be something like a natural cycle involved in the whole spiritual history. It will begin with the flowering of purely animal, first-order interest, directed to contingent goals of various sorts rather than their higher-order interestingness, and will then slowly rise above this to the cruder forms of self-interest. Then it will progress to those varied forms of what may be called social or tribal selfishness in which a man subordinates all other interests to those of some limited group to which he belongs. Here one has the beginnings of the impersonality or supra-personality inherent in all conscious, reflective desire, which we can see must tend to become stronger in the detached atmosphere of reflection. By a carrying further of the natural tendency involved in such desire we have the gradual emergence of generalized benevolence and justice: a desire directed to the satisfaction of everyone's interests and opposed to all narrowness and partiality. Concurrently with all this, there will necessarily tend to be a development of those sister forms of disinterestedness which are not concerned with persons and their interests but with the truth, possible truth and explanatory power of notions and alternatives, as in science, with the perspicuous manifestation of essence, as in art, or with sheer self-immersion in creative effort of whatever sort.

All this is one phase of the development of the human person, a phase in which, in the main, personal characteristics and interests become more and more definite, but in which they also become set in a framework of those impersonal interests which form the necessary, rather than the contingent, side of human nature. It is not necessary to imagine that the pattern we have sketched will always be followed: it is certain that it will not. The necessities of the spirit are never more than necessities of drift and tendency, and can be warped by stepmotherly circumstances, as well as by our own repeated exercises of choice and freedom, which on the many-life system will have taken place countless times before our present life. Each child born into the world will be the heir of innumerable, unremembered decisions, still effective in the form of character. We are not committed to a Humean view of causation according to which an action only is caused if it follows from antecedents according to a general pattern, nor is our notion of responsibility connected with that of a wholly fixed character or set of personal dispositions. The idea of free causality is that of an agency uncommitted but self-committing, guided but not obliged by its own former decisions, and which is fully explanatory, with or without additional factors, of any alternative it may actually realize. This is the notion of choice, of decision, as we have conceived the matter, that it can settle issues that nothing else can settle, and from the earliest period of conscious fleshly existence there will accordingly be choices made which will shape and perhaps warp further attitudes. Though life in subtler worlds will tend to iron out such warpings, there is no guarantee that it will always succeed in doing so. With the development of higher, wider interests, there is also, moreover, the possibility of perverse developments of the latter: corrupt and pitiless aestheticisms, cults of blind loyalty and obedience to impulse, of ruthless buccaneering, of torment and immolation senselessly imposed on self and others, etc., etc. We hold, however, that the achievement of a highly developed, strongly engaged personality, with great attachment to things and persons, and with at the same time a considerable deference for impersonal values of various sorts, and possibly their incorporation into a religion, is not only a normal outcome, in the sense of being how, in the light of absolute values, a man ought to develop, but also in the sense of being how men will in the main mass tend to develop, as the result of this-world and other-world influences and experiences. We need not here repeat that we see no error in a marriage, not tautological and definitory, but none the less essential and logical, between what should happen and what will actually tend to happen, which some, heroically confused, would regard as a dangerously optimistic form of 'naturalism'.

But at a certain point in human development there will tend to be a great turn, one of repentance, of metanoesis, a turn acknowledged in all religions but whose necessity can also be seen *a priori*. It is necessary, we may say, because it is part of the self-consciousness and self-existence of the absolute being without which nothing can either be thought of or be. The higher-order impersonal interests which have merely provided the framework for our strengthening personal attachments, will tend to take over altogether, and make personal interests their mere instruments and material. The impersonality involved in all our higher-order interests will develop its own zest, we shall love it itself and for its own sake, and we shall find something mean, paltry and restricted in the contingent personal goals on which it has first built itself. This development will be aided by innumerable this-world forays and otherworld retreats in which more and more store will come to be attached to the permanent otherworld outcome of this-world existence, and less and less importance to the limited, transitory aims and relationships which this-world living affords. This-world contingencies will dissolve as such, but the interpersonal, aesthetic, intellectual, moral and other deposit they leave behind them will become richer and richer: in the end these alone will be informed by essential zeal, and all else will be done only for them. The process is nigh inevitable, and only extraordinary accidents or deeply ingrained perversities of attitude can resist it effectively: we fall more and more out of love with this world and more and more in love with what is yonder. We become more and more seized with love for that necessary combination of all being and excellence which we have placed at the mystical pole of the cosmos, whether we speak and think of it in personal or in impersonal, in concrete or in abstract, in existential or nihilistic terms. We may again stress that even on this upward path new and peculiar forms of perversion necessarily open themselves:

there are higher forms of spiritual selfishness, ruthlessness and deliberate animality of which the history of human experimentation affords only too many instances. Nothing excludes the possibility that some of these evil stances may acquire great fixity in certain beings, may in fact end by becoming permanent blots upon the cosmos. But, by and large, the tendency of things must be to eliminate them: while first-order brutishness comes natural and easy, the higher depravities must certainly involve much exhausting effort. The innumerable damned whose wills are fixed at death in drear postures of evil are happily an unwarranted fantasy.

On the beginning and the end of the human cycle I have sketched I can, of course, only make most tentative suggestions. But there may well be forms of conscious life less bound up with long-lasting, exclusive forms of ego-existence than our own, and there is nothing in the prospective and retrospective dimensions of ego-life which excludes the possibility that we may look back to a conscious life which we rightly regard as our own, but which is rightly looked backward to by those who are now rightly regarded as others, and that we may look forward to a conscious life which we similarly regard as own own, but which is also similarly looked forward to by what are now rightly regarded as others. The logic of terms which are 'identical' at certain points of time and 'quite different' at others, which become one or cease to be one, is an extremely simple logic to develop, and only a perverse preoccupation with tenselessness has delayed its full formalization. (Though it may well be doubted whether sharply opposed notions like 'identity' and 'diversity' can have any but an abstract application to anything.) There is therefore no reason why there may not be forms of spiritual life much less parcelled out into discrete persistent units than the spiritual life of man, and the life of animals, on the one hand, and of glorified angelic beings, on the other, may afford good examples of this. Out of the life of animals human spirituality must probably have shaped itself by processes I am not competent to trace, but which explain and justify that deep respect for animals, and that horror at their sufferings, which is no mere Pythagorean quirk. The lessening of that horror in recent times, the toleration of the bull-fight or the factory-farm, are among the saddest phenomena of our age, against which even a detached philosopher must inveigh. And into some glorified superhuman form of continuous spiritual being we may well be

M

destined to go, again by processes that I am incompetent to trace. I only feel sure personally that something like a *parinirvana* must be a necessary final milestone to spiritual progress, a state where the spiritual contribution of a person becomes simply a node in the noetic cosmos, something that anyone who rises to that world can enter into and share, but which is not further continued in an exclusive personal history. Nothing prevents us from holding that the ego, which at lower levels may be the most basic and irreducible of appearances, may not, at higher levels, by a removal of appropriate contrasts, fade out in a manner which challenges us to call it an apotheosis, but which may just as well be described as the painless vanishing of an illusion. There are limits to what can be achieved along any line of separated personal development, ends to any story however beautiful, a time when such a story must simply take its place in the literature of the world. There is a death which we shall all, in our ultimate maturity, welcome: it is not the cessation of personal being that is to be lamented, but that we are not able to consummate it in our time and way. The *Sein zum Tode* which Heidegger saw at the root of human existence may well represent its ultimate sense: its seeming negation may, however, involve a blessed, positive richness and comfort, which the philosopher of *Angst* was far from conceiving.

The account I have been giving has throughout made mention of the mystical pole of the whole system, from which we periodically sally and to which we retreat. Our relation to this mystical pole could only simple-mindedly be regarded as one of identity: the very form and pattern of our sundered, transient being is not there at all. But equally it would be wrong to regard it as one of sheer otherness or diversity, underlined as this has been underlined in many forms of religion. The whole *nisus* of *our* being is towards the mystical pole in question; it carries to the limit the values that necessarily emerge out of *our* contingent purposes. There is, moreover, a line of retreat that can be followed towards it, and that has its necessary limit in various ecstatic experiences of our own: these we are concerned to regard as necessities of spiritual geography, rather than as anything of unique importance in themselves. The importance of an ecstasy depends solely on the worth of the soul that transcends itself in it. The whole process of development we have been sketching has, further, been regarded exclusively from the standpoint of the human spirit, and not from that of any life that may lie beyond it. What is, however, from one point of view the self-emancipation of man, may, from another point of view, be man's redemption by a life that transcends his own. It is the life and agency that may be conceived to be in and about the mystical pole of the cosmos that will concern us in our next lecture. We shall be as drily formal about it as possible, since we shall achieve no more by trying to be anything else.

THE LIFE OF GOD

In the present lecture we wish to complete the theology of which we made the abortive beginnings in Lectures IV and V. We tried to construct the object of religion as an idol of the cave, and found that it never became more than such an idol, a required synthesis that could not be effected, and that was always splintering into absurd, one-sided presentations. The religious object of our aspiration was one that embodied all the specific forms of value and embodied them in unity, but which did not embody them as an instance or particular case of them all, but as *being* the very values in question and being them together. It was also an object whose non-existence made no sense, which was completely *a se*, and which could not be conceived except as existing, though all other things required it in order to be. And it was, moreover, an existent transcendental, one that went beyond the distinction of the categories: it was as reasonable to speak of it as a character, a relation, an idea, an act, a process, an attitude, a manner, or a nothing as a thing or a person. All these requirements are necessarily formulated within the cave, but they cannot be fulfilled within it: they intend what they intend in an everlastingly empty manner. What exist within the cave are always instances of general kinds, things satisfying formulable conditions, and in their case there can be no question of a necessity of existence: the being of the instances adds something to the natures or essences they exemplify, and the latter could very well *not* have been exemplified in them. The this-world embodiments of types and values are, moreover, only embodiments of *one* type or value at the cost of *not* embodying another; sacrifice, one-sidedness, limitation is of the essence of this-world existence. This radical one-sidedness of realization can, of course, not be removed by any *series* or *system* of embodiments, however varied or prolonged. For, despite Spinoza, even when 'infinite things in infinite ways' are displayed before us, it is radically impossible to exhaust *all* things that could be so displayed: series and systems, however comprehensive, always give rise to further series and systems, and the notion of all possible series and systems remains an 'illegitimate totality'. It is likewise clear that any coincidence of categories is no more than an empty desideratum within the cave: there it is always mere verbiage to identify an idea with a thing, a thing with a relation, a process with a truth, etc., etc. Analytic philosophy rightly protests against such verbiage which, from its point of view, can only lead to a general disorganization of discourse.

The addition to this world, with its maximum distinction of categories, and maximum separation and fixity of individuals, of another world in which this distinction, separation and fixity gradually fade away, enables us to make better sense of the requirements of religion than is possible right within the human cave. The fading away of numerically multiplied individuality is a feature of much imaginative and thought-experience, where we deal with types rather than individuals: in dreams, e.g., individuals are always fading away into other individuals who *mean* the same to us in some respect, and there is no reason why there may not be a purely noetic experience in which everything that comes before us is typical, is general. The possibility of such noetic experience is of course parasitic upon the possibility of individual instantiation (or an approach to such) in other experiences, and Plato was wrong to make it independent in power and status, but this parasitism applies to everything in relation to everything else, and does not remove what is real and characteristic at each level. If there can be experiences of detached general patterns, there can likewise be experiences of detached values and disvalues, meaning by these intentional objects uniting descriptive content of high generality, e.g. equality of distribution, with the prescriptive and emotion-rousing forces necessary to all values. (That these two sides of genuine values have an *a priori* connection, is a point for which we have previously contended.) We are tempted to treat these detached values of justice, love, understanding, etc., as mere abstracta, which can mean nothing apart from their infinitely numerous, often incompatible instances, but this is to forget, not only that the particular is as dependent as the universal, but that the detached goals in question may be objects of love for a high-level *Noûs* or Mind which is essentially and not casually directed upon them, which in being directed upon them can be said to intend and love only itself, and which, in being directed upon them all undividedly, also unifies them all and holds them all together. We may, in short, place a pure and necessary love for the highest values at the heart of the cosmos, a burning flame of the purest zeal, and in this love subject and object will only be vestigially distinct: the love with which these values *should* be loved is the love with which they *are* loved, and vice versa, and norm and nature are one. And the highest values are all united, since the love of them all is indivisible, even if in concrete cases one must yield precedence to the other. The mystical pole of the world where this flame of love burns has further an intelligible necessity of existence which nothing in cave-life can possess. It is not the existence proper to instances, from the standpoint of instances it can even be denominated as a limit, a case of non-existence, but it none the less is presupposed by the sense and content of all instances and of all instantial minds. There can be instances of various sorts, some embodying one value and some another, and some deviating much or little from their ideal exemplars, but the whole framework of their possibility lies in the pure zeal of which we have been speaking, our thought being based on the quite unfashionable Platonic assumption that there is a two-way connection between value and being, nothing being capable of being which is not in some respect a specification or distortion of good, as nothing is good which does not in some perfect or imperfect or distorted form exist.

The flame of pure zeal we have mentioned, which is also a flame of pure insight, we therefore place at the centre of our mystical geography. It would, however, be both wrong and absurd only to place it there. A religious object which lies outside of the contingencies which radiate from it, and which approximate to it or fall short of it, would be a vain flame burning in the void, and would not, in fact, represent the highest values in union, since there would be countless valuable things, however one-sided and imperfect, that would not be part of it. As Hegel rightly saw, absolutes and infinites that merely lie beyond the conditioned and finite, are also merely another case of the conditioned and finite: the true absolute must embrace and annul the conditioned and finite, must leave no place for anything beyond itself. This is not necessarily a pantheistic opinion: it is rather, as Hegel said of

Spinozism, an acosmistic one, one that annuls the cosmos. It is the same vision which haunted the thought of Augustine when he found it hard to point to anything anywhere that was not, even in its defects, the product of some form of Grace. The mystical centre of the universe must therefore be thought of as one of those points which by their fluxion generate a whole geometry: it must be as much everywhere as at the centre. Each existent individual, even a corrupt and distorted one, must represent some specification of its pure variability, and this is what we sometimes feel when we see some rather poor object or person suddenly bathed in ineffable glory: there is always something in everything that resists every attempt to batter or abuse it, and which reveals the Most High *in propria persona*. The effort of the various things in the world towards this or that form or distortion of goodness may be regarded as *their* effort, *their* work, and we can treat the world's centre as merely inspiring them, as moving them through love. But we can just as well see in the pattern and behaviour of all individual beings, the infinite creativity of the mystical centre as well as its universal redemptive activity.

The use of words like 'creation' and 'creativity' requires much caution. They must not be taken to cover gratuitous creation *ex nihilo*, nor the Brahmanic exercise of *maya*, nor even the work of the 'productive imagination', which is the philosophical variant of these notions. We have accepted the principle of the Germanic theology, held by a long line of thinkers from the mediaeval mystics to Hegel, that a perfection that does not work itself out in creating and redeeming a world is a self-contradictory perfection, it is an empty abstract thing and not a true perfection at all. The contingencies and even distortions of finite being are as necessary to the all-creator as he is to them, the pure generalities of a perfect orientation are nothing if they do not terminate on actual objects they can transform: one must create, in order to be uncreate. There is no derogation from absolute perfection in its need for imperfect materials: nothing suffers derogation because it lacks powers that would involve absurdity and self-contradiction. Perfection must be carried out, concrete, and it can only be so in so far as it descends into the abyss of instantiation, decides among alternative contingencies, gives itself full being. The precise form of that being is arbitrary, but that there should be some such contingent, approximate expression of perfection, or at least that it should be in principle possible that there should be such, is not arbitrary, but unavoidable. The words 'creation' and 'creativity' have further disadvantages in that they carry with them pictures of a fabrication which precedes its products. The mystical pole of the world does not create in this way: its creation is rather a matter of presupposition, of timeless logical entailment. Its being can only deploy itself in a world of contingencies, ranging from arrangements of inert masses in space up to the highest development of personal and social consciousness in man. This presupposition might seem an external dependence, and so to derogate from absolute perfection. It is not, however, an external dependence, though the full proof that it is not, is seen only in the transforming, redemptive activity which pervades the cosmos, and which is shown in the emergence of life and mind out of inert masses, in the emergence of rational personality out of animality, and in the constant development of human beings towards higher and higher levels of detached, supra-personal interest which extends, as we hold, beyond the limits of this present life. It is in the fully liberated, enlightened, sainted human person—the Sage, the Messiah, the Buddha—that the ownership of the world and its phenomena by absolute perfection becomes fully evident. This contingent world is created by absolute perfection in the sense that it is its destiny, never wholly fulfilled in time, to be in all its windings, details and even imperfections, wholly mastered and dominated by absolute perfection, and that there never was a state in which it was not in process of being so mastered. This temporal vision may, however, well be short-circuited at a sufficiently high level of experience, so that something *like* a creation *ex nihilo* something *like* a conjured-up *maya*, something *like* the philosophical myths of the 'productive imagination', may well be found to have a strain of sense and truth. The cosmos of inert things in space, though not conjured up or dreamt up by anyone or anything, depends so absolutely on the absolute life that emerges through it, and that uses it to show itself to itself, that it may, not unfitly, be said to be the *maya*, the conjured-up dream-image of the latter: the 'conjuring-up' is, however, a timeless logical relation rather than a process in time. At the same level of insight, the cosmos of inert things in space may arguably reveal itself as the mass-display of innumerable undeveloped conscious lives, as in the cosmologies of Leibniz and Whitehead: what is the resistance and foil to the absolute must still *be* that absolute, and so must exhibit its essential properties, even if in some limiting deterioration.

The other-world system we have been constructing also renders intelligible that real transcendentality or surmounting of category-differences, which we have seen must be attributed to the mystical pole of that system. For the point of union in the whole system derives its character from its relations to the peripheral elements of the system, and from the relations between them which its presence can be said to effect, and in this sense it is intelligible that it can be most variously spoken of, that it can even be said to be a *coincidentia oppositorum*. As presupposing and involving the un-reflective, inert being of bodily masses, whether conceived as centres of sensation or not, the system's centre is the perfection of body, and it has all the blessed reliability and simplicity of bodily being, which often provides such a welcome contrast to the shifting tangle of personal relations. When Parmenides saw his absolute as a well-rounded sphere, his vision was estimable and not laughable. In the same way, obviously, the system's centre is the perfection of conscious personality, which is not to say that it is a conscious person or set of persons, nor one person or set of persons among others. In the same way, the system's centre is the source of all that interconnection among things and states of things which underlies space, time and causation: the system's centre is the bond, the relation *par excellence*. It is also the act of acts, since it is evinced in the origin and the steady redemption of all things. We need not be tedious and explain how it is also rightly denominated Love, or the Way, or the Truth or even the Perfection of Emptiness. This peculiar break-down of category-difference is intelligible precisely because it presupposes their non-break-down at the middle latitudes of the cosmos, just as a line or point can be the limiting form of many distinct and incompatible figures.

We may now attribute to the mystical centre of our system a cyclic alternation akin to the alternation between earthly life in the flesh and life in the subtle other world which we attributed to the soul. Here we are again following the traditional Indian cosmology, but there are traces of similar doctrines in the West, e.g. in the writings of Empedocles. The world must move from a period of contraction or *pralaya* to a period of expansion or *manvantara* in which the full diversity of creaturely being can be extruded. These two cosmic periods must alternate unceasingly because each is necessary to the other: the absolute perfection cannot be conscious of itself as absolute—through the medium, no doubt, of more or less elevated, adoring, finite minds—can give no meaning to its doffing of finite expressions of all sorts, to its own complete aseity and self-sufficiency, except in so far as it has put on all those finite masks or vestures, except in so far as it has given a seasonal independence to the beings whose claims it now sets aside. In the same way, the absolute perfection cannot engage in the infinite novelty and freshness of finite being except in so far as it has retreated from old patterns into the penetralia of its own innermost being, and so gained vigour for a 'new leap forward'. The cosmology which our Aryan ancestors left us is therefore in principle far removed from the unalloyed world-weariness which a sojourn on the hot plains of India must soon have induced: so far was it from hating *samsara*, that it was ready for an endless succession of such *samsaras*. The career of the various individual souls in a world-period, their graduation from passion and narrow egoism to reasoned impersonality, may further be regarded as part of the transcendent divine life of that period: the redemption by the central absolute of individual souls which in the end become its self-associated channels and instruments, is part of the outgoing and the ingoing life of the absolute itself. We may, if we like, further speak of two periods in the life of the mystical centre of the universe, a *theistic* period, in which it has all the properties of total 'otherness' beloved by some recent German protestant theologians, but in which, in virtue of the relative independence enjoyed by peripheral beings of all sorts, it is not really an absolute, not an all-inclusive being at all. This period is succeeded by the truly pantheistic or acosmistic period in which, as St Paul says, God is all in all. Theism of the protestant theological type is therefore bound up with the peculiarities of a particular world-period. It is an important doctrine since it preserves the axiological purity of the absolute in the time of its ontological demotion. The alternative to it are those somewhat dreadful forms of pantheism in which God vanishes into the all, rather than the all into God, and a divine licence is given to every human enormity, e.g. wild lust, cruelty, as in certain cults of Hinduism.

It is here important to advert to the notion of ecstasy which plays an essential part in the scheme we are constructing. The notion of ecstasy implies that, while we do not predicate identity of any finite creaturely being with the mystical pole of the universe, neither do we ever predicate sheer otherness of them. We allow the possibility that a finite creaturely being can *become* one with the mystical pole of the universe, can be brought into coincidence with it, which coincidence does not, however, exclude the possibility of a subsequent falling apart. Each finite creaturely being has its ecstasy, its appropriate going beyond itself into the mystical pole of unity, where it also becomes one with everything else, and this ecstasy is no strange emotional exaltation but a necessary limiting possibility of creaturely being, and also, in a reverse regard, of eternal, non-creaturely being. In the case of inert matter, ecstasy seems merely a thinkable possibility, though the sacrament of the altar perhaps furnishes a valid counter-example: stocks and stones, we may say, are too securely lodged on the periphery of being to retreat into their absolute source and re-emerge refurbished and shining. But conscious beings are capable of a transformation and reduction to that pure zeal for impersonal good which is also the core of their being, as of everything else, and, to the extent that this takes place, the distinction between conscious being and deity becomes altogether formal, like the distinction between an ellipse whose minor focus is zero and a straight line. In our 'highest moments' we feel ourselves to be mere extensions, expressions of an all-perfect absolute, and, since this absolute is not a person among persons external to finite persons as they are external to one another—thought at certain stages in cosmic history it may well seem to be so—there is no reason to think that there is anything intrinsically false in such feelings. The ecstasies we have mentioned extend to the ordinary ecstasies of devoted, dedicated persons of all sorts, though there are, of course, ecstasies of a more full-fledged, trance-like type, involving loss of ordinary consciousness for a period. Such trance-like ecstasies seem to have been enjoyed by Socrates, Plotinus, Buddha, St Teresa and many other great proficients of the path of unity. The importance of these full-dress ecstasies can, however, be much exaggerated, and nothing is so lowering to true spiritual tone as the mutual vying in regard to claims to have enjoyed *samādhi* or *satori* as is common among some Indians and some Zen Buddhists. Ecstasies will plainly differ in value according to the person who enters into them, and one whose conception of absolute perfection is thin and one-sided will have an ecstasy similarly thin and poor. Madame Guyon had many ecstasies, and was a genuinely devout, inspired woman, but it is agreed that she was also very stupid, and hence learnt little and communicated little through her ecstasies. Those who, as in our western civilization, hardly ever systematically practice ecstasy are not further from the mystical pole in consequence. The near-ecstasy with which Wittgenstein ends the *Tractatus Logico-philosophicus* is all the more precious on account of its roots in the dry technicalities of truth-tables and logical constants. The general merit of ecstasies is, however, itself logical: they set at nought the unmodifiable identities of certain formal systems, and force us to formalize better if we formalize at all.

We may now add to the general impertinence of our theological pronouncements, some attempts to detect a trinitarian structure in the mystical core of our universe: these attempts will, however, be modelled on Neoplatonic rather than Christian originals. To the mystical centre of the universe we must attribute a core of purely necessary being, which consists in nothing but the unspecific zeal for the whole round of impersonal values, which we have already said is not merely an attribute of deity but deity itself. This zeal will, however, be one with its own self-affirming consciousness, and in moments of world-dissolution or acosmism it will be *all* that there is to the life of deity. Not that it would, however, be possible without other outgoing phases in which it was *not* all that there was to deity: it is only by contrast with these outgoing phases that its universal dissolution is the dissolution of anything, and hence a real state at all. Secondary to this central hypostasis is the hypostasis which we have already recognized in our lecture on the the noetic cosmos: this will be a form of the absolute life widened to cover an intellectual grasp of all possible essences or ideal patterns, of whatever type or category, in all their systematic interweavings. In the form of life in question there will be a large element of contingency, for it will include, as we have held, all those patterns of natural kinds which might well have been absent or different, as well as all those qualitative and relational natures, e.g. colours, tonal intervals, etc., whose being remains obdurately contingent even when the existence of their instances is not in question. In the life of the hypostasis in question, time slows down to the point of utter arrest, without losing its internal order, which means, as we have seen, that this hypostasis counts rather as an unreachable limit, necessary to the understanding of states that come nearer and nearer to it, than as a reachable actuality. (The distinction between the unreachable and the actual is, however, quite blurred at this point.) The third hypostasis in our divinity will, however, involve change and movement as well as differentiation and contingency: it will in fact pervade and brood over the whole world-process in all the intricacies of its detail and history. Possibly it should be thought of as pluralized for many distinct cosmic systems.

The three hypostases of our rather poor account are not very remote from Plotinus's One or Good, his Divine, timeless Mind, and his reasoning, directive World-Soul. We do not ourselves doubt that Plato believed in basically the same trinity, as comes out in the passage from the Second Epistle so much quoted by the Neoplatonists, and that the doctrine probably went back to Pythagorean sources. Those who question these things do so because a modern Oxford or Cambridge philosopher would not have held a trinitarian doctrine that he expounded only in riddling words: we know, however, that Plato was not in this respect like a modern Oxford or Cambridge philosopher, if indeed he resembled such in any respect at all. We shall not attempt to decide whether Gibbon's gibe regarding the Christian Trinity—taught by Plato, revealed by St John—has substance or not. There is, however, one point in which the trinity postulated by us differs both from the Neoplatonic and the Christian trinity: in the order of dignity assigned to its members. In Neoplatonism the One or Good alone is truly self-sufficient: there is a one-sided dependence of the Divine Mind on it, and a one-sided dependence of the World-Soul on the Divine Mind. In Christian theology the equal status of the divine persons is officially stressed, but it remains the case that the terms 'generation' and 'procession' suggest a one-sided dependence of what we may call the 'later' persons of the trinity on the 'earlier' ones, and this is certainly part of the popular Christian picture. But in our theology which, as you will remember, stems from the Germanic theology, the priorities are precisely reversed. The Father, if so one may call our first hypostasis, produces the Son or second hypostasis, out of need rather than Neoplatonic superabundance: the pure zeal for absolute values would be a hollow sham were it not directed to their embodiment, at least in blue-print, in a possible cosmic order. In the same way, the Son or Logos or timeless blue-print of a world is a hollow sham if its pattern is not carried out in an actual process of creation and redemption, and this time-involved, existentially immanent work is essentially the role of the Holy Spirit, the third person in the Christian trinity. It is to this, the least emphasized member of the Christian trinity, that our emphasis is principally given, in which alone we see the complete concretion of absolute being. Divinity, if one may so express it, *is* redemptive activity, and whatever else it may also be said to be or involve, is only rightly attributed to it as part of such activity. Once in Japan I saw a shrine filled with innumerable images of the myriad-armed goddess Kwannon, each of which arms at each moment saves an entire world; I had a most valuable visual lesson in theology which I am now communicating to you. There is, however, always something false about stressing priorities in regions where factors logically belong together: one could at best say that my priorities were no falser than others.

It is here probably the place to consider more carefully the relation between two contexts in which the contingent content of the world can be taken as occurring: in embodied, finite separated things, on the one hand, and as part of the self-expression of the one mystical unity which underlies them, on the other. It is contrary to the whole notion of a mystical absolute that anything should be wholly and simply put outside of it, as having an independent nature or being, as doing or being anything in which that mystical absolute plays no part, or in which that part is merely remote, indirect, or hierarchically ancestral. These possibilities are not excluded because ruinous to finite things, with whose notion they might superficially seem to assort, but because ruinous to a mystical absolute itself. But, on the other hand, it is just as ruinous to a mystical absolute *not* to put finite things and their properties rather far from it: over a great range of the world and history—excluding, that is, rare moments of transfiguration or ecstasy—we do not wish the states of contingently existent things to be straightforwardly attributed to the mystical absolute, though they will of course have to attributed to it in *some* manner. The dilemma is how to attribute something necessarily imperfect to perfection, without either attributing it to something *else* which falls outside of perfection, or denying the genuine imperfection and frequent evil of the imperfect. Put in another way, we want the mystical absolute somehow to *be* all cases of finite instantial being, and also *not* to be them, its character as a something which is, rather than has, perfections being categorially different from that of things which merely have them. This dilemma assumes a most interesting and unhappy form in the philosophy of Spinoza, where all that is untoward in passion and self-assertion is held to be due to the 'mutilated' ideas in a finite mode of thinking, which ideas present things apart from their full context in the absolute unity of the one substance, but for which 'mutilated' ideas there is really no place in that one substance at all, since, however much a mode *A* may present some matter inadequately, it is absolutely united in the one substance with other conscious modes which present complementary aspects, so that there can be no proper place in the system for genuine mutilation. What we plainly want is an account which can find room *both* for a mutilated and an unmutilated view of things, and can combine them inseparably: everything must at once be attributable to the pervasive divine unity yet also to finite subjects at various logical distances from it.

The dilemma seems, however, to have arisen out of a persistent use of surface-categories, valuable and indispensable in dealing with phenomena on the world's periphery, in connection with relations in that inner, subtler world whose whole construction arose out of a need to transform such surface-categories. On the periphery of the world what comes before us can be 'pinned down' and identified for our common references in a sufficiently unambiguous manner, though by the use of varied, complex criteria of which modern linguistic researches have made us so conscious: perfect identity seems in no sense a limiting state to which only graded approximations exist. It seems an altogether-or-not-at-all state, and contrasts with diversity, otherness, which admits of no mitigation from closeness of resemblance or parity of origin. This kind of identity-or-diversity of this body to that body, of this embodied person to that person, etc., though not in fact perfectly achievable in the natural sphere—since only abstract aspects manifest perfectly clean-cut diversity—seems none the less definitory of that sphere and its contents, and serves also as the presupposition of all looser, more fluid notions. We can only loosen where something has started off tied and fixed, we can only liquefy where something has started off hard and solid. But, as we retreat into the inner reaches of non-physical experience, identity and diversity as we knew them become harder and harder to apply, and we are guided by their memory, rather than by their former precise intent. It becomes in fact more easy to operate with some concept of logical distance or 'alienation' than with sheer otherness, and, contrasting with this, a concept of logical nearness or approximation to identity. In that slippery otherworld environment, one may say, nothing can be trapped and embraced alone, or kept firmly apart from everything else, and procedures of identification and distinction no longer apply exactly.

It is with the relations of the divine unity, considered as we have considered it in its concrete, moving third hypostasis, to creaturely existents, and particularly to human spirits in various states, that we are here attempting to deal, and we may say that such creaturely existents are at most times more or less alienated from the third hypostasis in question, this alienation being marked for us by the 'oddness', monstrous or inconsiderable, of identifying them with the moving perfection in question, or of attributing their characters and activities directly to that perfection. It is queer and odd, e.g., to say of the Divine Substance of Spinoza that it is made of iron and can run from London to Edinburgh in six hours, but it is not so queer and odd to say of the same Divine Substance that it thinks of itself as underlying all modes, and hence Spinoza thinking the latter thought is less alienated from the Divine Substance than the Flying Scotsman performing the former feat. In the same way, perverse and evil developments are by definition the acts of things greatly alienated, fallen away from the divine perfection: if we attribute them to the divine perfection, as we are in some suitably remote manner obliged to do, we do so with intellectual as well as moral distaste, and with the theological perplexities which turn on the problem of evil, etc. The *difficulty* of performing the attribution in question is in fact, a precise measure of the alienation involved. Alienation is not, then, a relation without degrees like the identity and diversity which it replaces: a greatly alienated being is not a being wholly separated from the divine perfection, but only representing a remote extension of it, and its performances, like those of everything else, can with proper remoteness, be attributed to it. It is of the essence of a necessary absolute that there is nothing for which it is not, in the last resort, responsible, nothing which is not, in the last resort, itself. The queer power of stretching identity further and further till it nearly breaks is what we understand by 'alienation': if anyone finds the notion obscure, let him but contrast what happens in his eyes, head and hands with what happens in his toes, intestines or the small of his back. The extremities of our bodies are, on standard occasions, those parts of ourselves where we feel and are least ourselves, though it must be conceded that where we feel and are most or least ourselves varies from one occasion to another. This language of being 'most' or 'least oneself' must not be dismissed as subjective and poetic: it is, we have held, the language ultimately needed to deal with the mysteries and difficulties of the world, and is therefore to be preferred to an exact language which, in the last resort, applies to nothing.

Our reflections on alienation may here be used to throw light on the existence of evil and deviant forms, both in the absolute source of all being and in the contingent contents of the cosmos. Mere limitation of character and being, i.e. finitude, is not an evil: completed, concrete being is always necessarily finite, in the sense that it realizes one possible series of definite contents and thereby excludes countless alternatives. Even the divine unity, considered in and for itself, has a contingent as well as a necessary nature, even if in its case the distinction between the definite possibilities that it has realized, and those that it has failed to realize, is infinitely less important than it would be in the case of other things. It is impossible to exist without excluding possibilities of existence—even non-realization of anything positive is a limiting existential possibility—and hence limitation is in a sense the price of full existence, and is not as such evil at all. Nor is there intrinsic evil in the sort of limitation which gives something a defined place in a comprehensive scheme or system, in which it is made to fit in with or cohere with other things. In talking of 'fitting in' we are of course meaning infinitely more than the empty consistency of formal logic, which might as readily cover complete misfit or incoherence as complete coherence. Fitting in means that there are positive affinities between patterns which occur in the world, that they contribute to higher-order patterns characterized by the same good form and simplicity that we find in the lower-order patterns, and so on. What are, however, a root-case of evil are

N

circumstances in which fitting in is at points positively frustrated, in which one pattern simply clashes with another, prevents it from deploying itself fully, in which patterns are distorted, perverted, half crushed out of existence by other patterns. We can readily conceive what we may speak of as garden-universes, in which only easy maintenance of lovely arrangements occupy the happy gardeners that inhabit them, where everything is brought to the fullest realization of its nature and helps at the same time to make everything else do so. Such a garden-universe would have the qualities of a celestial 'Buddha-field' transferred to earth: it would have none of the grim, prison-like features of the human cave. We can likewise readily conceive a system in which the frustration of form by form, their mutual clash and distortion, achieves much higher levels than it does in our actual cosmos, in which there is perhaps not even a consistent pattern of ruin to comfort us aesthetically. As opposed to these limiting possibilities —which, from a deeper point of view, are probably not possibilities at all—we have a system like our cave, where the fitting in or clash of patterns is a matter over which no consistent pattern presides, which is, as we say, largely governed by chance. Such a loose, chance-governed system may be mediocre in the sphere of intrinsic value: it is plain, however, that it permits the emergence of conscious, human values that neither of the other systems permit. For all the higher human values, involving invention, construction and discovery depend on the existence of an order which, while not inherently shaped towards values, also permits their imposition. In a garden-world the best possibilities of gardening would be missing, and gardening, being personal and spiritual, is necessarily valued by man's spiritual nature at a higher assessment than the gardens it labours upon. It is plain, further, that a world, full of loose, variable, chance connections is not only a suitable field for constructive exercises of freedom in the direction of positive value but also for destructive, pernicious exercises in the direction of disvalue. But it is plain that the highest moral values only emerge when there is a definite possibility of actions that go against them: only if the direction of one's activity is not inevitably limited to them, but can be freely directed to them, can it achieve a remote analogy with the divine devotion which acts not out of anything instantial or circumstantial or dispositional or already there, but solely in virtue of being goodness itself. The highest moral virtues therefore presuppose precisely this rough-and-tumble, chance-governed world we inhabit, and this is necessarily a world in which there are many evil, purely destructive clashes.

If we turn from natural to moral evil it is plain, likewise, that the possibility of the highest moral goodness presupposes the possibility of the greatest moral evil: this may be to some extent guarded against, hedged around with difficulty, but not such difficulty as renders its practice, and the love of its practice, impossible. Moral evil is of a variety of sorts, its simplest varieties involving the subordination of higher interests to naked, primary interests, while its secondary varieties involve the preference of what interests the person himself to what interests persons in general. That such brutishness or selfishness may assume an endless gamut of subtler forms, enlisting all the higher forms of disinterest in the service of a glorified beastliness or self-interest, is a possibility we need not document, nor need we document its unaltered directive presence behind manoeuvres, often called 'hypocritical', in which this presence is the last thing to be confessed. But in addition to these primary and secondary varieties of moral evil, there are varieties in which deviation from the demands of the highest values acquires its own, higher-order zest, and becomes closely associated with the genuine values associated with personal freedom. In these tertiary forms of moral evil are the performances of the great sadists, the wanton deluders, the great plungers into monstrous depths of all sorts. That all these forms of moral evil exist is empirically well-attested and their possibility is part of the phenomenology of the moral sphere, but what concerns us now to stress is that these possibilities of perversion, even the most wanton ones, are involved in, part of, the possibility of the highest forms of moral value.

All this, however, can only be dealt with theologically in terms of the notion of 'alienation', which we were unfolding a little way up. Evil, natural and moral, is, in one way, *not* an expression of the essential value-causality of the universe, this is not active in it *in propria persona*, yet evil, natural and moral, is not the expression of some wholly other agent, otherwise it would not have the profound justification that we have just given it. In evil, natural and moral, we have, we may say, an agency alienated from that of the central value-source of the cosmos, but this word 'alienated' means that, while the ordinary notion of strict identity with the central agency in question certainly does not apply to the agency involved, any notion of strict diversity, otherness, is as little applicable. What we have, as I have said, is a graded situation where certain forms of agency can become less and less 'owned', more and more 'disowned', by the central causality of the universe, until, in the end, they are practically, but never totally, not its own at all. The S.S. man deliberately liquidating some innocent being in agony is so distant from the core of divinity, as to be practically an agent quite other than divinity. Distance from divinity is, however, also distant divinity, and this is reflected in the fact that all he does reflects perverted realizations of absolute values, e.g. of the personal life whose destruction he mocks, and that his possible existence is part of the highest saving justice and compassion. There is, we may say, something about the Most High irresistibly reminiscent of Pontius Pilate; he does, and must do, things that he must also officially disown. Calvinistic theology, employing the sole plea of 'unsearchableness', here does no better than the perplexed, practical Wotan in Wagner's *Ring of the Nibelung*. This is a point, however, where the desire to keep the hands or skirts of the absolute clean ought not to move us. A person can only keep himself clean from the corruptions of the society he lives in at a quite artificial, abstract level, and he requires to be both stupid and complacent to do so: really the surrounding corruption infects every tissue of his being, and could be avoided only by contracting out of life altogether. If such 'keeping clean' is impossible and undesirable for man, we must not think it possible for the central perfection of the universe. That the zeal at the world's centre is absolutely and incorruptibly clean is, in fact, only possible because it becomes more and more sullied as it moves out towards the periphery, because in variously alienated, sundered forms it can depart more and more from its central self. It must fall away from itself in order to be able to bring itself back to itself. The shocking character of what we are saying reflects only the creaks and groans of our logic and our language as we approach the final truth of things. If there is, and must be, a vein of sublimated immorality in all men whom we deeply love and admire, there is, and must be, a similar vein in the absolute.

The notion of 'alienation' may now, however, be used, not merely to express a relation but a process, and we need not be afraid to say, with Hegel, that the life of the divine absolute is essentially a process of *self*-alienation which is the presupposition and prelude to the reinstatement of a stricter identity. It is like two optic pictures wandering apart in double vision, yet brought back to entire fusion and coincidence. Only, whereas for Hegel the alienation in question is exclusively a this-world affair, on our view it covers another world or worlds as much as our own. The use of the term 'self-alienation' stress that there is a departure from a limiting form of the strictest identity, but also that this limiting form continues, as it were, to watch over the whole process, and to be responsible for it, and to re-emerge in its final outcome, and to be only fully what it is, true self-identity, when it is brought back to being itself out of alienation. There is here a great temptation to logical simplification in one direction or another. We are tempted to say that it can only be through ignorance, illusion, error, magical role-playing or what not, that what are at bottom the same agent can appear as different ones, and that the so-called reinstatement of the original identity is simply the realization that it was always really there. This is to ignore the fact that alienation is as necessary to unalienated self-identity as the latter is to the former. The differences, the distances between logical subjects in the world, their divergences from perfect sameness, are as essential to any emergent, absolute self-identity as the latter is to such differences. It is, one may say paradoxically, but not illogically, that it is only by moving away from itself, by in a sense not being what it is, that the absolute can come to be what it really is. But the acute logical discomforts engendered by these utterances reflect no surrender to an ultimate intellectual indiscipline: they reflect only our dawning sense of the working logic of alienation, and of its application both at the periphery and at the central heart of things.

This is perhaps also the place to speak a little of the total unconsciousness, the mental emptiness, which is often thought to exist at the centre of things, so that what we have there is not merely a physical but a spiritual void. Concreteness and definiteness of being and character and of mental orientation must persist, it would seem, in however attenuated a form, up to the limiting centre of things, and there, it seems, they must vanish altogether, just as there is no rational number which multiplied by itself yields the number 3, though there are an infinity of rational numbers which, multiplied by themselves, come as close as one

could wish to yielding the number 3. The 'negative theology' of
the west must be confessed to have great merits, in that it removes
from the core of the universe the finite thisness or thatness which
it can only have peripherally. The *Shunyata* or Voidness-doctrine
of the *Mahayana* has comparable merits, and has, in addition, the
authority of that supreme proficient, the Buddha. But, on the view
developed in the present lecture, the negative theology is more
misleading than illuminating. Having held that all forms of alienated existence, and the whole process of alienation and the return
from alienation, are essential to the central life of the cosmos, we
cannot make that life wholly void. Even its dismissal of positive
contingent content at the end of a world-period would mean
nothing if the content had not previously been posited: the world's
positive content, we may say, persists in its dismissal. Pulsating
richness rather than emptiness is, then, a suitable characterization
of the absolute, and it is their abstract concern with negativity
which has weakened the spiritual hold of the higher, non-
popular forms of Buddhism and Hinduism, causing the one to die
out altogether in the country of its origin, while the other became
overgrown with monstrous distortions. There seems scope here
for a reformed Christianity, blending its essential positiveness with
the subtler cosmology and methodology of the eastern religions.
At the heart of the universe we may therefore place a pure zeal for
impersonal good, everlastingly worked out in a series of possible
forms, and temporally active in the putting forth from and the
leading back to itself of an alienated world. At no point even
of ultimate retreat could there be anything in it not vibrantly
conscious and alive, as we well know in the brief instants when we
are taken up into it.

On the scheme we have been developing, the religions of earth
are all more or less misleading reflections of a life, relations and
processes which extend beyond the cave. Often they may start by
stressing the deep change in categories and being which the
higher life involves, as in Semitic statements of the self-existence,
uniqueness and glory of God. But often this is only a prelude to a
crude transfer of categories, appropriate at the world's periphery,
to the higher hypostases involved and to their relations to earthly
being. Alternatively, in an attempt to avoid all this, one may get
systems as elaborately negative, and as mistakenly destructive of
logic, as one gets in certain brilliant developments of Buddhism.

Obviously the oppositions of the common logic must be transcended if one is to go far on one's spiritual travels, but this can be done only by devising new and subtler uses of negation, identity, etc., covering wider possibilities that the common logic fails to envisage. Ultimately what one has must always be a positive doctrine, and should remain such even though it will have to be indefinitely modified as one's insight and one's nose for alternatives sharpens. All these religious developments may be said to be shadows of the religion yonder: it is not here, but in the upper world, that we shall worship and meditate as we ought.

RETURN TO THE CAVE

In the last four lectures I have been taking you on a conducted tour through a series of regions that I have not, in my clear memory, ever visited. We have been travelling imaginatively, but not I should wish to hold, fantastically. Now I am returning to the cave, in order to sum up and assess the value of the whole speculative expedition. It is important to stress that what I have written involves no use of, and no appeal to, any special sort of faculty, beyond the mystical faculties inseparable from human existence, which every man evinces in some degree, as every man in some degree evinces mathematical capacity, but which some possess so pre-eminently as to deserve the special name of 'mystics'. These faculties, we may say, looking back on the whole course of our argument, have nothing in their scope of vision or mode of operation, that is not severely logical, that may not, in fact, be regarded as the very crown and consummation of pure logic. Though they may seem, on the one hand, to involve an almost empirical encounter with an object unique, peculiar and profound, the properties of this object are all logical and categorial, even if they differ utterly from those attributed to common-or-garden objects: it exists of necessity, we cannot fully conceive of it without believing in it, it *is* rather than *has* the round of its essential characters, there is neither in it nor about it any application for the limiting notion of pure otherness, though there is room in it, and plenty of room, for what we have called a graded 'alienation', sometimes reduced almost to zero and sometimes stretched almost to breaking point, it requires this alienation which it also at a deeper level annuls, it admits of no consistent alternatives, and it involves various 'coincidences', of which the most impressive is that of the ontic modalities of what may or must be with the deontic modalities of what should be or ought to be. Whoever, in mystical feeling, approaches his absolute, whether seen in this emphasis or in that, has before him no garish empirical individual, decked out with a surprising array of characters that astonish because they might have been so different, but the Ancient of Days, the inescapable, the ever familiar, not unfitly expressed by the tautology 'I am that I am'.

These faculties further evince themselves, not so much by bringing any particular marvel before us, as by compelling us to see all contingent facts and phenomena in an astonishing, novel light, by changing the limits of the world rather than the facts in it, to recall a remarkable, mystical utterance of Wittgenstein's (*Tractatus*, 6.43). To view the world mystically is to decant all phenomena into a new language and a new logic, a logic quite different from that of the square of opposition or the syllogism or the propositional or functional calculus, but a pure logic, a purely formal, categorial framework, none the less. In that logic it is as reasonable to say with Meister Eckhart that this blade of grass *is* this stone or this wood, as in the ordinary logic it is reasonable to say that an A is an A, or that if p then p, and much more reasonable than to say, at Frege's level of surface-discourse, that the morning star is identical with the evening star. In that logic it is as reasonable to say that I ought to have pity on those whom I am ill-treating, because, in ill-treating them, I am really injuring myself, as, in the surface-logic which dominates ordinary ethics, I justify my utterance by the grotesque plea that I am thereby augmenting a total of happiness or other good that is enjoyed by no one at all. In that logic it is further right to attribute all that we do attribute to mutually exclusive things to 'something far more deeply interfused', which is not incapable of being ϕ *qua* ψ, while at the same time it is also not-ϕ *qua* χ, and so on. The kinds of utterance that we here permit ourselves presuppose the ordinary utterances whose rules they seem at times to violate, but it is only on a very superficial view of the transformed forms and categories that they introduce, that they can be thought of as absurd and self-contradictory. They in fact burst upon us with the same flooding obviousness as the most evident of mathematical truisms, and the fact that they make no impression on certain minds in certain moods has no tendency to prove them empty. Mystical writers often say that what they say or saw is self-contradictory, or make actual use of seemingly self-contradictory language, just as they often likewise say that what they are expressing is ineffable, but the fact that they believe themselves to be communicating something all-important shows that they do not really believe this to have the worthless emptiness of a mere self-contradiction, just as the fact that they utter it, and do so eloquently, shows that they do not really think it to be ineffable. Mysticism, like all things, can be developed in a self-contradicting, self-frustrating manner, but the fascinating task of a mystical theology is precisely to avoid this, to push towards the one consistent account of its absolute which, being consistent, also excludes any thinkable alternative—an absolute with alternatives would be no absolute—and so is not merely absolutely but necessarily true. The fact that an apprehension of a theorem in mystical logic may be deeply tinged with emotion does not show it to be void of cognitive content, of genuine alternatives for our thinking, even if these are not of a merely factual or contingent order. Even a theorem of the propositional calculus was called a *praeclarum theorema* by Leibniz, and the theorems of mystical logic, in which we ourselves as well as our symbols are transformed, may well excite an admiration and enthusiasm more intense. The theorems we are here dealing with reflect widely diffused, catholic, wholly normal insights, not only formulated by Plato, Plotinus, Aquinas, Spinoza and Hegel, but by Wordsworth, Shelley, Goethe, Dante, Wagner and many others. They represent, as it were, the horizon of human conception and vision, the open sky into which every unblocked vista terminates. That some should not be able to see this horizon nor its paradoxical, not nonsensical congruences, only shows that some men are incurably myopic.

Mystical logic has a claim to superiority based on the fact that it includes provision for an ordinary logic at the surface of things, and that it claims to express changes in depth of vision rather than changes in surface content. When in mystical logic we say this blade of grass is this stone, we do not wish to deny that it is, as we may put it, more intimately soft and green than it is hard and cold, of that it is *qua* shown in a blade of grass, that the absolute is more intimately green than *qua* shown in a stone. It has a claim to superiority, further, based on the philosophical discrepancies and antinomies with which ordinary ways of speaking and thinking are rife. But its application to the stuff of ordinary alienated experience is not smooth and easy, but rather forced and arbitrary, and one cannot help wondering what light is shed by deep identifications which make absolutely no difference on the surface? Is one not merely substituting the unwarranted, confusing difficulties of a new way of speaking for the familiar, tried difficulties of an old one? And does not one continue to have the same sorry, piebald, mutilated, patched together world of things, full of conflicts, puzzles and frustrations, because one claims to see in it the expression, or rather the procession, of a unity conceived in the transcendental terms outlined above?

It is here that our mystical logic leads to the strange extension that has occupied us in the last lectures. In order to work and to have significant application our mystical way of viewing things requires the existence of a whole series of states and experiences that will *bridge the gulf* between this alienated surface-world, on the one hand, and the mystical unity which explains its puzzles and appeases its stresses, on the other. These states and experiences will involve a *continuous passage* from the world of sense-given bodies, and of embodied persons, interacting and showing themselves to one another in space and time, but still profoundly separate and mutually irrelevant, to an order of things in which the corporeal, the spatially and temporally separate, the personally apart, the facts and values that have nothing to do with one another, etc., etc., are gradually attenuated and set aside, interpenetration and coincidence everywhere taking the place of side-by-sideness and mutual indifference, until in the end we achieve the mystical pole of unity, where distinctions lapse in the pure zeal of self-affirming rationality and goodness. These intermediate states and experiences are necessary to the significance of mystical utterances: without them the seeing of things in relation to an ultimate, deeper unity, as having the real mutual belongingness which their surface form belies, would, however much informed by ecstatic feeling, remain empty and verbal. And this is why developed mystical systems all include the intermediate states we have mentioned, and necessarily locate many heavenly mansions beneath the highest, or many levels of *Dhyana* before all is taken up into the perfection of wisdom or Nirvana. The apex of the whole system is nothing if not the limit of a whole ascending series, and, as in mathematics, the limit of the series is not profitably separable from the whole series when summed up in a final embracing intelligible manner. What we are now saying does not differ in sense from what we said previously, when we held that the persistent paradox of our earthly condition leads to the postulation of higher states in which that paradox would be lessened and removed. Then we were approaching the matter from the standpoint of the paradoxes and difficulties of this life, whereas now we are approaching it from the other glorious end which our mystical consciousness persistently sets before us. Neither this dispersed life in which, as Dante says[1], 'substance and accidents and their complexions' are scattered abroad over the universe, nor the opposed pole at which they occur 'as it were fused together', and 'bound by love into a single volume', could be anything at all were it not for the graded spectrum of states which connects them together and binds them into a unity.

We have therefore the position, unacceptable to many, that a pure logic pushes us towards a definite set of existential commitments, some going beyond anything we have encountered in experience, but which can none the less be confirmed in actual experience. The categories in terms of which we more or less successfully see our world or our part of the world, point to other categories in terms of which we do not with any success see our part of the world, but which apply to states and experiences beyond this life, and point ultimately to the categories of mysticism, which transcend, while also subsuming in themselves, all other forms of life and their categories. That the forms of thought and discourse should, however, point to an appropriate content has nothing surprising about it. The forms of ordinary talk in which the this and the that, the here and the there, the *meum* and the *tuum*, are central, imply, though they may not assert, a ready divorce of bodies, places and persons from one another, and their ready reidentifiability in many contexts and on many occasions, whereas the forms of otherworldly discourse imply, though they do not state, a much less ready divorce and reidentifiability of bodies, places and persons, the sort of fusion and interpenetration of dreams, in which, in the end, divorce and reidentification cease to be practicable at all. In both cases, moreover, we do not have a case of strict requirement, so that the forms would be impossible without the contents and vice versa, but rather a relation of graded affinity, some materials being more suited, more fitted to certain logical forms than others. No one doubts that certain data lend themselves better to mathematically precise treatment than do others, and in the same way certain experiences lend themselves

[1] *Paradiso*, XXIII, 85–89.

better to mystical treatment than do others. Our moments, e.g., of ecstatic personal passion afford better material for interpenetrative, mystical treatment than do our dealings with landladies, income-tax collectors and computers, and life at the levels where personal opacity is so attenuated that it is as right to say that we read people's behaviour in the light of their thoughts as that we read their thoughts in the light of their behaviour, will obviously be as thoroughly amenable to mystical treatment as it is unamenable to mechanical and mathematical analysis. There is nothing, therefore, at all absurd in supposing that the categories which inspire our mystical utterances are such as to call for a peculiar material to which they are specially adapted, and that this material will include much that goes beyond the things of this life, and that differs progressively from them. Or, to put the same thing as we put it in former lectures, there is nothing absurd in supposing that the anomalies and discrepancies of this life may call for a comprehensive ironing out in a progressively mystical experience that lies yonder. If there are, as we have held, 'heavens', as unbelievably interpenetrative as the noetic cosmos of Plotinus or the world of the *Avatamsaka-sutra* are described as being, and we can live and discourse in them, then the claims of mysticism and mystical logic will have been vindicated, whereas if we are never to encounter anything less parcelled, mutilated, ill-assorted, torn asunder and fortuitously assembled than the things of this life, then mysticism and mystical logic will be to that extent discredited or left unsatisfied. The phenomena of this life, and anything that merely continues their dirempted pattern, do not in themselves validate our mystical visions and utterances: they at best permit their imposition. But the phenomena of this life, fitly supplemented by suitable otherworld experiences, may make such a mysticism inescapable.

What emerges from what we have said is, however, a return to our original uncertainty and indecision. While we can elaborate a mystical, or an alienated, merely thisworld logic, and free it from all inconsistencies and develop its consequences fully, the final adoption of it, its acceptance as adequate and as 'true', depends on what will be encountered yonder, beyond the limits of this mortal life. *There*, if we ever are there, we shall be able to see that only one scheme of seeing and saying things covers all that is or could be, but *here*, where our understanding of possibilities is so shallow, we haver incompetently among several notional schemes, and are unable to give a firm preference to one over the other. If we see that 'a many' is only conceivable in the firm bonds of an absolute, self-explanatory unity, we still experience a truant longing to conceive what is condemned as inconceivable, a Russellian or Wittgensteinian or Humean world, where there are countless independent terms connected by bonds adventitious to the things themselves and to one another. Necessities may deploy themselves before us, but their *bona fides* never stands beyond question: we have no longer the simple guidance of the imagination, as appealed to by Hume, or a happy recourse to linguistic rules and the material mode of speech, as appealed to by Carnap. The theorems of mysticism, in particular, admit of no remote external understanding: teaching a doctrine of interpenetration and identification, they can be fully understood only when such identification either has been, or is on the verge of being accomplished: we ourselves, we may say, need to be or become the material of such theorems, and live through their logical connectives, their dissolving copulas, in our proper person. All this means that in this life the whole mystical vision hangs in jeopardy, however much it may be elaborated or expanded. This is, in fact, the condition of the cave, and the cave cannot be transcended even by the eloquence permitted to a Gifford lecturer.

What then, may we ask, has been the use of this long, argumentative excursus by which many auditors have been so plainly put off and some wearied? It has not been at all like those comfortable, modern discussions in which, whatever the yielding obscurity of the materials discussed, one has always the treatable hardness of words and their uses to deal with. The answer lies in holding that, even if the many mansions sketched by us, and the mystical goal beyond them, are a mere backcloth to this-world conditions, they are yet essential to their description and to the activities carried on in them: they are part of this world's phenomenology, a part not arbitrarily made, but constituted before us in a necessary manner. We cannot help seeing this torn, vexed, atomistic world as leading off and up into the pure zone of those blessed, limiting coincidences, much as the foreground of Palladio's stage at Vicenza, through cunning slopings and foreshortenings, leads up to the background of his perfect Renaissance city. And, as the charm of Palladio's background lies in the alternative pull of its nearly successful illusion, and the obviousness of the devices which both make it and undermine it, so the other worlds which enfold our own always tremble on the verge between poetry and enthusiasm, on the one hand, and sober prose and logic, on the other. Like Socrates at his trial, we always face two possibilities, two *a priori* likelihoods or εἰκοτά, on one of which the things of our world slope off to a real background which enables them to make mystical sense, and into which we shall ourselves one day enter, whereas on the other possibility we have merely a visionary picture masking a not unkindly encounter with nothingness. These two possibilities involve, however, the same intended goal or objective—whether bracketed or unbracketed is unimportant—and life in the cave is always lived in the light, whether authentic or visionary, of what lies beyond it. Faith and unfaith are not, in fact, so far apart in this case as they are in others: they succeed one another, in our alienated nature, like the pleasure and pain felt in Socrates' leg on his memorable last morning. What we must now again stress is that the light that seems to stream from beyond the cave, and the mystical prospects it sets before us, form no idle consoling background to our earthly enterprises, but are the necessary presuppositions of their being carried on at all. We shall end our lecture by recalling in summary much that has already been emphasized.

The first immeasurable benefit from our speculative upperworld visit is the blow which it deals to the forms and principles of the common logic, or at least to their unsupplemented, simpleminded use. There are of course things that we can 'pick out' from other things, and identify more or less satisfactorily on many occasions. There are of course clearly distinct lights in which such things can be viewed, and correspondently abstracted characters and relations which are in every way as definite as these lights. There are, further, the great natural facts, with feet both in the empirical and the ideal sphere, of repugnance and similarity. But even at the ordinary level we feel deep unease at the arbitrariness of the lines we draw between things continuously identical and things definitely diverse, and are always inclined to make identity narrower and stricter, or looser and more embracing. And this treacherousness of the subjects of our discourse makes for a corresponding treacherousness in predication and relation, for, while we can always maintain abstract diversity among predicates and relations *inter se*, such being the very nature of abstraction, we cannot satisfactorily stop a thing which has one of them from having another of them, even when that other predicate or relation quarrels with the first, and introduces a dimension of differentiation or alienation into the subject of our discourse. There is here always the temptation to postulate a fictitious part or element which has one of the quarrelling predicates or relations, and another fictitious part which has another, a mode of argumentation used by Plato to establish the existence of the parts of the soul, and by Zeno to establish the existence of innumerable points of rest in the course of a flying arrow. But a nobler and franker approach simply admits that lower, clearer forms of negation are always yielding to higher, subtler ones, and that it is possible *not* to be something both in the straightforward style of a lack or a privation, or in the subtler style of transition or differentiation, etc., in which subtler styles it is correct and not absurd to say that if one is *not* something one also need not lack some property in a simple, straightforward manner. Thus a moving arrow is neither here nor not here, in the sense in which being 'not here' means being at some other precise place: it is not here in a sense which covers the additional possibility of being in motion, of not being anywhere quite precise. In much the same manner, as argued before, futurity brings in a higher mode of negating the simple possibilities of positive and negative occurrence which confront us in the present and the past: there is a subtler not-going-to-happen which includes the possibility that the issue is as yet undecided, as well as the down-to-earth not-going-to-happen which means that it has been decided in the negative, and which would be better expressed as a going-not-to-happen. If we are forced into these subtleties even in our dealings with blameless physical matters in space and time, how much more certainly shall we be forced into them when we deal with the data of the interior life, where all is describable in terms of quarreling analogies, and where we can never get down to straightforwardly identifiable characters which have nothing analogical about them. The basic mental feature of intentionality involves something that has often been described as presence-in-absence or existence-in-non-existence: we can neither comfortably say that Desdemona's guilty passion for Cassio was something nor that it was nothing, nor that it was 'present in' nor that it was 'present outside of' Othello's mind. And in the higher reaches of thought we have states describable alike by their packed fullness of content and their utter emptiness, not less contradictiously, in fact, than the absolutes of religion and pure mysticism. The 'light' of attention is also a case of relief or of emphasis or of grasping, the active 'assent' of judgment is also a passive bowing to the might of fact, superficially conflicting characterizations if there are any.

If now, instead of dwelling on a few queer borderline cases, we conceive of worlds and experiences where hard-and-fast differentiations are continually breaking down, we shall become more and more willing to rise from lower and narrower, to higher and wider senses of negation, and to say of things that, in the *usual* acceptation of not-being-so-and-so, they are neither so-and-so nor yet not so-and-so, or even to say with the Buddhists that certain things are neither so-and-so nor not so-and-so nor both nor neither. The only thing wrong with the Buddhists is that they stop at this point, and are not willing to go on to a sixteenfold or a thirty-two fold negation and so on without definite limit. Only thus can they evade the elenchus which commits them to a one-sided thesis. For since negations in concrete thought are never absolute, but have positive presuppositions which can be dragged forth and further denied, we can escape between the horns of all but a wholly empty dilemma, and escape to new poises which will enable us not to come down on either side. Such evasion has long been practised in philosophy: where legitimate it is also obligatory, and is in fact the heart and soul of philosophical method. But in the upper world, and still more at its mystical apex, this continued rejection of a lower consistency, and this continued retreat to a higher consistency, is the very principle of its structure, and hence meditation on the possibility of that upper world and its apex will have the salutary effect of freeing us from the snares and delusive restrictions of the common logic. Illogical and inconsistent in a merely self-frustrating manner we need not and should not be, but we may and should cultivate a boundless willingness to look for the contrary in the seemingly contradictory, and to remain open to possibilities of a higher order than any that we have as yet envisaged or perhaps ever shall be able to envisage. This boundless willingness or openness is the true sense of certain mystical negations which, superficially violating the proprieties, can be said to have achieved a pregnant non-saying of the certainly as yet, and perhaps in principle, unsayable.

o

It is in the light of the upper world, likewise, that we may best understand that infinitely varied ampliative logic, which has had such infinite historical difficulty in freeing itself from the false support and equally false discredit of the common logic. The inferences worthiest of the name are those in which a conclusion does not follow with formal rigour from its premisses, but represents an unchartered, a not yet licenced, extension of them: inferences characterized by rigorous formal consequence are best regarded, to borrow a page from some modern philosophers, as mere displays, infinite no doubt in their richness and variety, of the working of certain content-indifferent, system-bound notions. Yet Aristotle, who above all men thought ampliatively in his treatment of lifeless and living nature, also assimilated his thought to that of a geometrical system, which though far from being formally rigorous in the modern sense, was yet making brave strides in that direction. And mediaeval and Cartesian thought was the glorious, interesting thing it managed to be only because its reasonings, however much cast in formal mould, constantly took steps and imported principles for which no formal, deductive warrant could be found. The protests of Bacon, and later of the empiricist and idealist logicians, seemed to have pushed formalism into the secondary position where its virtues and virtuosity could be profitably exercised, when lo, it staged a come-back, covering with an infinite variegation of tinkling symbols its essential, noble sterility. Men were so bemused by all this difficult magnificence, that it ceased to be plain to them that what was now being played out before them was not, in an ordinary sense, reasoning at all. And the issue was clouded by the fact that it was possible to formalize, and thereby to trivialize, each genuine piece of reasoning, by inventing a series of rules and premisses which covered by anticipation any inferential steps that one wanted to make. There came to be much lip-service to 'language-games', allegedly not trivial and formal, but genuine 'forms of life', but the rules which governed such forms of life were thought of as being merely conventional or contingently natural, and not as enshrining the very spirit and essence of the logical itself. It was the consequences of such games, the outcome of their strict or loose rules, which alone commanded interest: such and such was part of the way in which the word X is used, followed from the ways in which certain words X were used, etc.

That the use of words followed notional pressures, affinities between concepts which sprang from a deep and not a trivial identity, seemed the very essence of superstition.

Everyone knows, however, how certain states of affairs seem ready and appropriate continuations of others, the same thing carried a little further, even though there may be no formal fault in holding them not to be so continued, and that this is what ordinary men mean by the consistent and the logical. This was the consistency and the logic at work even in logic and mathematics, and in many *a priori* disciplines, before a half-century of effort had programmed their premises so as to yield all their conclusions, so that the latter were emptied of significance as of all inferential force. And this is certainly the consistency and the logic inseparable from the observed stuff laid before us by nature. A certain habit of being, and mode of proceeding, marks a distinct thing or node in the world-fabric, and dictates a continuation which, while differing from it, none the less will not differ enough from it to disrupt 'identity', distinct nodes in the world-process have a mysterious identity of kind which keeps them not so far apart in their further behaviour, styles of behaviour point inwards to characteristic styles of feeling, complex physical situations point inwards to thoughts that sum them up, natural convictions point to corresponding facts and vice versa, belief in something points to conduct appropriate to what is believed, and so on in innumerable cases. In all these cases we have phenomena which, while involving difference, distance, apartness, none the less have the profound kinship and mutual adjustment to which we only feel that we do full justice when we recognize an identity pervading them all, which nowhere breaks into that limiting independence involved in the notion of total otherness. This identity remains, however, a nebulous, groping concept at the level of this-world experience, and only unveils itself fully as we go on our speculative journey inwards into regions where distinctions between individuals and kinds, between thoughts and their objects, between inner private states and their bodily public manifestations, between full readiness and execution, and so forth, become less and less sharp, and all leads upward to that flame of pure zeal in which all these distinctions collapse into unity. The intermediate ascent is, however, necessary to the peripheral identity, which is otherwise 'merely mystical' in the vulgar, empty sense.

What we have been saying has been in a distant way said by many late nineteenth century Anglo-Saxon idealists with their belief in a single, seamless 'Reality', the subject of all judgments, all of whose nuances were 'internally related'. Only, if we may so put it, they sought absolute unity where it is not truly to be found, in the phenomena of this dirempted, alienated sphere, and their absolute reality accordingly assumed the painful form of a vastly extended total system, a sort of cosmic British Empire, with members bound together by strict Victorian causal determinism, beribboned with a few superadded links of sentimental teleology. Whereas, if we are right, this earthly sphere only hints at the genuine coincidences, the concentrated identity, which higher spheres will render explicit, and hence necessarily involves the gulfs, the indifferences, the limited independences, the mechanical encounters, the disruptive interferences, the distortions and perversions which it would be folly not to recognize in this life. Being Victorian progressives, the idealists in question found their fulcrum or centre in this present world, and, if some of their less guarded utterances may be held against them, they made London, with its Queen, Parliament, slums, clubs, docks, learned societies and far-flung connections, both their earthly and their spiritual Zion. Whereas the identity which pervades the world, and is expressed in all its continuities, is no unity of interlocking, separate parts, but an unextended, secret thing, like the Vairocana Buddha of Interpenetration to which the Emperor Shomu built his temple at Nara. We must find a fulcrum outside of this world if we are to lift the heavy load of puzzles which weighs on us in this world, and no therapy can hope to heal us if we are unwilling to be transported, even hypothetically, to the world's point of unity.

So far we have been showing the value of otherworld excursions for theory: we may now try to show it for practice. Practice plainly involves a realm of goals or values, the objects of desire or endeavour, and a contrasted world of reality in which they have to be executed or carried out. To a mind inured to the provincial arrangements of this life, nothing seems clearer than the distinction between the hard world of natural fact, which assaults us through the senses, and to which we submit with pleased, but sometimes with plaintive, masochism, and the strengthless world of our wishes, lost in a fine fume of fantasy, and only acquiring a wavering hold on the realm of fact through the fortuitous link of human muscles. To suggest that these two realms are inter-dependent, that the one exists to secure the carrying out of the other, seems infinitely silly and romantic, nor does it appear plausible to hold that desire, wish, is itself the living negation of the independence of the two realms, an ought which is also an is. But if we pass in thought only a little way up the speculative ladder, these provincial arrangements are eroded: there is no longer the plain distinction between the hard world of natural, sense-given fact and the inner world of desire. Desire writes itself large on the semi-sensuous landscape in beautiful or regrettable patterns, and the permanent, common goals of desire approach the perpetuity and the publicity of mountains. Values are certainly facts in that upper world, as all facts are living embodiments of values. This is even more true of the impersonal values studied in Lecture III, which arise in our earth-bound minds through an arduous anguished process, in which step by step we disassociate ourselves from the contingent material of our wishes, and from the particularity of our personal existence, and come to desire only what can and must be of interest *to* everyone and *for* everyone. Through this process we are led gradually to all those ideals of welfare, freedom, justice, beauty, knowledge, love and virtue which specify the *nisus* we are describing, and end ultimately by recog-nizing the unity of which they are the facets, and which *is* them rather than merely *has* them. Through this ethico-religious pro-cess, our practical life comes under the yoke of an infinitely per-suasive Logos, able to kindle the hearts and wills of others as it kindles our own, but still lingering in the mists of abstraction and aspiration, still reconcilable, even, with an ethic of decisions, recommendations and persuasive definitions. In our speculative upper world, however, impersonal values and their unity in a single infinitely inclusive, dynamic absolute, stand together like the grouped, glorified figures on some earthly altar. They are the supremely inescapable facts among the shifting, semi-subjective shapes of that upper world. And they may well have, at lower levels, the sort of magnificent semi-sensuous symbolization, that they have in the last cantos of Dante's *Paradiso*, a work written by one who was plainly better than an eye-witness. It is because, in that upper world, it would be totally absurd to oppose an impotent realm of ideal desiderata to the hard facts of actual existence, that we, even in this world, feel steeled against the assaults of all those who make values expressions of contingent personal preference. In the idlest personal wish, we have, not merely something that can cause something else by some secret physical mechanism or by Humean mental custom, but causality itself, naked, authentic, and intrinsically motive, and in those deeply serious suprapersonal wishes which are drawn, by a necessary attraction, to the just, the lovely and other forms of excellence, we have nothing less than the absolute, central causality of the universe, the pure zeal ultimately responsible for everything, in other words, *l'amor che move il sole e l'altre stelle.*

Practice further involves that deep concern for the personal interests and higher well-being of others, for which it is totally idle to seek a satisfactory foundation in the surface phenomena of the world. If modern philosophy has taught us anything, it has shown the utterly transcendent character of the stipulations by which a world of experient, mutually cognizant egos is set up, the total *a priority* of the whole notion of mental otherness, the impossibility of illustrating it in a medium whose structure involves it among other forms of alienation. Such a position can be used to undermine all deeper concern for the happiness and higher well-being of others, and only the contingent personal amiability of Wittgenstein and other modern philosophers disguises this fact. The lucidities of the Marquis de Sade may well succeed the sentimentalities of the solipsists and the behaviourists, and there are not a few signs of this coming to pass. But if, as our upper-world legend has put before us in not unimaginable outline, there are states in which the distinction of persons becomes largely a courtesy distinction, as often in dreams where we know people's thoughts or decisions before they utter them or act on them, and where the provenance and ownership of a thought is unimportant, and the difference between thinking a thought and thinking about it is quite blurred, and where sympathetic sufferings and personal sufferings have ceased to be plainly different, and the whole common stock of experience is so vast that, not its shared core, but its unshared fringes, its residue of apartness, alone creates a problem, all this is wholly different, and our concern with the feelings and visions of others becomes wholly justified. Only the seepage down from such higher levels explains the unmovedness of the *homo naturalis metaphysicus* by the arguments of the solipsist or the criteriologist: in the quietude of his being he underpasses the whole brilliant surface-discussion.

It is not necessary for us to underline the importance of those other-world penalties for injustice and cruelty which consist in practically becoming one's victims, and in reliving their mortifications and their torments, and the way in which they make personal what is impersonal. The many magnificent under-world descriptions of the Platonic dialogues make all of this clear. The Socratic doctrine that it is never profitable for anyone to do harm or injustice to anyone is, at the level of this-world existence, a trivial sophism, which confuses purely personal with absolute evil. But, in the deepest regard, it is the truth of the matter, for, since others are not really the absolute others that our alienated language would suggest, to mishandle and abuse them is to mishandle and abuse ourselves. The pains of hells and purgatories do no more than give ritual explicitness to this truth. It is also unnecessary to point out that our immense respect for the personality of men and even of animals indicates an extension of their being beyond the limits of this life: they may not be deprived of physical life on the specious excuse that, once dead, they will not repine at such deprivation, promises made to them must be fulfilled after death, etc., etc. Even if some of our taboos concerning euthanasia and abortion might seem unwarranted in an otherworldly perspective, they perhaps represent a strange compromise between such a perspective and the dubiety which is part and parcel of it. Whether or not the dissolution of the person at death is a genuine fact, it is something to which we are strangely obliged *not* to accommodate ourselves in our conduct, or not to accommodate ourselves *fully*. The athanatistic implications of many ordinary obligations have not been sufficiently studied by moralists.

We have said enough about the light thrown on theory and practice by the otherworldly Jacob's ladder we have postulated: let us now be Kantian and say something about its relation to art, beauty and the aesthetic. Concentration on this-world phenomena has reduced aesthetic philosophy to a shambles, where no general statement is permissible: there are no specific aesthetic emotions, no peculiar aesthetic objects, no rationally connected reasons for aesthetic approval or disapproval, not even a supreme value of the beautiful, which now is succeeded by a hydralike wealth of

independent heads like the dainty, the gorgeous, the classically
severe, the lyrical, etc. (I once heard Austin discoursing for a
whole afternoon on the 'dainty' and its contrast with the 'dumpy'.)
The practical effect has been to concentrate effort on the unexplored
interstices of the aesthetic, where the aesthetic goal can be
achieved in perverse and defiantly deviant ways. In reality that goal
is not altered when a man's glazed breakfast, pinned to a chair,
and set at right angles to the gallery wall, or the crushed entrails of
a motor car, replace the *Entombment* of Michelangelo or the
courtesans of Utamaro. In the little time left me I can only be
sweeping, and I shall simply say that, whatever their surface
differences of theme, material, form, method, etc., *all* the objects of
aesthetic appreciation can with illumination be said to express
precisely the same message, and that a mystical one. Hence the
rapt gaze of all who really enjoy beautiful sights and sounds, a gaze
that goes *through* what is immediate to a not easily utterable
target, and which is so much counterfeited by imitators, and so
embarrassing to the sincere but unmystical, that they prefer to
concentrate on technical or historical minutiae, details of contingent content, and quickly run away from the beautiful altogether.
The mystical message of all such objects is simply the overcoming
of alienation in overriding unity, such as occurs progressively as
we move towards the mystical pole of the cosmos. The alienation
of aesthetically esteemed objects lies in their contingent material,
their dealing with star-crossed lovers, or wild swan in flight, or
game and fruit, or what not, as well as with spatially and temporally
extended items organized in various ways: sometimes there are
two distinct tiers of inner significance and sensibly perceived form,
sometimes the inner significance is indistinguishable from the
outward pattern which may be said, paradoxically, to express or
bring out itself. The overcoming of the alienation consists in the
manner in which the contingent material and sensory items are all
made to co-operate and interpenetrate, so that one and the same
total character or pattern, whether sensory or notional, comes out
in all of them. The pattern or character which comes out may, of
course, be anything whatever, simple or complex, lowest-order or
higher-order or categorial. It may lend itself simply to aesthetic
treatment or may be superficially at odds with such treatment:
what is jarring, discrepant, bathetic, feeble, confused, decayed,
half-formed, jejune, patched together, loathly, etc., are, if seen *as*

such, as fit objects of aesthetic presentation as their more readily loved opposites. But, whatever it is, we always look through the character of pattern presented to a certain abstract triumph, the triumph of concentration over random dispersion, the complete worsting and utter subjugation of the latter, the sort of abstract triumph which occurs at the end of a world-period when inadequate, random forms vanish into the pure zeal which has breathed itself into them, and which now withdraws from them and makes use of them only to feel and know itself.

Aesthetic enjoyment may therefore be said to point to upper world conditions in which alienation is far more effectively overcome, and in which all existence becomes infinitely expressive. But existence at those levels is possibly *less* full of aesthetic delight than existence down here, since the ease of the medium gives a certain facility and absence of poignancy to the product. Beauty would seem, in fact, to be essentially a value of exile, which we experience down here when we look towards degrees of unity and interpenetration which cannot be achieved in a sensuous, spatio-temporal medium. But it is only because earthly organizations of material *suggest* the unity and interpenetration yonder that they acquire the right to be regarded as beautiful. It is because it suggests, rather than achieves, that our intercourse with beauty is also so often unsuccessful and painful, why our visits to our best-loved works of art are often a total failure, why our aesthetic sensibilities can be deranged by the slightest physical malaise or fatigue, why aesthetic impotence is a malady far more readily fallen into, and far more depriving, than the impotence of sex. The whole life of Ruskin, with its oscillating depression and final collapse, is an eloquent proof that the roots of beauty lie yonder, and that the attempt to take violent possession of it by mentally eating up all the buildings in Europe and every stone in Venice, can only lead to the dark night of the soul and to final madness.

Having suggested the relevance of the world to come to our theoretical, practical and aesthetic life here, I now wish to be a little more personal, and say something about one or two of the points of earthly existence, at which some people, and myself among them, do feel that there is a relative lack of opacity between earthly existence and upper-world being. There are an extraordinary number of extremely simple delights, which seem, as it were, to be the residue, of some earlier, untainted creation, and which involve, if only in symbol, that blending and interpenetration of essence in which upper-world being arguably consists. The breathing in of air, the touch and sight of water, being warmed by the sun or by fire, the eating of simple foods, repose under soft, clean covers, the touch and scent of flowers, the flow of unstrained human conversation: all of these have, and retain, something inherently marvellous, and seem as it were, to be natural metaphors for quite ineffable satisfactions. And I may further follow Wordsworth and refer to all those experiences of early childhood which certainly become more and more 'apparelled in celestial light' the further they retreat from us, and largely furnish the paradigms for our notions of the heavenly. Only I should not, with Wordsworth, lay such emphasis on meadow, grove and stream, glorious as these undoubtedly were, as on the domestic and social arrangements that then surrounded us, with their indescribable mixture of beauty, joy and trust. Modern existentialism has sketched the unauthentic 'they' which so tiresomely surrounds us in early experience, with its dreary judgments and its conventional prescriptions, but why not dwell on the authentic, the deeply accepted 'we', of which each of us was so intimately and so happily a part? In the structure of that 'we', a sound phenomenology or existentialism will surely distinguish the two primal figures, not loathsomely caught in some Freudian 'primal scene', but in those endless offices of sweetness and care in which parental being consists. And it will surely find room for a phenomenological characterization of the brotherly, the sisterly and the cousinly, and will perhaps find room for a special chapter on aunts, that interesting transitional category between maternity and random femininity, devoting perhaps a special study to the romantic aunt, who, dark, interesting and beautiful, brings into the nursery the rumour of strange voyages and amazing encounters, as well as sympathies almost unbearably touching. There should also, surely, be an existential chapter concerned with the 'home town', that blessed location whose streets served only to link one happy habitation with another, each a warm centre of family affection, of love between masters and servants, of domestic order and purity of life. Later in life, too, there are certain authentic reflections of the heavenly, if also of the purgatorial, in those experiences of early love where two worlds of experience seem magically linked, so that one can wander in astonishment among the strange landscapes, lights and jewelled trees of another's world, as also in those successive awakenings to whole worlds of human endeavour, and to human enterprises still in progress, and in pilgrimages with blessed companions to those cities, mainly Italian, which, like God, are not merely beautiful, but beauty itself. My selection of heaven-ward-pointing items has been highly personal: many others might have been mentioned, especially those that have to do with one's own children or with beloved persons who have gone beyond the shadows and deceits of the cave. I can only plead that the same personal selectivity is evident in the work of those existentialists and phenomenologists who have painted pictures of a human existence stained in care, guilt and anxiety, where the prospect of an ultimate nothingness is only one shade less dreadful than falling into the hands of a Kierkegaardian God. And I should further claim that, as values are the norms which give sense and possibility to the deviant and the evil, so the heavenward indications that I have mentioned are the normal, the normative ones, and that the dire pictures projected on to the cosmos whether by Danish melancholia or by central European social collapse are subsidiary and interstitial. What I wish to point out is that the whole of life is shot through with these astonishing experiences, no doubt differing greatly from one person to another, but which so deeply presuppose light streaming from beyond the cave that they make no sense without it.

I have now come to the end of these Gifford Lectures on *The Discipline of the Cave* and *The Transcendence of the Cave*. Though my audience has been exiguous—the most exiguous, in fact, in my whole experience—it has never been unattentive, nor, I think, uncomprehending, and I have greatly valued the opportunity of putting some of my less readily expressed fringe-convictions into moderately clear, coherent form. I am very grateful to the author-ities of St Andrews University for affording me this opportunity, which has also pleased me particularly as coming from Scotland. I am deeply proud of all my ancestors, whether English, Scottish, Suabian, Hanoverian, Dutch or French Huguenot, men blown by many motives to South Africa, but all also by that gust of the spirit which drives me too, but of none am I more proud than of that old Calvinist sea-captain whose name I bear, who sailed his

ship the *Alacrity* to St Helena, round the Cape and to Tasmania,
who so abhorred a graven image that his only portrait is a sketch
drawn privily from the rear, and who now reposes in the graveyard
of the Auld Kirk at Cullen. It is on account of these precious
Scottish ties, that I have not only ventured to tell you my mind,
but to open my heart.

INDEX

Abortion, 215
Abraham, 113, 116
Absolute(s), 18, 78, 81, 86, 90, 92 102, 105, 202
Abstracta, 36-7, 56-7, 77, 109, 142, 152
Abstraction, 39, 42-6
Acosmism, 81, 183, 186
Actio in distans, 130
Active intelligence, 139
Aesthetic(s), 34, 72-3, 148, 215-17
Agonies (other-worldly), 170
Alienation, 192-3, 195-7, 200, 216-17
Ampliative inference, 54, 68-9, 210
Analytic statements (inferences), 19, 31, 88
Angels (angelology), 23, 163, 177
Anger, 79
Anglo-Saxon Idealists, 212
Angst, 178
Animals, 156, 177, 215
Anschauung, 85, 124
Anselm, St, 78, 84, 86, 88-9
Antinomy, 20-1, 25, 32, 37, 91, 106, 119, 121
Apical phenomenon, 81, 107
Application, 38
A priori, 20, 80, 214
Aquinas, St Thomas, 84, 106-7, 124, 126
Arbitrariness, 74-5, 111-12, 165, 183-4
Aristotle, 42-4, 51, 93-4, 125, 136, 139, 144-5, 154, 210
Arupaloka, 126
Aseity, 82-6, 89, 91, 180
Asymmetry (of time), 25
Aunts, 218
Augustine, St, 116-17, 150, 183
Austin, J. L., 216
Avatamsaka-sutra, 158-9, 205
Awe (religious), 78

Bacon, F., 55, 210
Barth, K., 84
Being-in-the-world, 79-80
Behaviourism, 214
Being, necessary, *see* Existence, necessary
Belief 50, 110-11
Benevolence, 71
Bentham, J., 71
Berkeley, G., 39
Body, 18, 26-37, 49, 127-8, 133-4, 164

Boehme, J., 108
Bosanquet, B., 46, 84
Bracketing, 50, 82-3, 100
Bradley, F. H., 46, 84
Brahman(ism), 86, 108, 111, 167, 183
Brain, 27
Buddha, Gotama, 113, 116, 156, 159, 163, 184, 187, 198
Buddha-field (Pure Land), 172, 194
Buddhism, 82, 107, 110, 124, 139, 165, 167, 172, 187, 198, 209
Butler, J., 69

Calvinism, 196, 219
Carnap, R., 152, 206
Categories, 48-51, 151-2
Causality, 66-7, 75, 175, 214
Cave, 17, 20, 36-8, 102, 111, 113, 118-19, 162
Cézanne, P., 164
Characters, 48-9
China, 135
Christianity, 84, 95, 101, 114-17, 165-7, 198
Coalescence of egos, 163
Coherence, 50
Coincidence, 31
of opposites, 185
Collusion, 111
Compulsive experience, 50
Conscious light, 38-41, 53
Consciousness, 83
Constitution-theory, 46
Contingency, 93-4, 96, 99, 107, 113-14, 142, 146, 183-5
Contradiction, 21, 54, 126, 201-2, 209
in God, 155
Co-operation and communication (of minds), 31, 34, 36-7, 41, 46, 55, 77, 100, 118
Correspondence, 31
Coyness (of bodies), 33
Creation, 183-4
Cusanus, N., 106

Dante Alighieri, 202, 204, 213
Decision (in morals), 74-5
Dedekind, J., 24
Dependence-in-independence, 22, 31-2
Descartes, R., 30, 121, 152, 210
Description (pure), 19-20, 31
Dharmadhatu, 139, 158-9
Dhyana, 203
Dialectic, 17